EXPERIENCING JESUS' JOY

DR. JAMES B. JOSEPH
"BROTHER JAMES"

EXPERIENCING JESUS' JOY

DR. JAMES B. JOSEPH | "BROTHER JAMES"

ISBN: 978-1-935986-14-0
Library of Congress Catalog#: 2013375175
Author's Website: www.injesusservice.com

LIBERTY
U N I V E R S I T Y.
Press

Lynchburg, VA

www.liberty.edu/libertyuniversitypress

To God Be the Glory!

Foreword

Christ prayed that His followers would experience His joy, which was made full at the Cross. God invites every person of every generation to join Him in becoming a member of His eternal close-knit holy family. Upon acceptance, every member is asked to help others who are still living separate from God to know Him and join His eternal family and kingdom. Through the Holy Spirit, God develops love *for all* in the hearts of His family members and commissions each of them to be His representatives on earth. Like Christ, His followers experience great joy over every individual who is rescued from the deceptions of self-centeredness, selfishness, and Satan.

This book has been written to help those of you who want to understand more fully your God-given purpose in life and wish to experience more godly joy. As you realize more fully what God is asking of you and what Satan is doing to quench the leading of the Holy Spirit, you will be liberated to follow Christ more fully into spiritual battle resulting in more coming to know God and desiring to be part of His eternal family. Through God's children becoming more active in His Creation, God will become more fully known and trusted worldwide. Let's rejoice together as we follow Jesus bringing many into the Family of God!

– In Jesus' Service, Brother James

Table of Contents

1

Joy

Have you ever wondered if there could be more love, joy, and inner peace in your life? If you are not experiencing excitement and joy in your walk with Jesus, you should. Even if you think that you are not worthy to experience such joy, you are worthy through Jesus Christ and His redeeming death. Jesus wants all of His followers to experience an inner peace and joy that can only come from God, a peace and joy that is grounded in godly love that transcends everything of this world.

Just before being arrested to die for the sins of the world, Jesus prayed that all who followed Him would experience the same joy that He was experiencing by joining God and doing his or her part in the greatest rescue operation of all time.[a] [1] Without Jesus' victory over spiritual death, which had occurred through disobedience, no one would ever be eternally completed in God's image according to His likeness and live with Him forever.

Our Creator cares about everyone and has a great eternal life just waiting for all who listen and receive Him into their lives.[b] No one is accidently here. There never was an accidental explosion of gases or any type of accident that begat our universe and set it on an evolutionary path. There was and is an eternal creator who created the universe and all that is in it. He created you to be part of His close-knit holy family and wants you to join Him forever. If you choose to join Him, He asks you to bring others with you as you live out this part of eternity.

If you desire to experience more love, joy, and inner peace, *let God show you the spiritual importance of your participation in building His eternal kingdom and eternal caring family.* If you are willing to follow Jesus, God will teach you reality and grow a love in your heart for others that will bring you great inner peace and joy. You will join Him in rescuing as many as will listen from eternal disaster. Jesus' joy became full when He knew that the time

---

a: John 17:13; 15:8–11. b: John 1:12; Rev 3:20.

had come for Him to die providing salvation for all who would receive God into their lives. He knew that His death would provide a miraculous removal of sin and a righteous transformation for all people of all time who obediently listen to His heavenly Father.

If someone whom you love dearly was in dire trouble, what would you personally be willing to do to help? The writer of the letter of Hebrews stated that because of the joy of making it possible for all to be rescued, saved from the deadly consequences of sin, Jesus endured death on a cross with its suffering, despising the shame of dying as a common criminal.[a] His joy was made full through His sacrificial work on everyone's behalf because He was saving those whom He loves deeply. *There is no greater joy that you will ever experience than helping save those whom you love dearly from a present life of continual ongoing sin and an eternal life of suffering and shame.*[b] 2

If you allow God to develop love in your heart for Him and others, you will come to the place of joyfully enduring personal hardship and suffering in order to see people whom you have come to love experience God's salvation for the present and eternity! *Now* is the time for our generation to engage our culture and dispel the spiritual darkness around us. *Now* is the time for the Church to demonstrate clearly God's love for *all* through our actions as well as our words so that this generation will see God's desire for all to be part of His eternal caring close-knit holy family.

Jesus wants all who faithfully follow Him to experience the same full measure of joy that He experienced as He faced the Cross in order to provide salvation for all. There is no greater joy than rescuing someone you love from immediate and long term harm. Jesus has made a way for as many as receive Him into their lives to enter into His Father's eternal presence and become part of His eternal close-knit holy family. *The creation of God's eternal intimate holy family is the primary purpose of the entire Creation.*

In addition to praying for His followers' joy to become full as they became more active in God's ongoing creative work, Jesus prayed for God to guide and protect them.[c] He prayed that as we, His future followers, follow the leading of the Holy Spirit and do our assigned individual parts, we would personally know God

---

a: Heb 12:1–3.   b: Rom 6:22.   c: John 17:11, 15; cf. 14:12; 16:13.

more fully through His Word and our faithful experiences.[a] God created all to be caring individuals and in being so to experience Jesus' joy that comes only from being an active participant in His creation.

God created humanity in His own image according to the likeness of His own nature.[b] Although our nature has been corrupted through disobedience starting with Eve and then Adam, God grants everyone the freedom to make choices about contemporary and eternal relationships. Knowing that this high degree of freedom would result in disobedience and temporary separation for *all* from Him, God still chose this path for us. He desires all to enter into a close-knit mutual caring relationship with Him, yet everyone has the freedom to either accept or reject Him and His holy way of life. He is a loving kind creator,[c] 3 and He has made a way to remove all that is bad (evil/corrupt) from His obedient children, making them suitable for His eternal family.[d] 4 God is good and God is great. For those who allow Him to lead and shape their lives, at the point of physical death or at the Rapture,[e] He finishes perfecting each in holiness according to His moral image and each individually with their unique attributes enabling all to fulfill their specific roles in His eternal family.

Due to God's desire for each of us to make a personal decision on whether or not we will submit voluntarily to His leadership, He has allowed all to start off together on a wide road that leads to eternal separation from Him. This started with Adam and Eve's disobedience at the beginning of the Creation. Consequently, everyone travels on the wide road that leads to eternal suffering and shame. But, the Gospel proclaims that God has made a way for everyone to get off this widely traveled road without forcing any to do so. He continually works with all to help everyone know the reality of His love and desire for a godly change of heart. When one turns to God for a better life and subjects themselves to God and His standards, God starts showing them more and more reality including how good Heaven is without sin and how bad Hell will be with the absence of genuine love one for another. Yet, there are many led by Satan, who are working deceptively all of the time to convince as many as possible that this sin-filled life on earth is the best that life can ever be. *What a lie!*

---

a: John 17:17; cf. 8:31–32. b: Gen 1:26–27; cf. 3:22; James 3:9.
c: 1 John 4:16. d: 2 Cor 5:21. e: 1 Thess 4:15–17.

As we start responding to God's illuminating work in our lives, God shows us more and more of His nature and desired life style. The more that we listen to God and do His will, the more we know Him and desire to do even more of His will. As the Holy Spirit makes us all aware of our shortcomings in light of God's holy nature, each of us must come to a place where we are willing to admit that we possess a fallen corrupted nature and allow God to start transforming our lives. If we do not, we will never start experiencing firsthand the love, joy, and inner peace that come through following Him and His holy lifestyle. After getting to know God more fully, some are willing to put aside their self-centered view of life and make real commitments to follow such a caring creator and sustainer, who loves everyone dearly and desires all to be part of His holy family and great kingdom.

The primary reason that I wrote this book is to enlighten and encourage as many as possible to live out joyfully victorious lives "in Christ" instead of living empty lives without eternal purpose. Christ's followers should be living out their lives with a genuine concern for others demonstrating God's love as they continue to grow in their love for others becoming more and more like God. Being part of God's awesome family should bring love, joy, and inner peace to all who follow Christ. In addition to godly family joy, Christ's followers experience their greatest joy when they are rescuing those who are living empty lives now and headed for an eternal life of shame and suffering. Christ's followers experience their greatest joy when they join God in helping others to know Him, His way of life, and His desire for the very best for their lives.

Through a desire to please our heavenly Father coupled with a genuine commitment to follow Jesus, the Holy Spirit enlightens and empowers Christ's followers to accomplish their individual assignments within God's creative work. It is Christ's followers' duty, privilege, and great joy to help others understand more fully why God created them and why He allows suffering during their lives on earth. As more people begin to understand the purpose of the Creation, Satan's ongoing work to destroy God and all who listen to Him, the eternal consequences of personal choices, and God's perfect love for all, some will turn to God to join Him and His eternal family forever.

After reading this book, I pray that you will more earnestly seek God's plan for your life and enjoy the blessings of stepping out in faith more fully as you strive earnestly to do God's perfect will for your life. As you more fully and obediently follow the leading of the Holy Spirit, I know that you will experience firsthand more excitement and joy while working with God to build His and our eternal close-knit holy family.

If you have *not* truly committed to follow Jesus *yet*, let this book help you understand God more fully and His great love for you. Through this book, you will see that from the very beginning of the creation of the universe, God has been creating His own family that will live together forever truly caring for one another. It will also show you that God does not remove anyone's free will in order to subject them to Himself. ***Family subjection is voluntary!*** Self-centered Satan and many others have chosen not only to reject God's leadership but also to fight against Him and take away His Kingdom. But, for those who allow God to show them what is really going on around them, some eventually come to the point of realization that God is worthy of our obedient faithfulness. When we come to realize how much God has already done for us, it is much easier to submit to His lordship and follow Jesus. Finding your place in His family and kingdom and helping to build His family is an honor that God desires to bestow upon you.

Even if you do not feel worthy to accept such an honor at the moment, read on and allow God to speak to you through His Word as presented in this book. ***Understanding God's Word more fully will bring clarity about God's desire for your life.*** God has already done everything needed to guarantee the best for your eternal life. It is *your* responsibility to accept His invitation to live in peace, joy, and harmony with Him and others.

Whenever you are reading and you encounter super-scripted numbers, they indicate notes at the back of the book, which are there to help you look more fully at important words, phrases, or concepts. Whenever you encounter super-scripted lower-case letters, they indicate supporting scriptural passages, which are found at the bottom of the pages. In addition, there are subject and Bible reference indexes located at the back of the book. I have translated all Hebrew and Greek Scripture into English out of the appropriate sources shown in the bibliography.

2

—

The Creation

Have you ever wondered why God created Adam and Eve *with enough free-will to disobey Him* knowing ahead of time that they would? There were no surprises for God.[5] He knew before He created humanity with the high level of free-will that He designed into their nature that Adam and Eve would disobey Him. He knew according to His own nature and resulting standards that He would have to temporarily remove *all* future humanity from His immediate presence. Did you know that after God had completed the initial part of the Creation in six days with its perfect start, He stated that it was *tov meod,*[6] "good exceedingly," knowing that the whole creation would soon be caught in the middle of a major spiritual battle for each person's soul?[7] From an ongoing battle of evil trying to overthrow good completely, God knew that there would be many casualties. He knew that more would be lost than saved from eternal pain and sorrow.[a] Why did a loving Creator put together a creation that had to go through so much pain and sorrow?

The truth of the matter is this: God knows what He is doing and cares deeply about our pain and suffering. In fact, He has endured more pain and sorrow on our behalf than anyone else will ever endure. It is because He deeply cares for all that He has created us with so much freedom of choice that we are able to freely receive or reject Him and His desired eternal close-knit holy family. God knew that this freedom would lead the entire creation into corruption,[b] but without the freedom granted, there could never be an eventual *reciprocating* loving relationship within God's planned eternal family. With a love that is given by God and received by all who desire to live with Him forever, there will eventually be unspeakable eternal peace and joy for God and His holy family.[8]

———————

a: Matt 7:13–14. b: Rom 8:20–22.

Created According to God's Likeness

And God said, "Let **us** make Adam *in **our** image according to **our** likeness.*"[9] Gen 1:26a

Our first major clue about our place in God's creation can be gleaned from the first chapters in Genesis. As we read Genesis 1:26–27,[10] we see that Adam was created in the image and likeness of more than one individual. God said that Adam was to be created in "our" image according to "our" likeness, which is clearly depicted in the Hebrew text. As we study the entire Bible, we see that God is a "oneness," a single unity, consisting of three individuals, the Father, the Son, and the Holy Spirit. The words "Trinity" and "Tri-unity" are not found in the Bible, but they are used by many to describe the "oneness" of the Father, Son, and Holy Spirit. The night before He went to the Cross to die for the sins of all who would receive Him into their lives, Jesus prayed that His followers of all ages would experience the same "oneness" that He had always experienced with His Heavenly Father.[a] Together, He and the Father would send the Holy Spirit as the new Comforter in His place to guide and empower His followers.[b] [11]

There are places in Scripture, where the three are clearly active during a single event such as Jesus' baptism by John the Baptist when the Holy Spirit descended on Jesus as a dove and the Father said aloud for all those nearby that He was well pleased with His beloved Son.[c] [12] In reality, the Father, Son, and Holy Spirit are always involved together as a "oneness" working under the lordship of the Father with the Son being second in command over everything.[d] Jesus is the sent Son who obediently follows His Father.[e] The Holy Spirit follows the will of both the Father and Son.[f] Because Jesus, the Messiah, emulates His heavenly father so well, when you see Jesus in action, you have seen the Father in action.[g]

Adam is the first human being and his name is also used synonymously for all mankind.[13] Several things become apparent to us as we study the account of the initial part of the creation and

---

a: John 17:20–23. b: John 14:16–23. c: e.g. Matt 3:16–17. d: 1 Cor 15:28. e: John 8:28–29. f: John 14:16, 26; 16:7. g: John 14:7–9; Heb 1:2–3.

the fall of humanity. The first is that prior to man's disobedient act that separated him from God, he had a close relationship with Him. After God had created every type of animal after its own individual kind, He then created humanity *in His image according to His likeness*[a] to relate to Him and take care of planet Earth. Initially, prior to their disobedience (sin), one could see much of God's goodness projected by Adam and Eve as they lived out their lives communing with God and His creation.

From Satan's initial deception and Jesus' teachings later, we come to understand that Adam and Eve lost their close relationship with God after disobeying Him when tempted by one of Satan's many ongoing deceptions. When Adam and Eve disobeyed God, they were forced to leave His presence and experience evil in addition to the good that they had been experiencing. Due to Adam's and Eve's sin, all future descendants were also forced to experience *both* evil and good.

Adam and Eve's disobedience (sin) corrupted God's pure creation, which had initially produced caring individuals who would never harm anyone on any level. Sin produced an eldest son who killed his younger brother out of jealousy over God's favor. As we continue reading through the Old Testament, we see that Adam and Eve's initial disobedience opened the door for continual sin for all mankind bringing suffering to all. We are taught through the Apostle Paul that Adam and Eve's disobedience put mankind and *all* Creation on a path of corruption: a process of living and dying in which all physical things were marred and would come to an end through decay and destruction.[b]

In contemplating God's creation, we should keep in mind that *this is God's creation not ours*. He knew in advance the consequences of giving mankind the amount of freedom that He has given all. He also knew that many would be eternally separated from Him, but that some would turn to Him and His caring ways after being exposed to both good and evil.[c] [14] Here is where we start to realize how much value God places on free-will and its place in godly love:

> (1) we note that God insists that *we must make a choice*: if we are to live with Him forever, we must choose Him and His way of life over living out our lives for ourselves; and

---

a: cf. James 3:9. b: Rom 8:18–23. c: John 1:12–13; Rev 3:20.

(2) with eternity in mind, we should take note that God knows infinitely more than we and is working out a creation to bring as many free-willed children into His eternal holy presence and family as possible.

With perfect foreknowledge, God knew the outcome of all things prior to putting the universe physically together and decided to allow everyone to experience both good and evil.[a] He knew that some would learn from His continual revelation and their personal experiences to call on Him for help. *Knowing all things in advance*, He made a plan to save (rescue) as many as desired a better life. The Father, Son, and Holy Spirit worked out a plan of salvation in which They would experience death in our place and, in so doing, provide godly restoration for all who welcome Them into their lives.[b] 15

Molded & Shaped by God

And now, YHWH, you are our Father; we are the clay and you are our potter, and all of us are the work of your hand.[16] Isaiah 64:8; cf. John 15:2

Looking at Isaiah as a whole and the Scripture surrounding this verse, Israel is acknowledging their sin, asking for forgiveness, and *reminding God that He is the one who made them.* He should take some responsibility for their actions. This goes back to the very beginning of the Creation when God created Adam in His image according to His likeness with a tremendous amount of free-will. In a somewhat similar scenario, God's chosen people, Israel, were having a hard time living up to the agreement that their ancestors had made with God at Mount Sinai.[c] Adam and Eve's disobedience had separated them from God and created a corruption in man's soul whereby everyone following them was born into corruption with sin as part of their nature. Their disobedience caused all to start with sin in their lives and thereby go through *a process of refining* through the furnace of affliction.[d] Yes, this is God's creation and His pre-engineered plan. All ultimately go through some level of His refining process, and for

---

a: cf. Gen 3:22.   b. Isa 53; Gal 3:13–14.   c: Ex 19:4–8.   d: Isa 48:10.

those who choose Him and His way of life, they will be made whole through *His* redemptive work.

Even Israel, who was chosen by God to walk in His ways and represent Him to the rest of the world,[a] had to struggle regularly with the temptations that come with a fallen divided nature. So, even though it seems like godly living should be fairly straightforward knowing the damage that sinful actions cause, it is not. When you look at God's commandments for godly living, you realize that the goal of everything is to move as many as listen from a corrupted state of sinful self-centeredness to a state of holiness (wholeness/perfection), through which we truly learn to love Him and one another.[b]

Herein lies the problem: Adam and Eve's disobedience corrupted God's Creation to the point that all people are born loving themselves more than anyone else including our Creator who loves all beyond anyone's capacity to comprehend.[c] So learning to love God or anyone more than ourselves or even equally with ourselves does not come easily.

We can see through God's prophet Isaiah that at some point in her captivity and duress, Israel came to a place of wanting help. There was a group within Israel who knew that without God's presence and help, they were on an eternal road of shame and suffering. They knew that their present state of sinfulness had separated them from God.[d] God had told them at the beginning of His special relationship with them that whenever they committed blatant sin in the future, they *could* be restored–if they would come to their senses and repent. If they would start following Him again, He would restore their state of prosperity both physically and spiritually.[e]

Speaking through Isaiah, God told Israel then and people of all ages that they needed to wake up from their slumber[f] and come to a place in their lives where they were willing to return to a lifestyle that matched His holy righteousness.[g] [17] Knowing in advance what would happen throughout every moment of the Creation, God promised Israel and the world that He would send a savior.[h] For all who would repent and receive Him into their lives, His Sent Son would provide a way of escaping the corruption and resulting damage that Adam and Eve had initiated.[i] This savior

---

a: Ex 19:5–6.   b: Matt 22:37–40.   c: 1 Cor 13:9–12.   d: Isa 54:2–8; Dan 12:2.   e: Deut 28:9–47; 2 Chron 7:12–14.   f: Isa 51:17; 52:1–2. g: Isa 1:27; 30:15; cf. Lev 19:2.   h: Isa 56:1–2; Gal 4:4.   i: Rom 5:12–17.

would be both king of kings[a] and atoning high priest.[b] God's obedient children would eventually experience great joy.[c]

Completion Comes through Obedience

Jesus said, "*If someone loves me, he will keep my Word*, and my Father shall love him, and we shall come to him and make our abode with him."

John 14:23

God makes it clear through His Word that spiritual and physical wholeness come to those who respond to His love. God wants as many as will receive Him to experience His way of life providing eternal joy and peace. It starts by *returning* God's love, obeying His instructions for life, and remaining faithful to His direction and way of life.[d]

Because of God's unconditional love for us, we can learn to *obey* and *trust* Him. When we examine one of our best known scriptures regarding God's love for us, John 3:16–17, we see that eternal life is provided for all who *are believing (trusting)* in Jesus. It is important to note that the early Greek text indicates that those who are in *an ongoing* state of trust are the ones whom God molds and shapes more fully into His own moral image. Our salvation and transformation come through Christ when we make a conscious decision to live out our lives trusting God because of His great love and desired unity with us.[18] As we learn to return God's love *through interaction* with Him and others, *we gain experience in trusting Him.*[e] Ultimately, it is through our growing trust that we come to know God intimately. Biblical faith (trust) is not blind faith.[f] We learn to trust God by obediently entering into His assigned activities for us and *experiencing* His love for all through action.

Biblically, the writer of Hebrews defines faith as an assurance of things expected from God because of His faithfulness to His Word.[g] The words "***faith***" and "***trust***" are both derived

---

a: Isa 9:6–7. b: Isa 53; Heb 7. c: Isa 35:10; 51:11. d: Deut 30:15–20. e: Rom 10:10; Gal 5:6. f: Heb 11. g: Heb 11:1.

from the same Greek word *pistis*. The Greek is rooted in two ideas that many times are meant to be considered simultaneously:

> (1) it normally denotes a historical accuracy about something or someone; and
> (2) it denotes a trust in someone's character and ability or something's physical makeup in regards to its ability to complete its designed function.[19]

As we continue to walk with God, He helps develop our trust in Him because of His holy nature and ability to carry out His intentions,[a] [20] and we learn to reciprocate His love by obeying Him. Thus, our trust in God develops as we see and experience His faithfulness to help all people become whole. Scripturally, a "Believer" is an individual who has come to know Jesus as *both savior* and *lord*. The Believer (the Truster) trusts and obeys God because of His genuine love and His ability to carry out His desires.[21]

Our faith (trust) is developed more fully as we interact obediently with God. God does not want us to trust Him just because He is God, the mighty one who sustains us. Although God is strong enough to force everyone to do as He wishes, He does not do so because of the *high* value that He places on our willing cooperation. God wants us to love Him because of His unbiased love for all. God loved us first, and God is love.[b] [22]

God expresses His love through His actions as well as His words. God's actions are full of grace and righteousness toward all. God wants both our trust and obedience to come from the heart as we grow in our love for Him and one another. *If we interact with God* on an ongoing basis and join Him in His ministry to all, our trust and obedience *will grow*. With this improved understanding of the meaning and significance of the words "trust" and "obey," we can appreciate more John's use of these words interchangeably.[c] [23] Through our growing love for God, trust and obedience become part of our developing godly character. Trust and obedience toward God become an integral part of nature of the child of God who is going Home.

God has created all to live with Him in a loving caring community called ***Family***. God made it clear through His dealings

---

a: James 2:22.   b: 1 John 4:10, 16, **19**; Rom 10:10.   c: John 3:36.

with Israel, His chosen people, that any serious actions against others would cause one's death or exile. This is love in action. *Love does no harm.*[a] When Israel listened as a whole, the people lived in a fairly joyous peaceful prosperous environment. When they turned from God and His caring ways, their joy, peace, and prosperity disappeared as the corruption of sin within the world took its toll.

Nothing has changed regarding God's desired relationship with all of His creation. For as many as receive Him into their lives, He develops their love more fully and supplies joy, inner peace, and varying amounts of prosperity depending on each person's part within His global rescue operation. And, this is just a start. God has promised those who will return His love that He will take everything in their lives and use it to shape and mold them into Christ's image starting here-and-now.[b] 24 God completes His work in each of Christ's followers between the instant of death and meeting Him face-to-face.[c]

God's demand for true love from all of His children **is not optional**. Israel is God's example to all on the importance of godly living. If we ignore our Creator, we will end up living a life that brings much pain and suffering. Even in our sin corrupted world, if we listen to God, we end up living a life with much less self-inflicted pain and suffering and much more joy and inner peace.

Sin corrupts! We are living in a corrupted world and cannot clearly see the reality of our potential future with God.[d] But, if we listen to the teaching of the Holy Spirit, He will teach us something of this world and the world to come through God's Word and our interaction with God and others on earth.[e] If we consider God's work with Israel as His chosen people, and understand that sin is not acceptable because it brings harm to all, we start to understand what Heaven is like. Heaven is a place where God will have perfected our nature to be like His,[f] and as a result, no one will sin and cause harm. *Godly love does no harm!* Everyone in heaven will have perfect love for God and one another, and therefore, there will be no more pain nor sorrow.[g] God's desired relationship with us will become reality, and having been made complete without sin, we will experience the joy of being with our eternal *holy* Father and Family.[h]

---

a: 1 Cor 13:4–7. b: Rom 6:22. c: Phil 1:6; 1 John 3:1–2. d: 1 Cor 13:12. e: 1 John 2:27. f: glorification; Rom 8:17, 28–30. g: Rev 21:4. h: Rev 21:7.

3

Good, Evil, & Spiritual Warfare

Even if you do not believe in God, it is highly probable that you have sensed an ongoing battle of evil trying to prevail over good. Most have come to realize that there is a way of life that is beneficial and many ways of life that ultimately bring harm to themselves and others. The way that we live with others makes a real difference in the here-and-now and in the future. In reality, God has created the universe with real absolute standards for all life. When we follow His rules, we do good for ourselves and others, when we do not, we harm ourselves and others, which is bad, evil. Because God is communicating to all, on some level, everyone is aware of God's standards.[a]

Not only are most aware of the difference between evil and good, all participate in doing both. There is plenty of wrongdoing by all. No one is innocent. Everyone has fallen short of living out a perfectly righteous life according to God's standards *except Jesus Christ*.[b] Evil is recognized by most societies around the world, and due to the harm done through evil actions, more time is spent keeping current on the latest evil than on good. Whether speaking an unkind word, not helping someone whom God puts in our path, directly disobeying God's instructions for our personal lives, lying, cheating, stealing, killing, enslaving, sexually abusing, or doing some other form of evil, we all see and do some evil.

Evil vs. Good

Personally, we have all experienced times in our lives in which we have done something that has hurt someone else and have either felt immediate or eventual remorse. Even if someone has not been walking in spiritual awareness of God's presence and

---

a: Rom 2:14–15.   b: Rom 3:23; Isa 53:4–9; 2 Cor 5:21; 1 Peter 2:21–24.

continual teaching, most recognize the fact that we all struggle with self-centered desires. Whether we listen to the leading of God or not, He talks to all and moves as many as listen into a place of awareness that helps make good choices easier.[a]

We all need to listen to God more carefully, because He will help us look past our self-centered desires and block Satan's deceptions and noise. Satan's deceptions and noise are generated by many sources to include entertainment, technological gadgets, and even so-called friends at times. If we do not listen to God, we are controlled in some way by Satan, the Evil One.[b] God desires to develop our individual consciences and teach each of us our assigned good works.[c] 25 If we ignore or do not hear God's voice due to our busyness, distractions, or general disobedience toward Him, it is easy to miss out on what is really going on and miss the blessings that come from living out our lives within God's will.

Even with many in a state of hostility toward God and toward His followers,[d] God stays at work in everyone's life bringing as many as possible to a place of turning from self-centered ways to Him and His righteous way of life.[e] This is biblically called repentance. God wants everyone to come to a place in his or her life that allows Him to teach them about His genuine concern and love for all, which in turn encourages many to come to Him for salvation.[f] 26 But, for those who will not listen to God, who speaks to everyone from all societies and religious backgrounds, they will be accountable to Him for ongoing self-centeredness and disobedient action and end up separated from Him forever.[g] 27

Although many listen to God enough to know the difference between good and evil, there are many who have not listened well enough to know that *our world is caught in the middle of two powerful kingdoms at war*: the Kingdom of God and the Kingdom of Hell presently ruled by Satan. God and His kingdom are more powerful and will eventually put Satan and his followers in an isolated place forever called Hell or the Lake of Fire.28 But, until that happens, God has been using Satan to force everyone to evaluate the good and evil around them and decide on

a: John 8:31b–32; Rom 2:11–16. b: 1 John 5:19. c: Phil 2:13; Eph 2:10; 1 Cor 12:18. d: Rom 5:10; John 17:14–15. e: Lev 19:1–2; 2 Peter 3:9. f: 1 John 4:16. g: Matt 25:44–46.

which life style they desire for eternity. Because all of us live out our lives doing and experiencing both good and evil, each is required to make an eternal decision. Do we want a close relationship with God and those who are listening to Him, or do we want to reject God's lordship and way of life knowing that the alternative gives some freedom from His leadership but leads to a downward spiral toward eventual eternal shame and suffering.

Satan is out to deceive as many as possible trying to keep them in the dark so that they will never know God nor His Word. God on the other hand, wants everyone to understand reality and consider carefully that He desires all to receive Him into their lives. All who want to know Him and do His will come to know reality more fully over time and with God's help become less and less entangled in sin.[a] God wants everyone to see Him for who He really is through the reality of the universe, His written Word, and interaction with Him. He illuminates our understanding through the Holy Spirit.[b] As people become aware of both good and evil, God shows them the reality of His salvation provided through His Son's redeeming death, if they have any desire to do His will.[c] God wants all to understand Him and the ultimate outcome of His Creation, which produces two final kingdoms totally isolated from each other bringing peace and joy to one and pain and sorrow to the other.

As individuals start listening to God because of His great love and concern for all, God limits Satan's attacks and starts to mold and shape His obedient children into His image. On the other hand, for those who do not, God allows Satan to continue to deceive them into thinking that they are going to have a life of eternal peace *on their own terms*. Whatever one ultimately decides determines that one's *eternal destiny*. No matter where you stand, you should take note that our world really is in the middle of a major spiritual war with **eternal consequences** and that God eventually will separate those who want to be with Him and His way of life from those who do not.[d]

If you could look ahead in time and get a glimpse of both future kingdoms in their final states and see God and His perfected family living in peace and joy and Satan and his disobedient

---

a: John 8:31–36, 1 John 3:8–9. b: Rom 1:18–2:16. c: John 7:17.
d: Dan 12:2–God rescues (*malat*) those who listen to Him; cf. Matt
25:45–46; Rom 2:11–13; Gal 6:7; Rev 20:12.

followers continually hurting one another, what would you be willing to do for yourself and others in order to live with God forever? In reality, God has already made a way for you through Jesus Christ.[a] *If you really would like to know God better in order to follow Him, you will discover that He is as good as you have heard as He reveals Himself to you.*[b] In addition, He will help you live out your life in a way that immediately starts to bring love, peace, and joy because of your growing relationship with Jesus and eventually bring you complete into His eternal presence.[c]

Spiritual Warfare in General

> From now on, *be continually strengthened in the Lord in the strength of His might*. Put on all of the armor of God in order to enable yourselves to stand before the scheming of the Devil, *because our battle is not against blood and flesh*, but instead against the leaders, the authorities, the cosmic powers of this darkness, the spirits of evil in the heavenly places. Eph 6:10–12[29]

When Satan rebelled against God, he wanted to take over God's position of authority and control. He has been striving ever since to destroy God and anyone who is in alliance with Him. *The Creation is God's work!* As He enlarges His intimate close-knit holy family, Satan has fought hard against Him and His growing family. *When Satan encouraged Israel's religious leaders of Jesus' day to crucify Jesus, instead of getting rid of the Father's only Son, he unknowingly lost the battle to separate eternally **all** of God's children from their Creator.*

God teaches us through John 3:14–16 that Jesus' death on humanity's behalf *was necessary* in order to remove sin for all those who were trusting God for help in their present condition and redemption of their souls from Sheol (Hades). As we consider the entire creation, God teaches us in Hebrews 10:4–10 that Jesus' death removed sin not only for those who were trusting God in Jesus' day, but for all who learned to trust God from the beginning

a: Rom 1:16–17.   b: John 7:17; John 3:16–17.   c: Rom 6:22–23.

of time until the end of time at the end of Christ's thousand year reign on earth as king over all rulers.[a]

From the time of Jesus' death on the Cross and Satan's realization that he had just lost the battle for the souls of all humanity, he has been doing his best *to minimize God's victory.*[b] Satan has been doing his best since Christ's victorious death on humanity's behalf to distract, placate or intimidate, and mislead as many people as possible so that they will not take the time to figure out what eternity will be like without God's presence.[c] Over the centuries, as God has been building His eternal family and filling His eternal Kingdom with holy individuals, Satan has come to realize that his time is becoming short. Because of this, Satan has been escalating his attacks in the last couple hundred years. Satan is striving to silence God's obedient children on earth, and he is deceiving those who are not following God in order to hurt those who are.[d]

This Is Personal

If you are a committed follower of Christ, have you ever wondered why some of the good things that you wish to do seem so difficult to start and accomplish although part of you knows that it should be easier? Does it seem that during the times when you want to do some good knowing that God has put something special in your heart, you seem to be swimming in molasses instead of water? If this is the case, you have experienced spiritual warfare firsthand. You may have come to realize that many of your own doubts and hesitations coupled with circumstances around you were *not* just part of the natural order of everyday life. In many cases, they were caused by spiritual warfare going on in your life.[e]

Satan and his followers are constantly traveling among all of Christ's followers looking for ways to hinder or stop completely what God has laid on their hearts.[f] As God's children pray and seek God's will for their individual and collective lives, they need to be aware–as Daniel was–that this battle is not theirs alone. Although no human can see the spiritual realm, God has

---

a: Rev 20:1–10. b: 1 Cor 15:55–57. c: Rev 12:9, 12. d: 1 John 3:7–13. e: Eph 6:12. f: Eph 2:10.

incorporated His good angels into this battle over the souls of man
to work with His obedient children on earth. God's angels are
helping Christ's followers on a minute-by-minute basis.[a] Those
who follow Christ are used by God to help rescue souls as the
spiritual battle between the kingdoms of Good and Evil continue to
the end of this Messianic Age.

This Is Ongoing

During the reigns of Darius, King of Chaldea, and Cyrus,
King of Persia, God gave Daniel visions showing him future
events.[b] We see from Daniel's vision during the third year of
Cyrus, that there was ongoing spiritual warfare just as today. One
of Satan's angels, who was in a leadership position over Persia,
had slowed one of God's angels down for 21 days until the
archangel Michael came to his aid. Michael's intervention allowed
God's assigned angel to go to Daniel and give him insight
regarding God's plans in all that was transpiring.[c] This messenger
from God stated that he was going right back to continue his fight
against the same demonic leader in Persia as well as engage in
battle against one of Satan's angels who was heading up warfare in
Greece, as soon as he had given Daniel a vision from God.[d] Satan
consistently wages war with those who faithfully follow God.

Approximately five hundred years later, we learn that the
same type of ongoing spiritual warfare was continuing. Paul stated
that Satan had slowed him down when wanting to visit and
encourage the Thessalonians whom he had led to Christ.[e] Satan is
consistently waging war against God's obedient children causing
as much stumbling and suffering as possible,[f] but if we listen to
God, He will use our trials and tribulations to build our character.[g]

Daniel's account and Paul's warning about the bad angels
who are helping Satan should be a wake-up call for all of us. This
is not a game with simple consequences. This ongoing war
between good and evil has eternal consequences for all. In
Daniel's account above, God could have helped his angels

a: Heb 1:13–14. b: Dan 9–10. c: Dan 10:12–14. d: Dan 10:20.
e: 1 Thess 2:18. f: e.g. 1 Thess 2:14–16; 3:4; 2 Thess 1:4–5; cf. Luke
16:13. g: Rom 5:3–5.

overcome Satan faster or even immediately, but He works in such a way that His angels mature and become more skilled through experience just as He works with Christ's followers.[a] Christ's followers are required to do some things partially in their strength in order for God to develop their character.[b]

Jesus did not ask our Heavenly Father to remove any of His followers from the evil of the world, but He did ask the Father to protect His followers from the Evil One in His name. Christ's followers are part of His family and will be protected accordingly according to God's Word.[c] Whenever Christ's followers fall short in any given battle or circumstance, God, who dwells in His obedient trusting children, helps them overcome whether they physically live or die.[d] 30

Spiritual Warfare & Satan's Deceptions

Do not be amazed, for *Satan transforms (disguises) himself as an angel of light*. Therefore, it is not a great thing if indeed his servants transform/disguise themselves as servants of righteousness whose end shall be according to their works. 2 Cor 11:14–15

There is a common thread to all of Satan's scheming and attacks on humanity. Satan wants to take over God's top position of authority. He has turned a third of the angels in heaven against God[e] and now wishes to keep as many as possible on earth from knowing God. The truth of the matter is that whoever is not listening to God, is in reality fighting against God whether consciously or not.[f] Jesus said, "By their finished works you will know them."[g]

If Satan can keep people concentrating on themselves and their families, he has in reality keep them from knowing God and His love for all. If people start listening to God, some will obediently interact with Him, and God will develop within them a loving trust for Him due to His love and faithfulness. Those who choose to listen to God and obey Him will eventually come to

a: 2 Thess 3:1; Heb 1:14. b: Rom 5:3–5; Heb 12:1–3. c: John 17:11, 15–17. d: 1 John 2:25–27; 4:4. e: Rev 12:4. f: John 8:42–47; Eph 2:1–3; 1 John 5:19. g: Matt 7:16a.

know Him intimately. Intimately knowing the Father and Son results in salvation through a growing love and trust for them.[a]

Prior To Knowing God

In his battle for ultimate control over everything, Satan has been constantly trying to preoccupy humanity with itself, scare humanity into submission, and/or turn humanity from God through the introduction of many counterfeit gods and religious structures. Some of these counterfeits scare people into submission and others enable people to remain self-centered living for themselves and their families.

Our world is full of Satan's counterfeits for God. First take a look at the way that the world regards God. Because Satan has not been able to remove all knowledge of our Creator from humanity, he has created a myriad of religious institutions to confuse many. In reality, these false gods and religions satisfy many through deception and help keep them away from the one true God and connected to himself. The last thing that Satan wants is for people to know reality. In addition to riches, personal aspirations, entertainment, and even laziness, Satan uses individuals and fabricated religions such as Hinduism, Siddhartha Gautama (Buddhism), Mohammed (Moslems), Joseph Smith (Mormons), and Charles Russell (Jehovah's Witnesses) to distort reality and keep people from knowing their true creator. Even with all of Satan's cunning deception, he cannot disguise his deceptive false teachings because they *all* exhibit some of his personal attributes, some much more than others. If you come to know God and His Word, the counterfeits become easier to recognize.

Self-centeredness

If Satan can keep people thinking about themselves as the center of life, he has won. Due to the sin of God's first created, Adam and Eve, all are born into a self-centered, selfish world that is in constant rebellion against God and His standards.[b] Satan uses the desires of fallen humanity against itself. If an individual is

---

a: John 17:3; 1 John 4:16. b: Rom 5:6–10.

focused primarily on himself or herself, Satan is quick to remove anything that these individuals may have heard that is true about God from the forefront of their thoughts and replace them with substitutes.[a]

Loss of Familiar

If individuals start thinking about God as the Holy Spirit leads, Satan will try hard to make their lives miserable through many circumstances including the loss of friends and outbursts of the world. Satan knows that most people like what is familiar and will not move easily into unfamiliar realms to include friendships without a good reason.[b] But for those who step out in even a little faith, God is faithful to continue to draw them to Himself. He will teach them a better way of life based on a genuine concern for all.

Worldly Success

When one considers following Jesus, he or she may encounter an even greater hurdle than making new friends. Christ will start to reshape their priorities including redefining success, which may move Satan to tempt them with additional sources of revenue. If he is able to keep them distracted with additional resources that require additional time, many will lose their spiritual connection to God, which had started to develop, and go back to following other gods including money.[c]

Satan will do anything including offering additional monetary success to some in order to keep them from making a real commitment to God. It is amazing how good self-fulfillment through elevation of self looks until one learns from God how much better His way of life is. But, if the individuals who get this far in their walk with Christ make a commitment *to deny themselves* and join God in building His eternal holy family, God will continue to shape and mold them eventually bringing them closer and closer to Jesus Christ's perfect moral image as they lead others to God.

---

a: Matt 13:19.   b: Matt 13:20–21.   c: Matt 13:22.

Following Jesus

Through the Holy Spirit's constant teaching and guidance of God's rock solid written Word (the Bible), everyone who obediently listens to God and desires to know Him intimately will do so. Those who receive God into their lives will come to know Him and His eternal plan for peace and joy starting right now.[a] [31]

For those who start following Jesus wanting to live their lives according to the Fathers' will and ways, the battles normally intensify. Satan has already lost the battle for their souls, so he now must concentrate on how many more souls will be pulled from his grasp through the individuals who have made a solid commitment to follow God's leading. Christ's followers know that they are the light of the world and that God works through them not around them. They are the hands and feet of Christ.[b] If Satan can reduce Christian witness to the world by distracting them, he knows that he still has more opportunity to keep non-Christians in the dark and away from God.

Success, a Continual Temptation

If you have dedicated your life to serving Christ, you should not expect things to get easier. On the contrary, those who follow Christ will experience many spiritual battles that translate to tangible trials and tribulations in their physical life. Satan constantly tries to keep Christ's followers distracted from praying and actively seeking ways to lead others to God. If Satan can keep Christ's followers busy with worldly activities, he is reducing their witness and thereby the number of those turning to God.

In my own life, I have had many times when I became aware of God's desire for me to do some task that would help others both physically and spiritually. It seems that without fail all type of situations would come up to distract me from doing my assignment.[c] As I look back over approximately thirty years of following Christ with a genuine commitment, I pray that I have at least produced God's desired outcome fifty percent of the time. It

---

a: Rom 6:22; Rev 3:20.   b: Eph 4:4; 1 Cor 12:13.   c: Matt 6:25–33.

is so easy to be sidetracked, if we do not stay focused on Jesus.[a] I can recount everything from simple emergency repairs on our house or cars, to immediate family needs, to some other ministry needs, or even to expansion of current ministry or work that would try to pull me away from doing the current mission that God was asking me to complete. I am not alone in experiencing this type of spiritual attack.

For some, Satan will continue to use a common distraction that transcends time. He will temp Christ's followers with additional revenue for their families, if they are willing to give up more of their time serving God. Over the years, I have seen Satan use additional income to move many of my friends and acquaintances away from ministries that God had laid on their hearts. Many had become excited about what God had asked them to do. Before they became invested in God's work, they were faced with opportunities to make additional money for themselves and their families, and normally, there was additional work attached to that money. In many cases, they chose to forego God's ministry in order to obtain additional monetary security or simply to spend more on their own desires. Satan wins when we choose additional money over accepting God's assignments. We must all be diligent to listen to God, and then do whatever it takes to accomplish His will. I know from experience that God will see us through the spiritual and resulting physical and mental battles into success, if we are faithful to Him. In His perfect timing, He will supply appropriate physical blessings as well.[b]

No Pain, No Gain

Another common deception permeating our churches today is the idea that God does not want us to work through anything that is difficult. Many of Christ's followers are led to believe that if something is difficult, God must be shutting the door to that assignment. Some of Christ's followers just do not know any better, but there is a second group within our churches that do not know Christ and therefore have no clue about what it means to deny themselves, pick up their individual crosses, and follow Jesus.[c] This group of potential followers of Christ confuse those

---

a: Heb 12:1–3. b: Matt 6:33. c: Luke 14:26–27.

who are truly trying to follow Christ because Satan uses them to make complacency and other abnormalities look normal.[a]

The norm for a true Christian is ***to be radically different*** than the World and to truly listen to the leading of the Holy Spirit. All we have to do is look at the New Testament accounts of our forefathers as they ministered in the first century and realize that most went through many trials and tribulations as they served Christ. Following Christ is not suppose to be easy, but it is supposed to be rewarding! Following Christ will not be easy because the battle over the outcome of lives is ***not*** insignificant. There are eternal consequences for our actions. Although it is difficult to follow Christ, the outcome of faithful discipleship produces godly character, inner peace, and great joy.[b]

This is where real spiritual discernment must be sought from God and gained.[c] If we keep the big picture in mind, we know that the only success that has eternal value is that which helps others to see the reality of God and His loving nature so that some will change their attitude and way of life and start listening to Him. For every person who starts following God and His ways, there is great joy with God and those who are serving Him even in Heaven.[d] There is no greater joy for us than to join God in bringing people into His eternal family, which is also our eternal family. *What an honor* to be part of God's rescue mission that brings people close to Him and us and saves them from an eternal life of shame, suffering, and pain.[e]

Meaningful Relationships

If Satan cannot sidetrack Christ's followers from doing their God-given assignments through some form of additional work or adversity, he may try to keep them preoccupied from God's work through entertainment and/or entanglement in sins.[f] In America, I believe that the most benign type of diversion from God's will is entertainment. Whether it is watching television, going to live performances, interacting in sports or other

---

a: 2 Cor 11:14–15. b: Rom 5:1–5; Gal 5:22; John 14:27; 15:8–11; 17:13. c: 1 Peter 5:8–9; 1 John 2:27. d: Luke 15:7, 10, 32. e: Gal 6:22–23. f: Heb 12:1.

recreational activities, or just staying busy with our computers and other gadgets for personal fulfillment, *too much time* is expended without developing godly relationships. ***This is a sin!*** Christ's followers learn to minister to one another and others.

Consider the cycles of work and rest decreed by God in His Word. God has given us approximately one seventh of each week–including part of six days and one full day–for relaxing and building godly relationships through social interaction. Jesus said that God's decreed weekly day of rest was made for our benefit.[a] Satan has caused many to replace meaningful periods of work and social interaction with self-centered entertainment and/or technological activity that helps one feel productive but, in reality, only keeps one preoccupied. Many are now spending unnecessary long periods each day texting, e-mailing, internet browsing, gaming, and all sorts of self-absorbing activities that are contrary to building solid godly relationships. Is this the new opium of the twenty-first century? ***Self-centered activity and entertainment are easy; working hard and building meaningful godly relationships takes effort.***

As we come to know God and His desire for our lives,[b] we begin to understand the importance of a close-knit holy relationship with God and one another. Even within everyday routines, Satan is at work destroying godly relationships through many perversions of what God created for good.[c]

Consider food. God has created food to sustain our temporary physical bodies. Satan has caused many to substitute overeating, for godly intimate relationships. Overeating is easy, building caring intimate relationships takes work.

Consider drugs. God has given us the wisdom to use certain chemicals to assist the body. Satan has caused many to misuse all types of drugs as a substitute for godly caring relationships that serve one another. The misuse of drugs is easy, building caring relationships takes work.

Consider sex. God has created sex as one of our bodily functions in order to propagate His creation and eternal family while increasing intimacy between a man and woman within a life-long marriage relationship. Satan has caused many to substitute perverted forms of sex instead of building godly intimate caring

a: Mark 2:27.   b: Titus 2:14.   c: 2 Tim 2:22–26.

relationships. Perverted sex is easy, but building a godly caring relationship between a man and a woman takes work. A godly single heterosexual relationship is the basis of a sound family structure for the proper edification of our children and in reality the whole human race. A godly home is extremely helpful in learning to love God and man, but beware, Satan is out to kill and destroy as many caring relationships as possible.[a] *Listen to God!* He will help you build solid caring relationships and move you to help the lost and hurting of our world.[b]

There Is Nothing New Under the Sun

Reverence God and keep His commandments.
Eccl 12:13b

The writer of Ecclesiastes was dismayed at the end of his life after working hard and doing much. In reality, his efforts did not amount to much when looked at from an eternal perspective. Even if we work really hard and smart and acquire a lot, when we die we leave them to others who will do with them whatever they wish. This cycle will continue until God shuts down this side of eternity. John Ortberg has written a book titled *It All Goes Back in the Box*, which portrays this concept well using the idea of winning at any cost at Monopoly to illustrate the futility of winning in this world at any cost and not taking into consideration that when the game is over, all the pieces go back into the box. No one keeps the physical things that he or she acquires when physical death comes, but relationships are eternally important.

Solomon came to a point late in his life when he realized that what really matters is our response to God during this side of eternity. Do we learn to reverence God and consequentially abide by His standards and help others to know Him, which has eternal value,[c] or do we live foolishly and end up separated from God and forfeit an eternal life of peace and joy with Him and His eternal family? Satan has been tempting humanity from the beginning of the Creation to live foolishly and end up living a life with eternal pain and suffering.

a: 1 Peter 5:8. b: Rev 3:20; John 15:1–11. c: Eccl 12:13–14; John 8:31b–32; 17:3.

Disobedience and its deadly consequences showed up soon after God put the universe physically together. God had prepared a temporary place for the creation of His immediate family, our present world, knowing that everyone would initially be separated from Him for a short period of time due to Adam and Eve's upcoming sin. God allowed the *first death* for all, which includes separation from Him along with pain and suffering during a short time within eternity, in order to produce His free-willed, eternal close-knit holy family. His eternal family will never experience the *second death* decreed for those who choose separation from Him.[a]

Shortly after God created Adam and Eve and gave them responsibility to take care of the entire earth, Satan appeared to Eve pretending to be her friend and ally and told her a very destructive lie: he told her that she would not die if she ate of the Tree of Knowledge of Good and Evil.[b] After considering Satan's statement, the beauty of the fruit, the possible delicious taste, and the idea that she would become as wise as God, she ate of the forbidden fruit and Adam followed. *Satan had clouded their thinking through their personal desires and thereby blinded them to the consequences of sin,[c] which is death.[d]*

Disobedience to God's instructions always hurts God and His people individually and as a whole. We know from looking back at recorded events, not only did humanity suffer from Adam and Eve's disobedience, but the entire creation entered into a state of ongoing corruption, ongoing cycles of living and dying with corresponding suffering and shame.[e] From that moment on until the consummation of the creation at the final judgement,[f] the world lives with sin's destructive bondage affecting everyone and everything.

If one were to think that Adam and Eve's initial sin did only minor damage, and that it took time before man became corrupt enough to perform really hurtful acts, that would be wrong. ***Sin is always destructive!*** First, consider what happened with Adam and Eve. They lost their close relationship with God. The immediate consequence was death, separation from God. In addition, Scripture teaches that sin affects *all*. Consider what happened with their first children. Adam and Eve's first born son, Cain, killed his younger brother out of jealousy. Cain slew Abel

---

a: Rev 20:14–15; Heb 2:9. b: Gen 3:2–4. c: 1 John 2:16–17. d: Gen 2:16–17; Rom 6:23. e: Rom 8:20–21. f: Rev 20:11–15.

because Abel was walking more closely with God than he.[a] If Cain would have been listening to God, he being the older brother would have been doing everything in his power to protect his younger brother. As we continue on reading report after report of humanity's action after Adam and Eve disobeyed God, we see that time after time, horrendous sin was committed against God and man. It escalated to the point that God decided it was best to destroy all humanity except for eight individuals in order to preserve the last righteous man, Noah, and his family. In saving Noah and his immediate family, it allowed God to continue growing His eternal holy family through His ongoing creation instead of concluding the creation with Noah.[b]

So where was Satan in all this after deceiving Eve and Adam, which led to their disobedience toward God placing His creation in disarray? He continued to create as much havoc as God would allow. Consider what God teaches us through the Apostle Paul: our real battles are not against one another as much as against Satan who encourages those listening to him to harm one another–especially God's obedient children.[c] The book of Job gives us good insight. Prior to the Cross, we still see Satan going all over the world looking for people to harm and to prosecute. His role seems to be both legal prosecutor and instigator of evil. He comes in at appointed times and stands before God accusing even His best children of sin.[d]

Nothing has changed over the course of time regarding Satan's destructive ways. When Satan is not busy standing like some type of prosecuting attorney before God, he continues to cause destruction within God's constraints.[e] God has always had the final say on how much sin is allowed.

As we read through Job, we see that God used Satan's destructive ways to develop Job and his friends into more seasoned righteous children. And when it was all said and done, Job's maturing faithfulness toward God–in the face of great adversity– has given every successive generation a great testimony of God's faithfulness toward those who follow Him. The Creator of the universe will more than make up for His followers' losses now and in the future as He allows His obedient children to encounter trials and tribulations that mature them and lead others to Him.[f] [32]

---

a: Gen 4:1–10; 1 John 3:12.   b: Gen 6:9–18; 7:11–23; 1 Peter 3:20.
c: Eph 6:10–12. d: Job 1:6; 2:1; cf. Rev 12:10. e: Job 1:12; 2:6.
f: Job 42:10–12.

In reality, it is true for every generation that if one does not follow God's lead, Satan will be deceiving that individual into working against God and His Kingdom.[a] It makes no difference whether one is a school teacher, a nurse, a doctor, social worker, minister, or some one else who helps people as part of his or her life work, if that individual is not living under Christ's lordship, Satan will be misguiding and leading him.

Consider Jesus' conversation with some of the religious zealots of His day who thought that they were walking with God. Scripture is clear that even though one may appear to be doing God's work, unless he or she is actually listening to God and doing His will, that individual is not part of His eternal holy family.[b] Jesus told those individuals who were claiming to serve God in His day that although they were biological descendants of Abraham, in reality, they were following the Devil, Satan,[33] which made him their father whom they were honoring through their actions.[c] Jesus wanted them to understand the consequences of following the desires of the flesh through Satan's deceptions and thereby not carefully listening to God.

When you consider Jesus' ministry and all of the good that He did, how could so many supposedly godly people turn on Him and want Him crucified? Jesus very fulfillment came from doing His Father's will,[d] yet Satan led many of Jesus' contemporaries to a place where they were blind to the identity of the Son of God and in the end even openly stated that they had no king other than Caesar.[e] What happened to God being their king? Satan is very good at deception and continues to deceive even Christ's followers today whenever they slumber.

Today, many of our local churches are slumbering so soundly that they are ignoring their most important calling, which is to proclaim the goodness and purposes of God to those who do not know Him.[f] Somehow, Satan has blinded many in our local churches about the benefit to their families and world of walking in holiness and about the benefit of walking in perfection later in God's presence forever. *Satan has somehow deceived a fairly large amount of people who go to church on a regular basis to*

a: John 8:12; 8:43–44; 2 Peter 1:4; 1 John 2:16. b: Matt 7:21–23; John 7:17. c: John 8:37–44. d: John 4:34. e: John 19:15. f: Matt 28:18–20; Acts 1:7–8; cf. John 15:1–2.

ignore God's teachings on present sanctification and future placement in either Heaven or Hell. In fact over the years, Satan has convinced many to believe another lie that is worse than the one he told Adam and Eve because its consequences are eternal. As in the beginning, he has been calling God a liar.[a] He has been teaching that God has lied to everyone, and in reality, no one will experience a Second Death.[b] Through this lie, he states that everyone goes to Heaven whether they listen to God or not.

And, for those who trust God and know from His Word that there is a real Hell and a Second Death, Satan has come up with another lie and is now trying to convince some that eternity is not really eternal. He is attempting to convinced as many as possible that the Church has not understood God's Word correctly for the last 2000 years. Being in Hell for a short period of time will feel like being there for eternity due to the suffering and shame experienced, but no one will stay forever. ***What a surprise!*** Satan is at it again. He continues to lie in order to bring about death for as many as possible.[c] He is giving as many as will receive his latest lie a false license to live any way that makes them feel good during this time of eternity knowing that doing such will eventually lead them into eternal shame and suffering. Satan tells those who will listen to live for self now and enjoy themselves at the expense of others because their isolation from God and all that is good and holy will only be for a short season.

God's Word is clear: individuals who reject Him and His way of life during this part of their eternal lives will be isolated from Him forever. Anyone who does not start listening to Him during this part of their eternal life will be isolated from God and all who choose to live with Him in a place called Hell.

In reality, Satan has been rebelling against God for a long long time and getting as many as possible to do likewise. Everyone born physically automatically has to participate in this spiritual battle in which Satan is fighting against God and must decide what type of eternal life they want; everyone has to decide whose side they will join. Whoever does not choose to follow God and His way of life presently, in reality, has chosen to follow in Satan's footsteps and live separate from God and His holy family forever.

---

a: Gen 3:1–5.   b: Rev 20:11–15.   c: John 8:44.

4

Two Kingdoms at War

From the days of John the Baptist until now, the Kingdom of the Heavens is suffering violence, and violent ones are taking it by force. Matt 11:12[34]

The Law and the prophets stood until John; from then the Kingdom of God is being proclaimed *and everyone is forcing himself into it.* Luke 16:16[35]

Everyone is trying to force their way into Heaven! Today, Satan is still at war with those whom God created blinding and deceiving as many as possible. All humanity lives in a world caught up in war between two kingdoms, God's and the rebels', whose main advocate is Satan. Satan is a self-proclaimed ruler who decided before the Creation to overthrow God and rule everything.[a][36] God does not say in His Word that Satan will remain the primary ruler when He is permanently confined within Hell. But, throughout the Creation until Christ's thousand year reign on Earth and at the end of the Creation for a brief moment, Satan rules the world, those who are not listening to God.[b] Scripture teaches us that Satan has been rebelling against God and trying to take over His position of lead authority for a long time and will keep on rebelling until he is placed permanently in the Eternal Lake of Fire, Hell.[c][37]

As you study Scripture, you come to realize that God the Father has had everything under control from the beginning. He sent Jesus into our world to teach us further revelation and then died for all at just the right time.[d][38] God teaches us that this battle between His Kingdom and the Kingdom of Hell will come to an end in God's time when the Kingdom of Heaven is filled.[e] God's Kingdom is commonly called the Kingdom of Heaven, and

---

a: Matt 4:8–10; Eph 6:12.   b: John 12:31; 16:11; Rev 12:12.
c: John 8:44; Matt 25:41; Rev 20:10.   d: Gal 4:4; Acts 2:23; 4:27–28.
e: Matt 13:47–48; 22:1–14.

because of Christ's redemptive work, it is also called the Kingdom of His Beloved Son, the Kingdom of Christ.[a]

When Jesus became incarnate and ministered among us, He brought God's Kingdom to us.[b] Jesus taught the world that those who walk in God's kingdom ways are blessed.[c] When Jesus died on a cross for all humanity, He removed sin and its consequences for everyone of all time who learn to trust and obey God.[d] [39] After Jesus suffered death on everyone's behalf, the Father raised Him from the dead to become King of Kings for eternity.[e] Through His death, Jesus won the Kingdom of Heaven its decisive battle for all eternity.[f] [40] Without the Cross, no one from His Creation would have the possibility of being with God forever and being part of His close-knit holy family.[g] [41] But now that Satan has lost that crucial battle, he is working even harder to minimize God's overall victory.[h] *Woe to those who live on earth!*[i] Satan is trying to stop as many as possible from realizing and accepting the victory that Jesus has already won for all people of all time who learn to trust God and obediently start to follow Him.[j]

As we consider our participation in the battle going on around us, we all must eventually make a decision regarding our *eternal allegiance*. On this battle field called earth, there has been and continues to be many lying tongues teaching many false concepts about the nature of the one true God, YHWH. As we discussed above, there are many non-existent fabricated gods who stand in for Satan. They are presented to humanity as substitutes to replace YHWH. *Satan uses these shadows of himself* to distort reality and keep people from knowing their creator and His desire for an eternal close-knit holy family. Information on Satan's created gods and religious institutions can be studied through books such as Josh McDowell's *A Ready Defense*.[42]

Every teaching that takes individuals away from God's Anointed One, Jesus of Nazareth, and leads them to Satan through non-existent gods, money, and fame has the ultimate purpose of keeping people on the earth's wide road that leads to eternal suffering and shame. Satan's deceptions serve no other purpose

---

a: Col 1:13; Eph 5:5. b: Matt 4:17; 12:28. c: Matt 5:1–10; 7:21; 18:4. d: 2 Cor 5:21; 1 Peter 2:24. e: Isa 9:6–7; Rev 11:5. f: Rev 1:17–18; 11:15; 12:10–11. g: John 3:14–15. h: Rev 12:7–12. i: Rev 12:12. j: John 1:12.

than to keep those who are *not* walking in God's light from ever considering and knowing God, which brings salvation.[a] If Satan can keep those who do not know God from actually examining reality, he has won the battle for their eternal souls.[43] If the world stays busy following false teachings that either terrorize, promise perfect peace now, or appeal to people's present state of self-centeredness and selfishness, Satan wins.

God's Anointed One, Jesus, the true Messiah, came to lead people into the light of knowing reality and save them from eternal separation from the one true God who truly loves them. Jesus, the Messiah, came bringing abundant life to all who listen here-and-now and for eternity.[b] [44] Jesus is the only access to our Heavenly Father.[c] If Christ's followers stay focused on Christ and follow Him, they will not be deceived by Satan and will lead many into the light to meet God.[d] [45] But, as the battle for the souls of humanity rage, we understand from God that there are many who will stay in the dark in order to do things for themselves at the expense of others and that God will not force them to change.[e]

After the Cross

> After this, Jesus knowing that everything had now been completed in order to fulfill Scripture said, "I am thirsty." . . . Therefore, when He received the sour wine, Jesus said, "It has been completed," and having bowed His head, He delivered up His spirit.
>
> John 19:28–30

Now, after the Cross, it is different. Salvation is available to all who allow God's Anointed, Jesus the Messiah, to be lord and savior of their lives. Through Jesus' death on the Cross, He won the only critical battle for all humanity. Through His death and the miracle that it produced, everyone who ever lived from the beginning to the end of time could be made perfectly righteous before God, allowing them to live with God forever as part of His close-knit holy family.[f] [46] The greatest part of the pain of the

---

a: John 17:3. b: John 10:10. c: John 10:9; 14:6; Eph 2:18. d: Matt 5:14–16; John 15:1–2. e: Matt 7:13; John 1:9–13; 3:19–20; 2 Thess 2:10–12. f: Titus 2:14; Gal 3:13–14.

childbirth of God's eternal family was over.[a] [47] ***Satan knowing
that his time was getting shorter and shorter began in a renewed
intensity doing all that he could to hide the reality of Christ's
victory over death.***[b] [48] Satan is still effectively deceiving many
into thinking that if they desire to be in the Kingdom of God
through whatever religion or life style that they choose to follow,
in the end, God will accept them into His eternal presence.
Nothing could be further from the truth! God has clearly spoken
through His Word proclaiming that Jesus of Nazareth is the only
way, the only access, into His presence and kingdom. No one will
become a child of God through his or her own will, through the
desire of family members and friends, nor through any one other
than Christ.[c]

The only way to God is through Christ, and Christ teaches
that everyone who is born again–who is eternally joined spiritually
to the Father and Son through the Holy Spirit [d]–has received Him
as both lord and savior.[e] [49] If the Church does not follow Christ
closely, then it will not give off much light and consequently will
not be a good witness. If there are not many true followers of
Christ, those who follow need to work harder to produce abundant
light. Christ's followers need to listen carefully to God who will
in-turn empower them to proclaim clearly His love for all, His path
to salvation, and the reality of Hell for those who insist on having
things their own way.

It is really important that those who have committed to
following Christ strive to act according to Christ's examples and
desires. If Christ's followers work together in a godly manner,
those who have not committed to following God will come to
know two irrefutable facts through their ***words and actions***:

(1) the Heavenly Father sent Jesus Christ, His Son, into the
world to become its savior; and
(2) the Heavenly Father loves those who follow Jesus in the
same familial way that He loves Jesus.[f]

God beseeches all of Christ's followers to walk worthy of
their place in His family.[g] Jesus teaches everyone who wishes to

---

a: Ps 90:2; Rom 8:22. b: John 17:4; 19:28–30. c: John 1:12–13.
d: John 3:5–6; 14:16–17. e: Rom 10:9. f: John 17:21, 23. g: Eph
4:1–7; Col 3:1–17.

follow Him that they *are not able* to be one of His disciples if they are not willing to:

(1) deny themselves;
(2) pick up their individual crosses daily; and
(3) follow His example of life and His unique leading for each of his followers.[a] [50]

Knowing that Jesus has completed His work of providing salvation for all and that He is the only access to God and the Kingdom of Heaven, the Church needs to seek Christ's leading, live morally according to God's standards, and allow God to teach it to love more fully.[b] [51] Whoever seeks the Father's help in becoming a more effective follower of Christ is empowered through the Holy Spirit to help in His great rescue mission saving as many as possible from Satan's influence.

God empowers and guides those who are listening to Him. Since the Cross, Jesus personally guides, protects, and empowers His followers through the *indwelling of the Holy Spirit.*[c] [52] Jesus' followers from all Christian denominations need to keep their spiritual armor in good working order, properly fitted, and *on* at all times in order to see through Satan's deceptions and move according to God's will.[d] The full armor of God is supplied by God as individuals stay in a good working relationship with Him. As Christ's followers stay in a good relationship with God, God protects.

Resist Satan

When I consider a good friend and a former pastor of mine, Dr. Mark Corts, I remember a life that was anything but easy. God teaches us through the Apostle Peter to *resist Satan* and he will eventually flee.[e] [53] Christ's followers should never flee spiritual battles because they serve the one true God; He is able to overcome all enemies. God is able to overcome anything that Satan tries to do, and He is with and in all of His obedient children.[f]

Mark Corts was a follower of Christ who resisted Satan continuously doing what he knew to be right. He constantly had to

a: Luke 14:26–27–33. b: 1 John 4:20–21. c: John 14:16–17; Acts 1:8. d: Eph 6:10–15. e: 1 Peter 5:8–9. f: John 14:23; 1 John 4:4.

deal with spiritual battles within his charge, and for the last fifteen
years of his life, he had to deal with ongoing spiritual battles
intensified by physical illness. Mark wrote a book prior to his
death entitled *The Truth about Spiritual Warfare: Your Place in
the Battle Between God and Satan,* which discusses some of his
battles and spiritual warfare in general.[54] Because of his steadfast
work in proclaiming God's Word and his resolve to do God's will
at any cost, he became an effective contemporary role model. It
was through Mark's willingness to give of himself and follow
Jesus faithfully that I came to a place in my life at twenty eight that
I was willing to do likewise. I made a genuine commitment to
follow Jesus to the best of my ability.

Under Mark's teaching, various Bible classes, and personal
Bible study, Jesus not only became my active big brother looking
out for me, but He also became *my lord* and *primary mentor.*[a] As I
looked at Jesus' life on earth, I began to get a glimpse of what He
had given up in Heaven[b] and suffered on earth in order to make a
way for everyone's sins to be removed.[c] [55] As I continued to study
Scripture, the Apostle Paul became another mentor teaching me
what faithful service looked like. Paul was willing to give up his
religious prestige and endure hardship after hardship[d] in order to
proclaim the reality of the righteousness of God[e] and His atoning
work through Christ.[f] When it was the right time, Jesus revealed
Himself to Paul and corrected his understanding of God's plan of
salvation.[g] From that point on, Paul was willing to sacrifice
everything in order to help rescue those who did not know God but
were willing to listen to the Gospel as he proclaimed it through his
actions and words.[h] [56]

Jesus did only good as He walked according to His Father's
will and He suffered greatly. Paul suffered greatly after he started
following Jesus. Dr. Corts suffered much as he followed Jesus. In
general, all who follow Jesus will be asked to give up some of
what they could have had for themselves in this world, suffering
loss in order to overcome the schemes of Satan.[i] [57] Everything that
God asks of His children helps others to see God's love and

---

a: John 8:31–32; 1 John 2:27. b: Phil 2:5–8; Heb 2:9–11. c: 2 Cor
5:21; 1 Peter 2:24. d: 2 Cor 11:22–31; Phil 2:4–12. e: Rom 1:16–17.
f: John 3:16–17. g: Acts 9:1–20; 22:1–16; Gal 1:11–17. h: Phil
3:7–21; 2 Cor 11. i: Luke 14:26–33.

compassion for all, which in turn helps some to come to their senses and ask Him for help in changing their lives to match His.[a] Everything that God asks His obedient children to do will help others to see that there is a better way of life here-and-now and for eternity. Christ's followers will be refined in the process.[58]

I believe that Satan's two most effective forms of combat against Christ's followers are deception and intimidation. His greatest deception is tricking Christ's followers into thinking that they are not worthy of witnessing, not able to witness, and/or not needed. In reality, all of Christ's followers are called to witness, enabled to witness through the empowerment of the Holy Spirit, and worthy of witnessing through Christ's righteousness working in them.[b] [59] If you fear witnessing for any reason, ask God to give you discernment and empowerment. He will help you know when and how to witness in all circumstances. There are many helpful books and videos available that discuss the various ways to *intentionally* witness to others. A few such books and possible accompanying videos are: Bill Hybels and Mark Mittleburg's *Becoming a Contagious Christian,* Bill Hybels' *Just Walk Across the Room*, and Dick Innes' *I Hate Witnessing.*[60] If you seek God to help you tell others about Him, He will empower you and show you how to witness effectively with your unique personality.

Putting on the Whole Armor of God

When Paul used the metaphor of putting on the whole armor of God in Ephesians 6 as a way to be prepared to do spiritual battle against Satan and his accomplices, he wanted Christ's followers to realize that they need spiritual armor for such. It turns out that *if His followers walk according to God's will, they have adequate protection.* Like a good soldier putting on each piece of defensive and offensive gear in order to be prepared properly for battle, they will be able to overcome with God working in and through them as they faithfully follow Jesus.

---

a: Lev 19:1–2; 2 Cor 5:17–18.   b: Matt 28:18–20; John 15:1–5; Acts 1:8.

Look at Paul's list of pieces comprising the spiritual armor that all of Christ's followers are to wear:

(1) ***truth***, which makes up a carrying belt for all of their spiritual tools;

(2) ***righteousness***, which makes up a breast plate protecting their vital organs;

(3) ***preparedness to proclaim the Gospel of Peace***, which makes them effective witnesses wherever God leads;

(4) ***faith***, which provides a movable shield to be positioned as needed to stop Satan's deadly thrusts;

(5) ***salvation***, which provides a helmet covering their heads so that they do not suffer loss of ability to see, hear, and understand what is happening; and

(6) ***knowledge of the Word of God*** through the teaching of the Holy Spirit and willingness to follow His leading, which empowers each with both an offensive and defensive sword in order to clear the way for truth to be known.

Handling the Word of God correctly through the instruction and leading of the Holy Spirit allows Christ's followers to defend themselves against Satan and to overcome Satan's deceptive practices against those walking in darkness. And last but not least, at all times staying in contact with God ***through prayer***.[a]

Even if we live righteously, study God's Word, and follow the leading of the Holy Spirit, a holy life does not mean that we will not someday become a casualty of war. Like Jesus, God the Father is working good out of our losses including our physical lives for the ultimate building up of His kingdom and holy family, which is also *our* kingdom and eternal close-knit family. God will bring good out of every pain and suffering that His children experience.[b]

Heaven or Hell?

Have you ever wondered why God does not just take each of us into Heaven and show us around and then take us to Hell and do likewise so that we could make an informed decision of where

---

a: Eph 6:10–18; 1 Thess 5:14–22.   b: Rom 8:28; cf. Col 1:24.

we want to be for eternity. When I was young, I did. It seemed that manifesting the two would be an easier way to convince many to follow Him. But, as I got older, I realized that God does not want anyone making a decision to follow Him based on *things* but instead on the eternal relationship that He offers all. Although Heaven is going to be a great place to call home, a place that will make even the best places on earth seem mediocre, God wants us to make our eternal choice of family and friends based on a desire to live with Him in a truly caring community. If we do not submit to our loving Heavenly Father and allow Him to complete our transformation into His moral and family image, we have automatically chosen Hell for our eternal home.[a] [61] What does Scripture teach about Hell?

Hell

> If an eye of yours causes you to stumble, cast it
> away; it is better for you to enter into the Kingdom
> of Heaven one eyed than having two eyes to be cast
> into Hades where the worm does not die and the fire
> is not quenched. Mark 9:47–48[62] (cf. Matt 7:13–14)

Satan has already made his eternal decision to separate himself from God and overthrow Him if possible. If Satan could kill the Father, the Son, the Holy Spirit, and all who are associated with Them, he would. But, the good news is that God is not only filled with loving-kindness toward those who receive Him, He is great and *able to maintain control.* Satan cannot change what God sets in motion, and God desires for there to be two kingdoms: the Kingdom of Heaven and the Kingdom of Hell. God is insuring that He and those who choose to be part of His eternal close-knit family have perfect love with its resulting joy and peace. He will not allow any disruptions in the new Heaven, but the kingdom called Hell will be full of agony and despair.

When we look to God's Word to understand the living conditions of the Kingdom of Hell more fully, we come away with a deeper desire to help as many as possible make it into the Kingdom of Heaven. Hell is a very disturbing and hurtful place.

---

a: 2 Thess 2:10–12.

Once one is placed there in shame, he or she stays forever.[a] We learn from Scripture that those who are placed in Hell for eternity undergo eternal pain and suffering that affects them both physically and mentally. We see metaphorical imagery depicting physical pain compared to being burned continuously by fire and an eternal worm devouring the flesh but never completing the task.[b] [63] We also see the pain of Hell as something similar to having just experienced the loss of a loved one who is very dear to you causing much "weeping and gnashing of teeth."[c] [64] There are also other metaphorical images of general humiliation, shame, and discomfort including metaphorical imagery of sleeping on a bed of maggots and using a giant worm for a covering.[d] We do not have explicit statements regarding the pain, suffering, and humiliation of being in Hell forever, but we do have enough metaphorical imagery that shouts loudly, ***"beware, stay out, pain, danger, and humiliation ahead!"***

When one rejects God, their pain and suffering starts immediately after physical death,[e] while waiting in lower Sheol (Hades) for their final judgment in God's court. All of the disobedient wait in Hades until the great judgment day at which time they will be formally charged and judged according to their actions,[f] [65] and then they will be sentenced to the *second death*, which is total eternal separation from God in a place called Hell, Gehenna, the Lake of Fire,[g] which burns forever.[h]

Considering terminology, most of our modern English translations of "hell" come from translating two Greek words, *Geenna* (Gehenna) and *Tartarosas* (Tartarus).[66] First, we learn from Scripture that Hell (Gehenna) is not the same place as Sheol, which is called Hades in the New Testament.[i] [67] When Scripture is examined, we find Sheol (Hades), as a place of waiting for the final judgment.[j]

Before Jesus died on a cross for the sins of all, Sheol was the place where *all* went when they died,[k] because everyone had to wait for Christ's atoning work. Until He came, all waited in

---

a: Dan 12:2; Matt 25:46. b: Isa 66:24; Mark 9:47–48. c: Matt 8:12; 13:42; 25:30. d: Isa 14:11; Dan 12:2. e: Luke 16:23–25. f: Matt 25:45; Rom 2:13; Rev 20:12. g: Rev 20:11–15. h: Matt 25:41, 46; Rev 19:20. i: Acts 2:27, 31. j: Matt 11:21–24; Luke 16:19–31; Rev 20:14. k: 1 Sam 2:6; 2 Sam 22:6; Ps 88:3; 89:48.

either upper or lower Sheol. Upper Sheol contained those who had come to trust God during their lifetime while lower Sheol contained those who had not.

We learn from 1 Samuel 28:15, that King Saul actually was able to interrupt Samuel's life in Sheol in order to talk with him about future events. It appears that King David had some understanding that God could and would raise some out of this temporary holding place in the future.[a] The prophet Daniel also proclaimed a future resurrection of those in Sheol with some obtaining an *eternal* life with God and some obtaining an *eternal* state of disgrace and contempt.[b] God gave further wisdom through one of David's psalms declaring that in addition to David's expected resurrection, God's Anointed One, the coming Messiah would be raised from the dead of Sheol without suffering bodily decay.[c]

The Old Testament writers knew of two areas within Sheol: the higher was reserved for the faithful and preferred over the second, which was further down in the depths of Sheol and reserved for the wicked.[d] From Jesus' promise to one of the criminals with whom He was crucified, He promised him that he would be with Him that very day in the upper area, which He called "Paradise."[e] [68] In one of Jesus' teachings, He gives us further insight into Sheol's two areas prior to the Cross: the first area contained those who had learned to trust God during their mortal time on earth. They were living with Abraham, Isaac, and Jacob without suffering as they waited for deliverance.[f] [69] The second area contained those who did not listen to God and were already living in agony.[g] The latter group is still presently waiting in lower Sheol for the final judgment at which time they will be taken out to stand trial before God and then placed into the Eternal Lake of Fire called Hell, which is the Second Death.[h]

Those who lived in the upper area, Paradise, prior to Jesus' saving death on the faithful's behalf were set free and brought into God's presence when Jesus ascended from His three days in Hades.[i] Ignatius (A.D. 37–107), an early Christian writer and martyr, said that after dying on a cross, Jesus went down into Hades alone but ascended with a multitude having tore down the middle-wall, which had been dividing God and man.[70] It appears

a: Ps 49:15; 86:13. b: Dan 12:2. c: Acts 2:22–36. d: Deut 32:22; Prov 9:18. e: Luke 23:43. f: Luke 16:22, 25–26. g: Luke 16:22–24. h: Rev 20:14. i: Eph 4:8–10; Heb 2:9; 2 Cor 5:6–8; cf. 2 Cor 12:1–4.

from Paul's testimony, that Paradise was moved into an area called the Third Heaven,[71] which God allowed Paul to visit and hear things that encouraged him, but that he dared not repeat.[a] Those who were trusting God prior to the Cross were able to finally be made perfectly righteous allowing them to be in God's immediate presence after Christ finished His atoning work. Now, there is only the lower depth of Sheol containing those who are waiting for the great day of judgment, which is coming to all who reject God.[b]

The New Heaven

> I heard a great voice coming from the Throne saying, "Behold, the dwelling of the [one true] God is with the [saved] people, and He shall dwell with them, and they shall be His people, and He shall wipe away every tear from their eyes, and death shall be no more, nor sorrow, nor weeping, nor suffering shall be any more; the first things have passed." Rev 21:3–4; cf. 2 Peter 3:10–13

Peter said that the god and father of our Lord Jesus Christ deserves to be blessed by all. He said that it was God the Father who has caused Christ's followers to be spiritually born, justified, and glorified. It was God's righteous work that made it possible for those who lived their life trusting God to have an imperishable inheritance in heaven.[c] So, what do we know about the new Heaven from Scripture?

Although He does not give a lot of detail about the new Heaven and the new Jerusalem, God gives enough information to inform all that it will make even the very best on earth of any age seem mediocre. Have you ever visited a city suspended in space or sitting on part of the earth that extends vertically 1500 miles high? With our present limitations, we feel that we are doing good to build buildings that extend upward one quarter to one half mile.[72] But what about building a city that shows the glory of God in its dazzling splendor starting with its size:[d] it is 1500 miles wide,

---

a: 2 Cor 12:1–6.   b: Rev 20:13.   c: 1 Peter 1:3–5; Rev 12:7; John 3:5; Rom 1:16–17; 8:30.   d: Rev 21:11.

1500 miles deep, and 1500 miles high. That is the outer dimensions of the New Jerusalem![a] This city is home for all of God's children in Heaven with its gates open all of the time in an eternal state of peace within Heaven.[b] The walls of the city consisting of jasper have twelve foundations made of precious gems while much of the city including its streets are made of pure translucent gold.[c] The city has three gates on each of its four sides individually made out of gigantic pearls.[d] There will be no lights, because God's radiance will illuminate everything and the Lamb will be its central source of light.[e] Wow!

The Relational Aspect of Heaven

. . . For *our citizenship exists in heaven* from which we are awaiting a savior, the lord Jesus Christ, who *shall transform our body* of lowly nature *into a similar form to the body of His glory* according to the effective working of His ability and the subjecting of all things to Himself. Phil 3:20–21[73]

Beloved, *right* **now** *we are children of God*, and it has not yet been manifested what we shall be like. (But), we know that when He is manifested, we shall be like Him because we shall see Him just as He is. 1 John 3:2

Now, what about God's desired relationship with us? We know that God has created us to be part of His eternal close-knit family, and if we receive Him into our lives as *both lord and savior*, God's desire becomes reality for us.[74] God has created each of us to be an intimate family member experiencing perfect peace and joy with Him forever.

In Jesus' personal revelation to John for His followers, we take note that in our future Heaven, God is *with* His children.[f] God does not distance Himself in any way from His children, but instead, He is right in the midst of His family. Each individual who

a: Rev 21:2, 16. b: Rev 21:25. c: Rev 21:18–21. d: Rev 21:21.
e: Rev 21:23; 22:5. f: Rev 21:3.

learns to trust God will be transformed into a likeness of His very nature.[a]

Part of being like Christ with similar resurrected bodies means that the miracle of Jesus' death on the Cross will become reality for all who learn to trust God from the beginning of time right up to the final judgement.[b] In Heaven, all sin has been removed, which began with the first man Adam, along with any propensity to sin.[c] Without sin in Heaven, there will be no more pain, sorrow, and death.[d] God's children will drink from the Waters and eat from the Tree of Life abundantly.[e]

When we consider Jesus' prayer the night before He died on the Cross as the Savior of the World, we should take special note of the fact that He stated that *He was sharing His glory with all who were and would be trusting in Him.* Through His desire to share His sonship and personal attributes with His followers,[f] [75] He was insuring our close-knit holy unity. All who become part of God's family are guaranteed perfect unity with Him, the Father, and all other family members.[g] Jesus was praying aloud so that His followers and future followers would come to understand how close-knit God desires His family.[h] [76] How close is this unity?

When we look at Jesus' journey for our salvation, it becomes apparent that He went through three changes in the process of saving us. First, the Father and He worked out a transformation from the purely spiritual to the physical realm.[i] This transformation allowed God to speak to His fallen creation on a more intimate level than at any time prior. The Son, who had been identical to the Father in nature and make-up now took on a much lower form of life culminating in His death on everyone's behalf.[j] This was a joint venture of the Father, Son, and Holy Spirit that allowed God to speak to us face-to-face.[k] A second change occurred after suffering humiliation, a terrible beating, and suffocation on a cross. Jesus took away sin for those being saved and suffered separation from His heavenly Father as punishment.[l] Then came the third change, the Father raised Jesus up in a newness of life cleansed of all of our sin,[m] in a new resurrected

---

a: Phil 3:20–21; Rom 8:29. b: Heb 10:10–14; cf. 1 Peter 3:18.
c: Rom 6:22; 8:28–30. d: Rev 21:4; 22:3. e: Rev 21:6; 22:1–2.
f: John 1:14; 20:17. g: John 17:22–23. h: John 17:20. i: spirit &
truth: John 1:1–2; 4:24; incarnation: 1:14. j: Phil 2:5–8. k: John 14:9.
l: Matt 12:39–40; Heb 2:9; 9:22; 10:10. m: 1 John 2:1–2, 29; 3:5.

form. After suffering for all humanity, Jesus would never die again.[a] Jesus took on the completed state of Creation,[b] a perfected spiritual humanity, and now is working to bring as many as listen home to be eventually completed in a similar state.[c] [77]

As we consider Jesus' physical-spiritual make-up (ontology) after the resurrection,[d] we note that Jesus could walk through walls,[e] He could change His appearance,[f] people could touch His body and feel substance,[g] He could eat food,[h] and He could ascend in that body from this realm into the very presence of His spiritual Heavenly Father.[i] The capabilities of the resurrected body are awesome transcending the physical and directly interacting with the spiritual. All who faithfully follow Jesus will have a resurrected body with their own unique personal features but similar in nature to Jesus' resurrected body. They will have the same abilities to operate in both a material and spiritual world simultaneously within the new heavens and earth to come.

We, His followers, are going to have resurrected bodies,[j] which are going to be similar to Jesus'.[k] Jesus is sharing His glory in order that we may all be an equal part of the Father's eternal family removing all divisions.[l] [78] This is why we are going to be able to be an intimate part of God's family. God has promised those who follow Christ that they will be transformed into the same state of Jesus' final transformation. Nothing will divide God's children. In addition, as socially responsible family members, each will take on their assigned responsibilities and corresponding authority.[m]

This is why Heaven is going to be so great. Have you ever considered what it would be like to live somewhere where everyone loved you to the point that you did not ever have to worry about somebody trying to hurt you spiritually, mentally, or physically. In heaven, to use an earthly phrase, "we will have each other's backs," and we will not be hiding from God because of our shame of doing wrong and hurting others (sin). We will become fully transparent no longer being afraid of what others might do in the future to hurt us, and we will joyfully serve one another as we

---

a: Heb 6:20; 7:24–25. b: Col 1:15–18. c: Phil 3:20–21; 1 John 3:1–3.
d: 1 Cor 15:1–9. e: John 20:19, 26. f: Luke 24:13–35; Mark 16:12.
g: Luke 24:39; Matt 28:9; John 20:17. h: Luke 24:41–43; John
21:12–15. i: Acts 1:9. j: 1 Cor 15:50–53; 1 Thess 4:13–17. k: Phil
3:20–21; Rom 8:28–29. l: John 17:22–23. m: Rev 3:21.

take on our assigned responsibilities. We will all be serving one another in perfected love without any sin under the lordship of the Father and Son. We will be living in a world where our Heavenly Father and Eldest Brother have saved us from the bondage and corruption of sin in order that we may experience a perfect life of love, joy, and peace with Them and one another.[a] [79]

Heaven is going to be great! It will not be great because of how great the metaphysical realm will be but because we will finally be able to know God perfectly and be in His presence forever. At this point in time, we can only imagine what it will be like to speak in casual meaningful conversations with our Heavenly Father, Jesus Christ, the Holy Spirit, and all who ever obediently listened to God over the ages. Although it seems too good to be true, those of us who are following Christ are looking forward to that day when we will actually realize our close relationship with God and one another.

For those of you who have not really committed to following Jesus up to this point in your lives, I want to encourage you to journey with me a little further and seriously consider following Jesus. Although many who are not following Jesus know that something is wrong and desire something better, Satan has been deceiving them into thinking that they cannot change.[80] *This is a lie!* God gives everyone multiple chances to turn to Him and obediently follow Him and His way of life. It is God who helps Christ's followers change.

God is worthy of our submission. If you come to that conclusion and desire to become part of His eternal intimate holy family, we will pray together to receive Him into your life prior to finishing this book. If you are already following Jesus, I pray that the rest of this book will encourage and build your spiritual resolve helping you achieve greater levels of joy and effectiveness as you continue to serve our loving Creator and all humanity.

---

a: Rom 8:21, 35; 1 Cor 2:7–9; Gal 5:22–23.

5

——

God's Eternal Close-knit Holy Family

When speaking of solitary individuals, "one" is a lonely number and that reality is valid for God's planned eternal holy family as well as humanity.[81] In spite of the many forms of life created at the beginning of the Creation, God said that it was not good for Adam to be without a suitable mate, and therefore, He made a mate for Adam whom he could relate to and share his life.[a] Similarly, we see our Heavenly Father working with His beloved Son creating a people in Their image according to Their likeness who would be suitable eternal companions for Jesus.[b] [82] A people whom the Father and Son could relate to, share their lives, and join them in their good works. They are asking all people to join them in a mature godly relationship,[c] which in turn provides great joy and inner peace. Having a godly relationship with God and others produces good works.[d] [83]

During everyone's earthly life, God lives closely with *all* as loving parents often do watching over their children carefully.[e] Yet, He cannot fully share His life with us until we mature. Similarly as adults, we cannot live on the same level of intimacy with our young children as we can with some of our adult children and mature close friends. To make a close, mature, and eternal relationship possible, our Heavenly Father is at work in a special way developing those who listen. As we submit to God's leading and holy way of life, He develops us daily encouraging us to join Him in His good works waiting for the time that He will bring us into His eternal presence.

In a somewhat similar manner, we patiently work with our children as they are developing, waiting for the day that we may obtain a close mature relationship with them as adults. The major difference is that we are happy if our children's sin is reduced

———

a: Gen 2:18. b: Gen 1:26–27 (see pp. 8–9); Rom 8:29; 1 Cor 1:9.
c: Matt 12:50; Rev 3:20–21; 21:3. d: Eph 2:10; Titus 2:14.
e: Matt 23:37; Luke 13:34.

when they mature, but God insists on total sin removal. This is the main difference between God's development for us and our development for our children. God promises all who follow His leading that He will *totally transform* their moral character to be like Christ's and through the miracle of the Cross they will enter into Heaven *without any* sin. What a miracle! Because of Jesus' atoning death, those who listen to God will enter into His eternal presence clothed in His righteousness.[a] [84]

God's Desired Intimacy

Does God seem too distant, righteous, and glorious to want a close relationship with you? Because of our sin, it is easy for all of us to consider a distant relationship with God, but to think that God might actually want to live with us in a close relationship just seems illogical in our present sinful rebellious state. It seems that if we get too close to God, our sin will tarnish His reputation and glory. But, just the opposite is true: God's willingness to work with us in our sinful hostile state shows His true nature of pure love that is demonstrated through His justice tempered with grace.[b] [85] In fact, as Jesus ministered on earth, it was common for Him to associate with known sinners. Because of His willingness to associate with flagrant sinners, His reputation seemed to have been tarnished by some who did not understand how godly love works to lift all.[c] [86] But, in the end, God's glory will be clearly seen by everyone.[d]

God's Intimate Family Follows His Will

One day when Jesus was teaching about the Kingdom of God, someone came to Him and told Him that His mother and brothers were outside and wanted to speak to Him. This became an opportune time to teach those around Him about the closeness of God's eternal holy family. Jesus asked the one who had made the request on behalf of His biological family who His mother and

a: 2 Cor 5:21; Rom 8:28–30; 1 John 3:1–2. b: Rom 5:8–10. c: Matt 9:9–13; 11:18–19. d: Rev 22:5; Phil 2:5–11; 3:20–21.

brothers were. He then proceeded to answer His own question by stretching out His hand toward His disciples and saying, "Behold, my mother and my brothers! *For whoever will do **the will of my Father in Heaven**, he is my brother and sister and mother.*"[a]

With this teaching, Jesus wanted those who were present and all future disciples to reconsider the idea of family. Although our biological families are normally closer than any other earthly relationship, Christ's followers are in reality closer to God and one another than any biological relationship. Yes, we all have a God-given responsibility to take care of our immediate family members,[b] but Jesus is teaching all who listen that His Heavenly Father is the head of all and that His followers comprise a very close-knit holy family that is closer than relatives through blood lines. Jesus is so close to each of His followers that whenever someone does something good or bad toward any, they are also doing it directly for or against Him.[c]

Eternal Brothers

This close-knit family unity is far superior to even the best family unity on earth due to our present fallen nature. There is also one major difference. On earth, there are millions of small family units. This is not so in heaven. There is one God and Father of all and one Family of God.[d] 87 Jesus said that in heaven there would be no marriages,[e] but instead, His children would be like the angels in this regard. As one studies God's Word looking toward Heaven, one notes that there are many references to brothers but not brothers *and* sisters. This is because there is no longer a need to reproduce. God's eternal family will be complete. The earthly function of creating additional children through small family units ceases. Everyone–whether male or female on earth–who learns to trust and obey God will be perfectly completed and reconciled to God as one of His sons.[f]

---

a: Matt 12:49b–50; cf. Luke 8:19–21. b: 1 Tim 5:8. c: Matt 25:31–46. d: Eph 4:6; 2:19–22. e: Matt 22:30; Luke 20:35–36.
f: Matt 5:9; Luke 20:35–36; John 20:17; Rom 8:14, 19; Gal 3:26–28.

Free-Will

Although He wants a close relationship with all, God does not force anyone to be part of His eternal family.[a] He continually works with all to bring as many as possible to a place of understanding, a place where individuals start to understand their ongoing personal sin and have a desire to turn to Him for a better way of life.[b] When our Heavenly Father sent Jesus to live among us, He provided us all with an example of His love in action.[c] After Jesus' death on the Cross, He also became our one and only *access* to the Father.[d] [88] If we learn to return God's love, we also learn to love one another.[e]

Free-will plays a strong role in God's desire for fellowship with us. God has set life and death before all people asking everyone to obey Him and follow His ways because of His genuine concern and love. God will bless both now and in the future all who listen to Him.[f] Although God desires and strongly encourages all people to join His eternal close-knit holy family, He does not force anyone to do so.[g] God gives all people the ability to accept or reject His love and authority. But, beware, a large amount of freedom does not give anyone a license to do whatever he or she wants without eventually costing everything that is worth anything.[h] [89] God is sovereign. He has the final say.

If we do not allow God to develop us into good social beings and remove our sin, He separates us from Himself and His obedient children for ever. If we do not listen to God and join Him in shedding light on His great work–*the initialization of the Creation . . . to the Cross . . . to the Consummation of the Creation in Heaven* with its perfect fellowship–we will not ever become part of His eternal family. Instead we will end up isolated from God and His family in a place called "Hell." The penalty for transgressing God and fellow man is death, eternal separation from God.[90] Any remnant of sin in anyone's life would take away from *perfect unity* in Heaven. God will not allow any divisions in heaven.

---

a: Rev 3:20.   b: 2 Peter 3:9.   c: John 15:13, Phil 2:1–11; Heb 1:3; 7:25. d: John 10:9; 14:6.   e: 1 John 4:12, 19.   f: Deut 30:15–20; Mal 3:8–10; Rom 6:22–23.   g: 2 Peter 3:9; 1 Tim 2:4.   h: Matt 25:45–46; 1 John 3:14–18; Rev 21:7–8.

Give-and-take relationships based upon social family equality require free-will within the family. Until an individual allows God to teach him or her the nature of godly love in order to be a functioning social being within God's family,[a] he or she will continue in a self-centered lifestyle. Everyone who starts to listen to God starts growing in godly love. From the moment that someone truly commits to following Jesus, he or she becomes a new creation reconciled to God and the rest of His close-knit eternal holy family forever both *legally* and *socially*.[b]

Authority: Our Legal Status as Sons of God

He came unto His own, and His own did not receive Him. *But, as many as did receive Him, He gave to them authority to be children of God*, to those who were believing/trusting in His name. John 1:11–12

The Apostle John's first point made in this Scripture is that the majority of people in general rejected and continue to reject Jesus Christ's presence in their lives as both lord and savior. John's second point is that *Jesus officially makes those who receive Him as lord and savior legal children of God*.[91]

Paul, a skilled lawyer of God's laws, who lived in a world of Hebrew, Greek, and Roman culture and thought, used similar Greek terminology stating that Christ's followers have the same legal rights as Christ Himself. In his letter to the Romans, Paul stated that Christ's followers were children of God and *fellow heirs with Christ*, who would eventually be glorified with Him. They were eagerly waiting for the realization of their *huiothesia*, "adoption as sons," and the redemption of their bodies, their purification from sin.[c] [92] In his letter to the Galatians, Paul stated that those who are chosen by God are received into His eternal family through *huiothesia*, "adoption as sons."[d] [93] In Ephesians, Paul stated that prior to the physical implementation of the creation according to God's kindness, He predestined those whom He called to *huiothesia*, "adoption as sons," through Jesus Christ.[e]

---

a: John 13:34; 15:9, 12. b: 2 Cor 5:17–18. c: Rom 8:15–17, 23.
d: Gal 4:4–6. e: Eph 1:3–6; 2:4–7.

Oneness: Our Relational Status as God's Children

> Jesus praying, "And *the glory* that you have given
> to me, *I have given to them in order that they may*
> *be one just as we are one*; I in them and you in me
> in order that they may be made complete into one
> with the result that the world may know that you
> sent me and that you love them just as you love
> me." John 17:22–23; cf. John 14:19–21

     Part of Jesus' prayer, as stated above prior to His arrest and crucifixion the next day on behalf of all humanity, gives us the clearest meaning of what our relationship will be like with God as His children. It reveals God's inner thoughts regarding the close-knit nature of His growing eternal holy family and His great love for all. If this thought seems foreign, talk to God and ask for His help in understanding this close-knit holy relationship.

     This part of Jesus' prayer gives us the clearest meaning of what our relationship will be like with God as His children. Jesus said that those who obey Him are both His brothers and friends.[a] Jesus also taught His followers that *if someone did not have any desire to do God's will, they would never really understand who God is and what He has done through His son Jesus Christ.*[b] In fact, it is only those who actually have a desire to do God's will and allow Him to mold and shape them in a godly way who will end up in His holy family.[c] [94] ***Following Jesus is a radically transforming experience*** *compared to following the ways of worldly living.*

     On Jesus' first ascension to the Father after suffering in Sheol (Hades) for you and me, Jesus told Mary Magdalene to go to His brothers and say to them that He was ascending to His Father and God, who was also their Father and God.[d] In the first-century Mediterranean world, the word "god" and "sustainer" were synonymous for most of the gods, which the people thought of as utilitarian in nature. For the most part these imagined gods were considered as beings greater than mankind who would for the most part help them through their daily life struggles. This included

---

a: Mark 3:35; John 15:14.   b: John 7:17.   c: Matt 7:21.   d: John 20:17.

such things as keeping their fires going, giving fertility to their livestock, guiding and guarding them while they traveled, and protecting them during battles.[95] Jesus' heavenly father was also Jesus' eternal sustainer just as He is ours. So what does John 17:20–23 teach us about Jesus' relationship with His and our Father?

When Jesus prayed that all people of all time who believe (trust) in Him may be "one," united with God and one another, He illuminates the meaning of eternal life and salvation declared in John 3:16–17. Jesus is praying for all who learn to trust and obey Him out of love to be united in the same special way to His Heavenly Father. When we look to God's Word for a better understanding of "oneness (unity)," we are reminded that God said, "Let us make Adam in *our* image according to *our* likeness." The Father, Son, and Holy Spirit's unity is so close that Israel considered their God, which was written in the plural form, "our gods," as *ahad*, "one" entity, one God.[a] [96] In the Hebrew language, we see the word *ahad* used to express this idea of close unity for Adam and Eve. They became "one flesh" through marriage.[b] [97] In other circumstances, Israel's men were described as coming out together as "one man" to overcome wrong and adversity.[c] [98]

It is clear from Jesus' teaching to Nicodemus that it is critical that one be born a second time. If one is to see and enter Heaven, one must be born a second time–this time into God's holy family.[d] Jesus had taught His disciples that no individual could be born spiritually into God's family through the will and/or action of man, but solely through God's will and action.[e] When Jesus told Nicodemus that God loves all people so much that He sent His Son who helped Him with the Creation to die on a wooden cross for their salvation, He was telling Nicodemus that God's love is different than the love of the World. Although God's children were in direct rebellion against Him,[f] [99] He still provided a way of peace and joy for them. His creation was rebelling against His peaceful plan for their lives and thereby transgressing Him and one another. But, that did not stop God from loving the World and making a way for all who would learn to trust and obey Him to be born anew into His eternal holy family being justified by the

---

a: Deut 6:4; cf. Mark 12:29. b: Gen 2:24; cf. Matt 19:5. c: Judges 20:1, 8, 11; 1 Sam 11:7. d: John 3:1–8. e: John 1:12–13. f: John 1:10–11; 3:19–20; 15:18–19.

redeeming death of His Son on the Cross. When Christ entered the world through the power of the Holy Spirit becoming incarnate as a baby in Mary's womb, He came to show us how to live holy lives proclaiming God's love, and then He died on a cross on our behalf. From the beginning of the Creation, God has been at work on our behalf with a plan *in place from the beginning* based on His righteous ways and effort, not man's.[a]

Jesus Shares His Glory

What is this unity that Jesus desires for all who learn to trust and obey Him? Jesus shares His glory with all who learn to love the Father and Him so that we may be united in the same way to the Father, the Son, the Holy Spirit, and one another as He is united to the Father. *John 17:22–23 unlocks the door to our understanding of all other Scripture and gives us tremendous insight into our identity as children of God through Jesus Christ.*

Through His prayer, we see Jesus asking that His disciples be protected under His Father's name thereby showing that His followers are *an intimate part of God's eternal holy family.* Jesus asked the Father to protect those whom He had entrusted to Him,

> Holy Father, *keep them in **your** name*, which you
> have given to me, in order that they may be one just
> as we are. John 17:11b

In addition to this request, Jesus declared a powerful truth to encourage all Believers throughout all time by illuminating the truth of their present and future relationship with God and one another,

> *I have given them **the glory** that you have given me*
> so that and with the result that they may be one as
> we are one (in perfect holy unity), John 17:22

Jesus' first request [b] asked the Father to be the protector of His disciples (followers) by putting them under the same umbrella that He is under, the Father's name. He and His followers are

---

a: Gal 4:4; Rev 13:8; Rom 1:16–17. b: John 17:11b.

members of God's household. Jesus asked the Father to bring all of His followers into His family as reconciled brothers. His request to "keep them in your name" *places all of His disciples into His Father's household.* As we look at John 17:22, we see ***Jesus sharing His glory*** and thereby allowing us to come into His Father's household ***with the same unity that He already has with the Father.*** With the Holy Spirit, they share an intimate godly unity under a single family structure.[a] Jesus has provided a way for His faithful brothers and sisters on earth to be fully reconciled as His eternal brothers.

The glory that Jesus is sharing with His followers stems from His relationship with the Father and His resulting character. Jesus is like His father, who is full of grace and truth. Jesus' glory as described in John 1:14 is similar to the Father's glory described in Exodus 33:18–19 & 34:6.[100] It is Jesus' sonship *and* loving character that comprise His glory and attracts individuals to Him much more than His beauty or power. His nature attracts some to Him as a multicolored spectrum radiating from a diamond or a rainbow in bright sunlight might attract some.[b]

Many fail to understand the importance of Jesus sharing His glory with all Believers. Jesus' glory is derived from His relationship with the Father and His resulting nature. Jesus was the only son, and therefore, He possessed honor and greatness, which is part of His glory, because of His unique relationship to the Supreme Authority of all. Yet, the greatest part of His glory that attracts us is His nature; Jesus has a nature that is identical to His Father's, who is full of grace and truth (cf. John 14:9; Heb 1:3).

> And now, *glorify me, Father, with your glory* that I already possessed before the world existed with you. John 17:5

When Jesus asked the Father to glorify Him with the glory that He already possessed before They created the world, He is equating His own glory with His Father's glory. He said "your glory." Jesus' family position and character are both derived directly from His Father.[c]

God did not create anyone or anything *for* His glory. God's glory is based on His eternal glorious nature and *is demonstrated*

---

a: cf. Eph 2:19.   b: Exek 1:28.   c: Luke 18:19; John 20:17.

through His creation.[101] His total character, which includes His
attributes of strength, justice, and love, contributes to His glory.
Because of His nature, God is glorious! In Isaiah 43:7, the prophet
Isaiah said that the way that God works with those who are called
by His name and whom He has continually worked with, manifests
His glory.[102] Isaiah went on to say that those who are called by His
name are His witnesses to the whole world telling others about
YHWH's (Jehovah God) faithfulness, which contributes to His
glory.[a]

If we pay attention to the leading of the Holy Spirit, we
begin to love the Father because of His righteous and loving
character; He is holy, sinless. The part of His glory that draws us
to Him, is not derived primarily from His power but from His
unselfish loving nature, which is shown in His two greatest
character traits, grace and truthfulness.[103] His grace and
truthfulness originate from His unbiased love for all. He is
compassionate and patient toward His stubborn and disobedient
children.[b] He tempers His justice with love as He works to change
our character to be like His, which God has promised to finish by
the time that we meet Him face-to-face.[c]

Through the eyes of the apostles, we can see that Jesus has
the same type of glory that His Father has,

> And the Word became flesh and dwelt with us, and
> we observed *His glory*, glory as of an only son from
> a father, *full of grace and truth.* John 1:14[104]

The very nature of Jesus' glory is easy to miss if we think
only in terms of power. Jesus' glory is like His Father's glory and,
therefore, full of grace and truth. A major clue to the specific
meaning of what Jesus prayed to His Father can be deduced from
the fact that He is sharing His glory with *all* who follow Him of all
ages with the result *that its quality enables perfect unity*. Gifts of
the Spirit such as power, wisdom, knowledge, miracles, healing,
proclamation, prophecy, and tongues would not in themselves help
us form a perfect union and are not shared equally with all Christ's
followers.[d]

The glory that Jesus is sharing with all of His disciples
enables them to live in perfect holy unity with God and one

a: Isa 43:10. b: Rom 2:4; 2 Peter 3:7–9. c: Phil 1:6; Rom 8:28–30;
1 John 3:1–2. d: Acts 1:8; 1 Cor 12–13.

another just as Jesus already lives in perfect unity with His Heavenly Father. Therefore, when Jesus said,

> *I have given them the glory* that you have given me
> *in order that they may be one as we are one,*
>
> John 17:22

we come to realize that He gave up His *exclusive* position as the Father's *only* son. Jesus is sharing His sonship and His Father's nature of grace and truth with His followers. We recognize that the very essence of Jesus' glory, which He shares with all Believers,[a] is derived from His Father's nature.

As we consider the fact that Jesus is sharing His character and position as the *only* son of the Creator with all who trust and obey God, imagine how that would have sounded to the people of the first century as they considered how much more important it would be to be the son of the Most High in comparison to being the only son of their greatest leader, the Roman Emperor. If you lived in the first-century Mediterranean world and the Emperor had only one son, you would have had a great respect for him knowing both his present and future positions. It brought great joy to all who were listening in the first century when they heard that Jesus Christ, the only son of the Most High, had given up His exclusive right of sonship and shared it with all who followed Him. He had done so in order that all who trusted God could have perfect unity with God and one another. What a wonderful part of the Gospel Message!

The Father Has No Favorites

> There is neither Jew nor Greek;
> there is neither slave nor freeman;
> and there is not male *and* female;
> because *all of you are one*
> *through Christ Jesus.* Gal 3:28

The relationship that exists between the Father and every Believer is that of a loving Father and an obedient, *only* son.

---

a: Rom 8:17; 1 Peter 5:10.

Normally, an only son in good standing receives favor and full inheritance from his father. Regarding being loved as a child, our heavenly Father treats all of His *obedient* children equally as if each one were His only son; *God does not have favorites.*[a] God has created each individual uniquely different emotionally and physically including such attributes as eye, hair, and skin color. *He has created everyone different, yet He wants all to work together in great unity.* God's unbiased love encourages us to love all people equally.[b] [105]

To fully grasp this unbiased father-son relationship between our Heavenly Father and each of us who follow Christ, we take special note that the original relationship is between our heavenly Father and His *first* son.[c] In Jesus' prayer, He says that *those who love and obey Him will be loved just as the Father loves Him.*[d] This unbiased relationship brings great joy to all obedient disciples. In this give-and-take relationship, it gives the Father great pleasure to fulfill the welfare and desires of His Son. There is great joy and glory associated with being an obedient son of the Father. This relationship is based on that of a loving father and a son *who is obedient to his father.*[e] [106]

Because of this great relationship between the Father and Jesus, Jesus is the heir to all that the Father possesses.[f] Yet in spite of what Jesus personally possessed prior to the Creation, He graciously shares His inheritance with all Believers of all ages.[g] Those who learn to trust and obey God will have this same close father-son relationship.[h] Our heavenly Father loves each of us *as if* we were His *only* son—just as He loves Jesus.[i]

The moment that we fully receive Jesus Christ into our lives as our *savior* and *lord*—which means turning our lives over *completely* to the potter so that He can finish the good work that He started in us—we begin to realize our Father-only-Son relationship. Once we are born from above, it is a done deal.[j] [107] Even in our present state of sin, we become our Father's justified children who are learning to be more and more like Christ, who eventually will be completed in Christ's likeness.[k] God tells us

---

a: cf. James 2:1–5. b: Rom 2:11–12; 1 Peter 1:17. c: Col 1:17–20; cf. Rom 8:14, 28–30. d: John 17:23, 26. e: John 5:19, 30; 14:31. f: Col 1:16; John 16:15. g: John 17:22; Rom 8:17. h: John 1:11–12; 12:36; 14:6, 21–24. i: John 17:23. j: John 5:24. k: Rom 8:28–30; Phil 3:20–21.

that when we have been born of the Spirit, He places part of Himself in us, His Seed, which is the Holy Spirit.[(a)] When we submit to God and His way, He begets us spiritually into His family and we can no longer continually . . . continually . . . continually sin.[(b)] [108] Similarly in the physical realm, we know that our children receive part of our character through our seeds (husband and wife) that are joined at their conception. In this sense, the Holy Spirit is the seed of the Father in all Christ's followers.

As soon as the Holy Spirit unites with us, we become part of God's eternal intimate holy family and our increasingly greater walk within God's eternal plan allows the World to see God working in us. Where Jesus is, the Father is.[(c)] [109] The unity between the Father and the Son is so close that if you know one of them, you have seen both.[(d)] Where Christ's followers are, Jesus and the Father are.[(e)] Jesus introduces us to a third individual who is united perfectly to the Father and Him, the Spirit of Truth. If you have seen Jesus, you have seen the Father. If the Spirit of Truth lives in you, the Father and Jesus live in you.[(f)]

The world continues to hear the Gospel from the Father and the Son through Jesus' obedient followers who are assisted by the Spirit of Truth, who is dwelling in them.[(g)] The Father and the Son working together in perfect unity have sent the Spirit of Truth, the Holy Spirit, to comfort and guide all of Christ's followers similarly to the way that the Father sent the Holy Spirit to help Jesus during His earthly ministry.[(h)] [110] *When Jesus asked the Father to give His disciples a comforter to replace His physical presence,[(i)] He was making this special Father-only-Son relationship* **immediately** *possible for all of His disciples through the indwelling and empowering of the Holy Spirit.*

Early Church Understanding

How did the Early Church receive Emmanuel, "God with us" and the closeness that God desires? Satan has been at work

---

a: Eph 1:13–14. b: 1 John 3:9. c: John 8:28–29. d: John 14:7–11.
e: John 14:23; Matt 25:40; Acts 9:4. f: John 14:16–26. g: John 13:20;
17:18. h: Matt 3:16–17. i: John 14:16–17; 16:13.

from the beginning of the Creation to keep people in general from drawing close to God. But, he works even harder against those who start paying attention to God's invitation into an eternal close holy relationship with Him. In his studies, Constantine Scouteris discovered that the Early Church Fathers had a sound understanding of God's desired closeness through the apostles teachings on Christ.[111]

Regarding Jesus' prayer for unity among Believers, Scouteris stated that the New Testament presents Christ's followers with the possibility of realizing that *Christ's communion removes in the most radical way any worldly communion*. Christ's communion is the creation of a new relationship, a relationship involving God and Christ's disciples. He went on to say that John 17 has two major themes:

> (1) the godly unity desired by Christ for His followers is not only for His immediate disciples but also for all future disciples who will learn to trust Christ through the apostolic preaching; and
> (2) all disciples participate in Christ's divine glory.

Scouteris wrote that these two points became a solid foundation for understanding God and His desired unity.[112]

From Ignatius' letter to the Philadelphians around A.D. 107, Scouteris stated that a radical change had occurred after Christ's ascension for God's children: their focus had moved from a subject-object relationship to one of *participation* with God.[113] God had made a way through Christ's atoning death for a closer relationship. When one looks at Origen's (A.D. 185–254) work titled *De Principiis*, one observes Origen teaching both a future perfection into a divine likeness and unity that Jesus had prayed for (3.6.1) and a present practical unity that expresses itself in Christ's followers being like minded in godly unity (1.6.2).[114]

In light of our early Greek Fathers, Scouteris sees God the Father as an accessible divine person who generates the Son and causes the Holy Spirit to proceed establishing a unique unity based within His kingdom. The Father has given of His divine essence to the Son and Holy Spirit and in return they respond in freedom and love with absolute obedience to the Father's will.[115] He went on to say that the Early Church Fathers could now promote unity of

God's people through the unifying force of Christ. In the person of Christ, all distinctions and divisions were and are abolished.[116]

Scouteris went on to discuss Gregory of Nyssa's (A.D. 330–95) teachings regarding the divided nature of each individual due to sin derived from self-centeredness. This divided nature due to sin deprived mankind of any possibility of living in godly fellowship with God or others. But, Christ's self-sacrifice has the potential of reestablishing God's original desired harmony bringing those who listen back into a perfect unity with Him and others.[117] By becoming a real individual with a concrete human nature, Christ, who was of the same nature as our Heavenly Father, took on the nature of humanity and transferred godly unity to the human level enabling the unity that Jesus prayed for all of His followers.[118]

C. H. Dodd having studied the terminology of being "in the Father" and being "in Christ" from a first-century Mediterranean perspective, came to the conclusion that individuals living in the first century would have understood this type of wording to denote a unity that transcends human unity, a close godly unity.[119] He said that Jesus' prayer shows a completed picture of unity for the Father, Son, and the Son's followers with love being the key. *It is love* that leads Jesus' disciples to obey His commands just as He obeys His heavenly father's commands out of love for Him.[120] The idea of "God in us" represents the most intimate union conceivable between God and men.[121] Bruce Milne, writing about Christ's twenty-first century followers said that Jesus had prayed for a unity that does not merely reflect but actually participates in the unity of God–the same unity of love and obedience that binds the Son to the Father.[122]

Fully Reconciled

Now, that we understand more fully that Jesus is sharing His unique sonship and character with all Believers, let us re-examine a passage from Scripture that paints a vivid picture of God's love. Do you remember the ***Prodigal Son*** story that Jesus told in Luke 15? The younger son left home with his share of the family's wealth and went off into a foreign land. He selfishly spent it all on himself and his superficial friends. Eventually, after running out of resources and seeing that his false friends did not genuinely care about his welfare, he realized that those who were righteous and truly loved him were at home and not in the foreign land that he had entered. ***When he came to his senses*** with the help of God and realized how good his earthly father was and how selfish most people were, he wanted to go home. He knew that he had wronged and hurt his father deeply. Because of His disobedience toward his father, he hoped that his father would at least let him live with him as one of his servants. Living as a servant for his father would at least allow him to live in the presence of a caring, righteous man and allow him to have his daily physical requirements met. His father might give him the necessities of life as a worker, but he did not expect his father to think of him as a son after what he had done.

After coming to his senses and going home out of his own free-will, what did his father do? *His father did not receive him as a servant.* Instead, he told everyone that his son who had died was alive again, his son who had been lost was now found.[a] *His father did not hold his son's past sins against him.* There was no condemnation. *With the son's change of heart, his father cleared the records of all past wrong.* **Praise God! That story applies to as many as will listen obediently to Him.**[b]

Many of us are still trying to go Home as servants because God has opened our eyes to our personal self-centered, selfish ways of thinking and our corresponding sins. This may make us feel as if we must be eternally separated from God, but praise God! He loves us unconditionally and continues to encourage us to receive Him. Because of His great love for us, our Heavenly Father has made a Way for us to come Home justified fully and glorified like our eldest brother, Jesus Christ. He is encouraging all to come to their senses and hurry Home.

God's Grace Is Hard To Believe

The Gospel is a message that brings *such good news* that many are afraid that it cannot possibly be true. But, it is true, and it

---

a: Luke 15:24.   b: John 3:17; Rom 8:1, 28–30; 1 Cor 2:9.

is *never too late* to receive Jesus Christ as your personal savior and lord. Whether male or female, when we make a conscious heart-felt acknowledgment of repentance of our sins and receive Jesus Christ as savior and lord, we are *immediately reconciled* to God as His sons with the same inheritance as Jesus Christ. God receives *all* who follow Jesus as His eternal children *with all the rights of an only child, a son.* Those who follow Jesus are not reconciled as the Most High's servants.[a] In fact, Jesus not only calls His followers "brothers" but also "friends."[b]

When Jesus agreed to share His glory with all who follow Him so that they would become "one" with the Father, Him, the Holy Spirit, and one another, He was not guiding His followers Home to be servants! They are going home as *fully reconciled and transformed sons of the Most High.* The Father has made a way for his obedient children to come Home through Jesus Christ fully reconciled as the lost son did in the exceedingly reckless lost-son account. When any of us accept God's Way home, which is through Jesus Christ, we are fully reconciled to our Heavenly Family even more fully than the *"lost-son"* was reconciled to his earthly family. To make our reconciliation and going home complete, our Heavenly Father promised that He will complete our transformation into Christ's image prior to meeting us face-to-face.[c] [123]

Are you getting a little nervous because God is calling as many as will listen into His close-knit holy family? Being part of God's intimate eternal holy family places one into a mutually close relationship with the Father. It sounded like heresy to Israel's religious leaders in the first-century when Jesus told them that He was God's son, because by proclaiming to be His Heavenly Father's son, He was proclaiming to be a member of God's immediate family. He had made Himself equal in family membership to the Father.[d] [124] The religious leaders considered our Heavenly Father a father in name only.[e] They knew that Jesus was saying that God was his literal heavenly father. Later the same religious leaders said that Caesar was their only king.[f] Jesus is literally God's son and that makes Him equal in relational stature although not in authority to God the Father. Those who follow Jesus also become literal sons of God, and therefore, become equal

---

a: Gal 4:7. b: John 15:12–15. c: Phil 1:6; 1 John 3:1–2. d: John 5:18. e: John 8:41. f: John 19:15c.

to the Father in relational stature as family members ***under*** His authority.[a] [125] As stated above, there will be a day when we will meet our Creator face-to-face and begin a full mature relationship with Him and all other individuals who follow Jesus Christ.[126]

Does it look like the deeper we dig, the more we have taken away from God's glory by our up-and-coming mature and intimate relationship with Him? No, the deeper we look, the more we realize how gracious our Heavenly Father is in making us equal family members with Jesus and Himself. Knowing that we are far from perfect makes it very difficult to accept this pure love-relationship with Him that is based on equal family membership. God's planned and perfect holy relationship with us leaves *nothing to separate us from Him* in the future when all sin is removed from our individual lives and we stand before Him clothed in the righteousness of Christ.[127]

Most of us are intimidated easily and would have a hard time even communicating with some national figure much less with the Most High. Yet it is true, God is calling all who listen to Him into a pure, mature relationship with Him and one another because of our current ongoing close relationship with Jesus Christ, our big brother.[b]

If we become whole and complete like Christ as an equal member of our Heavenly Father's family, surely we will lose our awe and reverence for the Father, the Son, and the Holy Spirit. ***ABSOLUTELY NOT!*** Jesus tells all that He has made a way for His followers to come Home as fully reconciled and transformed brothers similar in nature to Him. He said that He wants His followers to be "one" with the Father and Him just as He is "one" with the Father. When we begin to understand that the main purpose of the Creation and the Cross is to create an eternal close-knit holy family for the Father, Son, Holy Spirit, and one another, we should receive God into our lives and submit to Their lordship. We along with our other family members should eternally love, praise, and obey the Father and Son.

Christ' followers will have gone through God's refining process to become complete with God's grace and truth embedded in them. They will never turn against God as Satan and one third of the angels did. Christ's followers are being matured to have great

a: John 10:34–36; 20:17.   b: Rom 5:1–5; 1 John 2:28.

grace and truth as Christ in addition to sharing His inheritance and excellent name.[a]

God is going to finish the good work that He has started among those who learn to love, trust, and obey Him. Jesus has a proven track record.[128] Just look at His ongoing obedient, mature relationship with our Heavenly Father. Looking at Jesus' actions and words gives His followers great confidence that they can also live without anything separating them from a holy, full-time, and caring relationship with God and one another.

Everyone needs to consider carefully the wonderful gift of love and life that God offers through Christ Jesus. God's Anointed One, the Messiah, has *fully* and *eternally* reconciled all of His followers and all who were trusting God prior to His earthly ministry to the Father and one another. Those who learn to trust God, which includes following His Sent Son, will be completely transformed into God's righteous image. **Yes!** *God's reconciled children are equal with Him in family membership status,* but equality in membership *does not mean* equality in authority, responsibility, ability, nor power.

If someone does not learn to trust and obey God out of a returned love, *they will remain the children of disobedience,* the Devil's children. Satan's children will all be eternally separated from our loving creator and father.[b] [129] The more fully that one understands God's love for all and knows His qualifications for being our savior and lord, the easier it becomes to submit fully to His authority. Our heavenly Father loves us deeply and so does our eldest brother Jesus Christ, who is the Father's appointed savior for all who learn to trust and obey Him.

Knowing that Jesus willingly shares His position as the "only son" of God with all who submit to Him as lord and savior should motivate everyone to joyfully follow Jesus out of heart-felt love. With family membership, Jesus' followers join God in the creation of His eternal close-knit holy family. For those who join God for eternity as intimate members of His holy family, *they experience great joy on earth* as God leads bringing as many as will listen into His marvelous presence and light.

---

a: Heb 1:1–4; Rom 8:17.   b: John 8:34–47; Rev 20:11–15; 21:8.

6

Jesus Is Lord As Well As Savior

You (Jesus' disciples) are proclaiming me, *"**the**
Teacher and **the** Lord,"* and you are speaking
correctly, for I am. John 13:13; cf. Luke 6:46

Have you ever considered that our most faithful teacher
was also active in creating each and every one of us? Through the
Father's guidance, Jesus Christ put the entire universe together.[a]
This great teacher and leader is the Son of the living God,[130] who
works in His followers in perfect unity with the Father and Holy
Spirit.[b] Jesus teaches His followers truth (reality) so that they may
mature and become free from the bondage of sin, which originates
from self-centeredness and selfishness.[c]

Jesus Christ is *not* just another good man. Jesus Christ is
not just another great prophet. Jesus Christ *is* the son of the Living
God who worked in close unity with His father putting together the
total Creation including the heavens, earth, and humanity.[d] [131]
Jesus is the force who is literally holding the Creation together.[e]
The Father has appointed Jesus Christ, our Eldest Brother, to lead
us *for eternity*.[f] ***Jesus is lord as well as savior!***

Jesus' Farewell Discourse and Prayer

Jesus' farewell discourse and prayer is different in one very
important aspect from all other leadership farewells recorded in
God's Word. In His farewell discourse, *Jesus never relinquishes
His authority to a successor.* After completing His last supper with
them, Jesus speaks to His disciples before going to the Cross. He

---

a: John 1:1–3. b: John 14:23. c: John 8:31b–32; 18:37. d: Matt
16:13–17; John 1:3,10. e: Col 1:16–17. f: Eph 1:19–21.

knows that He is responsible to continue teaching and leading all who are willing to learn to trust and obey Him. John gives us this account of Jesus' commandments and exhortations to His disciples and His requests to the Father for His disciples of all ages as recorded in John 13–17. Let us compare Jesus' farewell discourse to other farewell discourses recorded in God's Word.

The practice of commandment, exhortation, and prayer for one's loved ones at the point of death is a well-attested practice. Being responsible for the lives of their loved ones, the dying authority figure passes on his most valuable thoughts and concerns to those who will follow him. Before a final prayer or blessing, the last set of instructions and exhortations normally includes confirmation of the individual who will assume responsibility for the guidance and care of the family or nation. Examples from the Bible include: Isaac's blessing of Jacob;[a] Jacob's commandments and blessings to his sons and their families who became known as the nation of Israel;[b] and Moses' exhortations, commandments, and prayer for the blessing of each tribe of Israel.[c] In the Gospel of John, we see Jesus engaging in the same type of action. In His farewell discourse, Jesus gives His disciples one new commandment, "Love one another just as I have loved you."[d] He also exhorts and encourages, "Let not your heart be troubled, for we (Jesus and the Father) will come to you through another Comforter, the Spirit of Truth."[e] [132]

The *major difference* between Jesus' farewell discourse and prayer and all of the other biblical farewells is that *Jesus never relinquishes His authority* as the highest leader of the Church to another individual. Although dying leaders normally appointed new leaders to take their place, Jesus deliberately did not appoint a new leader, because He expected to become the **risen** Lord in just three days. Indeed, He knew that after His ascension, He would continue to teach and lead His people through the Holy Spirit, the Spirit of Truth. Jesus said,

> I shall not leave you orphans; *I am coming to you.*
> Yet a little while, and the world will no longer
> observe me, but you (pl) will observe me; *because I*
> *am alive, indeed you shall live also.* In that day you

---

a: Gen 27:2, 27–30. b: Gen 48–49. c: Deut 1–4, 32; 5–31; 33.
d: John 13:34; 15:12, 17. e: John 14:1, 16–17.

will know that I am in my Father, and you in me, and I in you . . . 26 *But the Comforter, the Holy Spirit, whom the Father shall send in my name, He will teach you all things, and He shall remind you (about) all that I spoke to you.* I am leaving peace for you; I am giving you my peace; not as the world gives do I give to you. Let not your heart be troubled nor afraid. John 14:18–27

Jesus Christ Is the Son of the Living God

Our eldest brother *is* the Son of the living God.[a] He is working in perfect unity with the Father. Yes, Jesus Christ is *not* just another good man *nor* is He just another great prophet. ***Jesus Christ is the son of the Living God*** who helped His father create this *temporary* world in order that ultimately They would create an enlarged eternal close-knit holy family.[b] We can learn a lot about our savior and His great qualifications to lead us through Paul's letter to the Colossians. Look at what God teaches us through Paul.

Jesus Christ is the ***Beloved Son*** of the Father who has redeemed us from our sins.[c] Jesus is loved very much by the Father. Jesus is the ***Image of God*** who cannot be seen with human eyes,[d] [133] yet we can see the Father's nature by observing Jesus.[e] He is the ***Firstborn (Eldest)*** having the rights of the firstborn over every creature,[f] [134] yet He shares His rights with every one who trusts God.[g]

Jesus is the ***Master Craftsman***,[135] creating all things seen and unseen in Heaven and on Earth. We were created through Jesus for fellowship with Jesus.[h] [136] Jesus is the Word,[137] the Origin, the Source, from which the Creation came.[138] Jesus was before all,[139] ***the Eldest***, and it is *through Him* that all things continue. Literally, Jesus has built the universe and all that is in it and holds it all together.[i]

Jesus is the ***Head*** of the Body, the Church,[j] [140] and sits at the right hand of the Father in power forever.[k] Jesus is the

---

a: Matt 16:16. b: John 1:3, 10; Heb 1:2. c: Col 1:13–14. d: cf. John 14:7; Heb 1:3. e: John 12:45; 14:9. f: Col 1:15. g: John 1:14; 17:5, 22. h: Col 1:16. i: Col 1:17. j: Col 1:18; 1 Cor 12. k: Eph 1:20–21.

beginning of resurrected life, the ***Firstborn from the Dead***.
Because Jesus is the first, the oldest son, and continues to obey our
Heavenly Father faithfully, He has the greatest eternal
responsibility and corresponding authority over all matters.[a]

Jesus is the ***Sinless Reconciler***, reconciling us and *those in
Heaven* to the Father through the Cross.[b] [141] Prior to the Creation,
our Heavenly Father and Jesus Christ agreed together to make an
atonement for our disobedience.[c] [142]

The Father sent Jesus Christ to die on the Cross potentially
for all people, and then He raised Jesus from the dead and set Him
over all powers and authorities in Heaven and on Earth forever.
Today, this same Jesus delivers all who come to trust and obey
Him from the destructive plotting of the Evil One, Satan, the Devil
who was a murderer and liar from the beginning.[d]

Jesus *is* the Son of the one true living God.[143] During Jesus'
earthly ministry, many Jewish leaders *ignored* His identity and
rejected His authority *because of their hardened hearts toward
God.*[144] Their hearts had become hardened as they took matters into
their own hands and stopped listening to God. They would not give
up control over their fellow man, which they had wrongfully
taken.[e] Therefore, the Father removed all of their responsibility
and corresponding authority including that which He had
originally given them.[f] [145]

Throughout the centuries following Jesus' earthly ministry,
many have continued to *ignore* His identity and *reject* His
authority because of hardened hearts. Those who hear and receive
Jesus Christ hear and receive the Father. Those who hear and
receive Jesus' disciples hear and receive Jesus.[g] [146] The Father has
and is speaking to all who listen through Jesus, and presently Jesus
is speaking to all who listen through the Holy Spirit, Scripture, and
His Body, the Church.[147]

Jesus Alone Is Savior Providing Access to the Father

When Jesus said that He is the Way, the Truth, and the
Life, and that no one is able to appear before the Father except

a: Col 1:18; 1 Peter 3:22. b: Col 1:19–20; 2 Cor 5:17–21. c: Acts
2:23; 3:18; Rev 13:8. d: John 10:10; Rom 10:13; John 8:44. e: Matt
21:33–39. f: Matt 21:43. g: Matt 10:40.

through Him,[a] the Sent Son was making it perfectly clear that eternal life with the Father only occurs for those *who are in close association with Him*. Jesus made it clear, while teaching about the Kingdom of God, that those who did not receive God into their lives would never enter into His eternal presence. In one of His sermons on a mountain, the apostle Matthew tells us that Jesus stated emphatically that on the Day of Judgment there will be many who will say that they had called Him "lord" and had done many things in His name. Yet, they had never really started obediently listening to His Father nor following Him. They had never really started following His will for their lives. For those individuals, Jesus will declare, "I have never known you; depart from me you who have been working contrary to the Law (the Word of God)."[b] [148]

The apostle John not only remembered Jesus saying that He was the *only way* to God, but he also remembered Jesus using the metaphorical image of being *the one and only* "door" declaring that He was the only point of access to the Father.[c] [149] Jesus taught His disciples that those seeking a relationship with God must come through Him in order to be saved,

> *I am __the__ door!* It is through me that if someone enters, he shall be saved—indeed he shall come and go and find pasture. John 10:9[150]

Jesus taught that the way to God included **obedience** and **corresponding effort** on the part of individuals. If one follows the normal course of building their own security without paying attention to God, they are *in reality* following the broad road that leads to eternal shame and suffering void of God's eternal presence. When individuals listen to God, He teaches them how to build an eternal future of great worth in His eternal Kingdom.[d] Obedience to Jesus' leading is the *one and only* path that leads to eternal life with God, because Jesus is metaphorically both *the only* "gate" and *the only* "door" leading into the Kingdom of Heaven.[e] God tells us this same truth through the apostle Paul as Paul teaches the Gentile Believers that they and their Jewish brothers and sisters in Christ have the same access to the Father,

---

a: John 14:6.   b: Matt 7:21–23; 12:50; cf. Rom 2:11–16.   c: John 10:17.   d: Matt 6:31–34.   e: Matt 7:13–14; Luke 13:24; John 10:7.

which is *through Christ* and was finalized through Christ's redeeming work on the Cross.[a] [151]

Although our redemption cannot be attributed directly to our activities because none of us perfectly live out our lives according to God's moral standards nor do His will perfectly, it does depend on our commitment to do His will. God wants us *to want to listen to Him* because of His love and faithfulness toward all.[b] For those of us who listen to Him, we are commanded to strive to walk in His will according to our noble calling and do those good things that He has assigned to each of us prior to forming the physical world.[c] [152] In order to be part of God's eternal family, we are told that God wants us to participate with Him while living on earth. We must get to know both the Father and Son personally through our continual communication (prayers) and obedient actions.[d]

To walk with Christ requires effort! Prior to doing God's will, one must make a conscience decision to put God first. In fact, Jesus says that unless we are willing to put God first and even deny ourselves as the center of our own lives, we *cannot* be His disciples.[e] If we are truly going to be considered a follower of Christ by Christ, we must:

> (1) freely deny ourselves in the sense of giving up our right to remain lord over our own lives;
> (2) pick up our individually assigned crosses each day making an effort to expose Satan's deceptions and declare God's love through our actions and words; and
> (3) actively follow the will of the Father and Son.[f]

Each follower of Christ must willingly give everything back to God, the originator of all, and be willing to own everything collectively with Him.[g] [153] This does not mean that Christ's followers own nothing personally on earth, but it does mean that they cannot hold onto things disregarding God's will. What each follower owns personally with God should be directed by God, who is the true provider for all. Each individual who has any desire to follow Jesus must make a conscious decision to follow Jesus on His terms in order to be empowered as a follower.

---

a: Eph 2:18. b: Matt 7:21; John 7:17; 14:23; Rom 3:28. c: Eph 2:10; 4:1–3; Rom 2:11–13. d: John 17:3. e: Luke 14:26. f: Luke 14:26–33; Matt 16:24; Mark 8:34–35. g: Rom 8:17.

When Paul speaks of being in close association with Jesus, he commonly uses the phrase of being "in Christ."[(a) 154] If one were seeking justification by "doing the works of the Law" without having faith in the Messiah, that one would fail. Scripture is clear that no one has perfectly followed God's will and ways,[(b)] and therefore without Christ, everyone would stand guilty in God's court of law. The consequences of failing to live a perfectly righteous life is death,[(c)] an eternal separation from the Family of God, in order to keep perfect peace within the Family of God.[(d)] But, the Good News, the Gospel, proclaims that God Himself provides redemption from sin for all who learn to trust Him through His own righteous work on humanity's behalf.[(e)]

In Galatians, Paul makes it clear that those who are trusting God and His righteous acts on their behalf are in close association with Christ. They are "in Christ."[155] Paul states that those who are "in Christ" including the Gentile followers[(f)] are in such close association with Jesus that it is as if they are wearing Christ as their clothing.[(g)] Being in close association with Christ means that no dividing barriers are allowed among His followers. In addition, all of His followers are going to receive the promise made by God *to Abraham's descendants*.[(h)] Christ's followers are justified before God through Christ's atoning death and are continually fulfilling the righteous requirements of the Law through Christ by learning to love their neighbor through the leading of the Holy Spirit.[(i) 156] The true People of God are "in Christ" and learning to bear one another's burdens through the leading of the Holy Spirit.[(j) 157]

In his letter to the Saints living in Rome, Paul taught that those who are "in Christ" will be glorified at the end of this age with Christ as sons of God.[(k) 158] As he started bringing this letter to a close,[(l)] Paul put it this way, "And you (pl.) do not owe anything to anyone except that you are to love one another; for the one who is loving another has fulfilled the Law."[(m)] Love does no harm. Paul encouraged the Roman Saints to follow God's moral guidelines that were given to Israel over fifteen hundred years earlier on Mount Sinai. Then Paul concluded by saying that the

---

a: Rom 3:24; 6:11; 8:1–2; 12:5; etc.   b: Rom 3:23.   c: Rom 6:23; Gal 3:10.   d: Rev 21:27; 22:15.   e: Rom 1:16–17.   f: Gal 3:14.   g: Gal 3:27.   h: Gal 3:18, 28–29; 5:6.   i: Gal 5:14–18; 6:12.   j: Gal 5:16; 6:15–16.   k: Rom 8:1, 14–17.   l: Rom 13:8.   m: cf. Matt 22:37–40.

one who truly is learning to love is not working evil toward his or her neighbor, because love is the fulfillment of the Law.[(a) 159]

When he wrote from his imprisonment in Rome around A.D. 62,[160] Paul taught the Believers at Philippi to live out their lives "in Christ" with great humility considering how Christ humbled Himself in order to serve humanity.[(b) 161] In Philippians 2:1–2, Paul gave some of the desired attributes of those who are in close association with Christ by asking the Philippians *to fulfill his joy by being of the same mind, having the same love, and being united in life.* Paul went on to tell Christ's followers at Philippi that although he was formerly walking as a Pharisee "according to the righteousness that is in the Law," he gladly gave it all up "not holding onto his righteousness derived from (works of) the Law," counting it all as rubbish in order that he might gain the righteousness that comes from God, which is "based on faith."[(c)]

In Ephesians, which was written approximately the same time as Philippians, Paul addresses some of Christ's followers in Asia using the same terminology, "in Christ," to denote their close association with Christ.[(d) 162] The mystery of God has been revealed through God's redeeming work through Christ. Everyone in close association with Christ, *both* Jew and Gentile, are joint heirs of God's promise to Abraham.[(e) 163] For those in Christ, Jesus' death on the Cross has effectively removed the ongoing hostility that existed between the Jew and Gentile for centuries.[(f)] In the coming ages, the surpassing richness of God's grace will be shown to those who are "in Christ."[(g)] Similarly, Christ is also in a very close relationship with His heavenly father. With this in mind, Christ's followers are to be kind, tender hearted, and forgiving toward one another.[(h)] In reality, Christ's followers are God's "workmanship having been created *in Christ Jesus* for good works."[(i)] Although "good works" are continually being completed by Christ's followers, no one receives salvation through them because salvation is a gift of God.[(j)]

---

a: Rom 3:31; 13:10. b: Phil 2:5–8, 12–16; 3:20–21. c: Phil 3:2–11. d: Eph 1:1, 3, 10, 12, 20; etc. e: Eph 3:6. f: Eph 2:13–16. g: Eph 2:7. h: Eph 4:32. i: Eph 2:10. j: Eph 2:8–9.

Peace, Joy, and the Holy Family of God

Come to me all who are laboring and are burdened,
and *I will give you relief.* Take up my yoke upon
yourselves and learn from me, because *I am gentle
and humble in heart*, and you will find relief for
your souls. For *my yoke is merciful and my burden
is light* (easy to bear).[164] Matt 11:28–30

So, what does it mean to be "in Christ" and a household
member of the family of God? Because God truly cares for us, He
asks us to give Him our anxieties, trading our heavy burdens for
lighter loads. There is peace and joy for every individual who
allows the Creator to be part of his or her life as both lord and
savior.[a] For those who accept Jesus' salvation and lordship, it is
Jesus Himself who is yoked with them making sure that the load is
not more than they can bear. God will not load anyone with
ambitions toward building self-centered empires. Jesus Christ will
guide His followers into building what really counts for eternity:
caring holy relationships between God and man and between man
and man. God teaches all who learn to love Him that there is
something much greater than self, a pure non-selfish
interrelationship with God *and* other obedient members of His
family. Jesus leads us through learning experiences that transform
our lives forever. He teaches us to love all people, and we learn to
live as intimate holy family members of God ministering to all.[165]

Families are social units that should provide proper
development and support. The family's primary role is to provide
each new member of society, the child, with its core training in
social skills and moral behavior. This training becomes part of that
member's very being, their "self." A proper family continues to
provide support for its members throughout all phases of life.

A biblical family structure on earth is suppose to be similar
to God's eternal family structure. A husband is the head of the
family and should love his wife as Jesus loves the Church, which
means that a husband should learn to love his wife to the point of
being willing to lay down his life to save her.[b] A husband must

a: Luke 6:46–49; John 15:8–11; 17:13, 23; Rom 5:1–5. b: Eph 5:25.

learn to consider his wife's welfare as important as his own. Although the husband is the head of the family, he is never a dictator just as Jesus is lord but never acts as a dictator. Men must allow free-will to work within their families just as God allows free-will to influence all humanity. Free-will brings some pain, but when mutual love is at work, great joy and peace between those participating become reality. A husband and wife should interact in a mutually beneficial way building their family–just as God works with all creation working with those who will listen building our eternal family with mutual effort.

In response to her husband's love, a wife is to submit to the authority of her husband and help him in every way possible. The husband is the head of his wife as Jesus is the head of the Church.[a] [166] Jesus put his love for us into action. He died for us and *continues* to lead us! Although wives are to submit to the authority of their husbands, they are not inferior to men in any way. God tells us clearly that all men and women of all nationalities and walks of life are equal to each other through Christ.[b] [167] Christ has made us *free* and *equal* **through the Cross**. Let us view our freedom as an opportunity to serve God and one another caring for all.[c] [168]

The family of God is continually developed and directed through Jesus Christ in accordance with our Heavenly Father's will. Of course, there are rules for members of God's family just as there are rules in any social or business organization. Order originates from God, chaos from Satan. There cannot be peace in any organization without some form of order including levels of authority. We cannot have completeness–neither individually nor corporately–with its accompanying joy and peace without allowing God to develop us for present good and our future place in His family.[169] If we listen to God, He will prepare us to take our individual positions within His family. We all have been created with beneficial gifts for the entire family. As we become people of grace and righteousness, God is able to incorporate us more fully in helping to build His eternal kingdom and family.

If we are "in Christ," we *are presently, right now,* children of God and have been called into a fantastic relationship with God and Christ's followers. We *are* loved by the Father just as Jesus is loved, and we are coheirs with Him in everything.[d] Yet, we are

a: Eph 5:22–29. b: Gal 3:26–29. c: 1 Peter 2:16. d: Rom 8:14–17; 1 Peter 3:7; Rev 21:7.

clearly not equal with Jesus in authority, responsibility, nor power: Jesus has more responsibility than any of us, and He *is* our lord forever. Let's remember that Jesus helped create and save us, continually guides us, and is our good and perfect eldest brother.

As we learn to trust and obey God, Jesus shares some of His responsibility and authority with us.[a] We learn to work with Him in many ways ministering to people in our communities and all over the world. God does not call all people into full-time ministry, but He does ask *all* people to join Him in *being light to a darkened world*. Those who are following Christ are to help those who do not know God know Him. If we are committed to following Christ, our Heavenly Father gives us the resources, talent, and frame of mind to carry out the good works that He established from the beginning.[b] [170] The part of our work that has eternal value is that part that helps others spiritually know God better and thereby overcoming the deceptions of Satan. God's work through Christ's followers allows those who are not working with God to see His goodness at work. Whatever good work God has set in place for you personally, feel assured that He has also provided abundantly the empowerment, resources, talent, and frame of mind needed for you to complete your assigned work.[171]

Whatever your relationship is to God, be on the alert, because Satan is the father of lies and deception, who sometimes even works through individuals disguised as Saints.[c] [172] Whether you are aware or not, Satan is out to destroy you personally. If you are striving to follow Christ, Satan is trying to keep you separated from other like-minded followers in any joint ministries that God may have for you. Satan knows that if he can keep God's children divided, he has a much better chance in reducing their effectiveness.[173]

But, if you are one of the many who have *not* made a commitment to follow Jesus yet, I want you to consider carefully what you have learned and pray that God will help you come to the place of knowing Him well enough to step out in faith and start following Jesus. As you read further, ask God to help you see through Satan's deceptions and beyond your own self-centered world view far enough to come to the place that you know Him

---

a: 1 Peter 2:9; Acts 1:8; Rev 3:21. b: Eph 2:10; Titus 2:14. c: 1 Peter 5:8.

well enough to trust Him with your life. Ask Him to help you come to the place that you know Him well enough to truly turn your life over to His leading. God is truly worthy of our loyalty and obedience considering that He:

> (1) wants the best for all;
> (2) loves Christ's followers just as He loves Christ; and
> (3) is able and willing to mold and shape each of Christ's followers into the perfect sinless nature of Christ keeping His designed uniqueness intact for each.

If you are willing to follow a loving Creator, ask Him to reveal Himself to you. ***His nature is glorious!***

7
―
Scripture & Church Organization

Does it really make a difference in the way that churches decide to organize? The answer is yes. Some church hierarchies are organized in ways that allow Jesus to lead His overseers more fully while others quench the Spirit and become very rigid. First and foremost, the local churches and the Church universal are part of the same family. Christ's followers are the Family of God. Yes, there is flexibility within Scripture for Gods' family structure, but local churches should organize to operate as a part of the Family of God with Jesus Christ being the head.

This book does not intend to give a history of how churches organized over time, but instead, it shows the basic organization that Jesus left in place through His first-century apostles. It is always good for all churches to look occasionally at the simplicity of Jesus' organization model and reconsider their own structures in light of His design. Godly understanding starts by examining God's Word.[a]

Scripture: The Word of God

Originally, the Church of Jerusalem was the final earthly authority on what God's Word meant. If there were theological questions, church officials could ask the leaders in Jerusalem the meaning of Scripture and the general will of Christ for His Body. The leaders in Jerusalem were not official heads of state over the many local churches springing up all over the world in either a micro or macro management style. The Apostles individually and collectively offered encouragement and correction to the local churches springing up everywhere. *Jesus Christ was and still is the active head of the Church, which is comprised of all local churches!*

---

a: God enlightens and empowers His followers of all ages.

At the time of Jesus' death, Scripture, which consisted only of the Old Testament, was being understood through the teachings of Jesus. Jesus' closest disciples knew what Jesus had taught and how He interpreted Scripture. After His death, resurrection, and forty days of additional teaching, Jesus's disciples continued to teach Scripture through an understanding that was derived from Jesus' teachings.

In addition, after Jesus' ascension, Paul personally encountered the risen Jesus, turned from his old way of life, and started to follow Him.[a] God used Paul and his past study of Scripture[b] combined with the new revelation from Jesus to teach many the meaning and practical application of the Old Testament. Others such as Luke learned from Jesus' disciples and accurately wrote down what Jesus had taught and how He was leading His Church toward the completion of the Creation bringing as many as would receive Him into God's family.[c]

It did not take long after Jerusalem fell to the Romans in A.D. 70 for local churches all over the world to seek copies of the writings of Jesus' closest disciples, Paul, and others such as Luke to study and gain understanding of God's Word, the Old Testament. Within a short time, prior to the end of the first century, the Gospel writings and letters from some such as Paul and Peter had become as important as the Old Testament. They were recognized on the same level as the Old Testament, which divinely helped everyone understand the fulfillment of God's Word through the life, teachings, death, and resurrection of the Messiah.[d] Through the leading of the Holy Spirit, Christ's followers knew that God had inspired these authors in order to give the Church a clear understanding of His Word.[e]

From the very beginning, Satan started attacking the Church with false teachings that Jesus' initial apostle had to oppose and correct.[f] [174] Later, we learn from second century leaders of the Church, that they also had to contend with heretics such as Marcion and Valentinus. Those who had been called to oversee regional areas such as Irenaeus, recognized the dangers of unchecked heresy and wrote accordingly to help others identify

---

a: Gal 1:11–17. b: Acts 22:3; Phil 3:5. c: Luke 1:1–4; Acts 1:1ff.
d: 2 Peter 3:14–16. e: 2 Tim 3:16–17; cf. 2 Peter 3:15–16. f: e.g.
2 Cor 11:3–4, 13–15; 1 John 5:13–14.

and stop those who were either altering or misrepresenting Scripture (*Heresies* 3.15.1),[175] which by their time consisted of the New and Old Testaments.

Toward the end of the fourth century, Satan had not let up in his assault against the Church, which included trying to distort Gods' Word, and therefore the churches of the western Mediterranean world officially agreed upon a specific list of authoritative New Testament Writings. *This generally accepted list of twenty-seven authoritative works had existed unofficially in most areas for over three centuries under the leading of the Holy Spirit.* In his A.D. 367 Easter address, Athanasius, bishop of Alexandria, included this list. Under Augustine's guidance, the West collectively agreed that these books were the authoritative Word of God at the councils of Hippo in A.D. 393 and Carthage in A.D. 397 & 419.[176]

The same twenty seven books that were compiled by the Early Church and endorsed by the 4th century Church comprise our contemporary New Testament. They along with the Old Testament are still considered by Christ's followers as God's authoritative Word. *It was the Son of the Living God, Jesus Christ, who gave proper illumination of the Law and the Prophets showing how God's Word had pointed to His coming and ongoing rescue operation for as many as would listen.*[a] It is Jesus' words and work as stated and illustrated in the New Testament that give the Church its foundation from which to follow the leading of Christ through the illumination of the Holy Spirit.

First-Century Church Organization

As we examine the organizational structure of the Church in the New Testament looking for guidance for our current ministries, we note that many evangelized cities had a council of elders appointed by Jesus. These councils were initially set-up by His apostles. The apostles also provided initial encouragement and guidance to each of the cities' individual leaders and collective councils. It can be seen through Scripture such as Acts 15 that Christ's followers living in Jerusalem gave the final rulings on doctrinal issues that came up before the Church Universal. We note that God did not specify any specific form of worship in the

---

a: Matt 5:17.

New Testament for individual assemblies. In addition, we observe
great cooperation among first-century Christians.

    Through Jesus' leadership through the leading of the Holy
Spirit, His disciples started turning their world *right-side-up*
reconciling many to their Heavenly Father.[a] *It is clear from
Scripture, that even after Jesus' ascension, He continued to
guide the Church through the Holy Spirit.*[b] Each community
acted as a *particular part* of the living organism called the Body of
Christ, which was constantly helping others in all walks of life. In
the earliest stages of Church growth, we observed the apostle Peter
acting as a spokesman in Jerusalem. Later, Peter was forced to flee
for his life,[c] and we note that the apostle James was appointed as
Jerusalem's spokesman.[177] As the Church grew, an important trend
appeared: *Jesus continually expanded the leadership of the
Church to accommodate its growth.*[178]

    As we evaluate the early Church's growth, we take special
note that *Jesus remained the leader*. We observe Jesus working
through Paul and Barnabas appointing elders on their second pass
through Lystra, Iconium, and Antioch of Syria.[d] When Paul
traveled to Jerusalem on his third missionary journey, he stopped
in Meletus and summoned the elders of Ephesus and reminded
them that *Jesus through the Holy Spirit* had appointed them as
overseers.[e] We learn through these accounts that elders
(presbyters) of a city-church council were the same as overseers
(bishops) and pastors.

    There are six basic terms used throughout the New
Testament showing four levels of organization. The six terms and
four levels of organization are: Lord; apostles; overseers–who
were also called elders and pastors; and deacons. Let us look at
each level of leadership so that we may more fully understand the
way that our lord Jesus Christ organized the Church to work in our
individual communities and around the world. *The first level is
straightforward: Jesus remains the lord.*

---

a: 2 Cor 5:18–21.   b: e.g. Acts 1:8; 2:4; 9:3–16; 10:19–22.   c: Acts
12:1–17.   d: Acts 14:21–23.   e: Acts 20:17, 28.

Apostles

The general meaning of the term *apostolos*, "apostle," refers to one who is sent and officially represents the sender. This term has a dual meaning of being sent *and* being equipped (prepared) to function correctly as an official representative.[179] We observe that this term was used in the book of Acts and in Paul's letters to designate a group of Jesus' disciples who were responsible for evangelizing cities and establishing the corresponding councils of elders for each individual city.

The New Testament shows us that the first level of leadership directly under Jesus consisted of men, who were called apostles, whom He personally appointed.[180] Through Paul's letters, we note that Paul, Silvanus, Timothy, and Apollos were apostles in addition to Jesus' closest disciples while on earth.[181]

As we read Paul's letters, we come to realize that beyond the apostle's responsibility to evangelize specified areas, he was also responsible for establishing and guiding the councils of elders.[182] We know from the book of Acts that through the guidance of Jesus Christ through the Holy Spirit, Paul and Barnabas appointed overseers (pastors) to look after the Believers of the various cities where they had already ministered.[a] In addition, we have an account where Paul asked one of his co-workers, Titus, to appoint overseers for all of the cities of Crete where they had ministered.[b] In one of Peter's letters, he is encouraging the overseers of the Eastern Mediterranean World to guard, guide, and develop Christ's followers with joyful hearts setting godly examples.[c]

Overseers & City-Councils

Many cities and smaller communities had elders who were helped by deacons to oversee and coordinate the day-to-day ministry of local assemblies. Several of Paul's letters were addressed to these individual city-councils of elders who were working together to transform their respective cities for Christ.[183]

---

a: Acts 14:21–23. b: Titus 1:5. c: 1 Peter 5:1–3.

Paul consistently used the terms *episkopoi*, "overseers, bishops," and *presbuteroi*, "presbyters, elders," interchangeably to represent the leaders of local assemblies (churches). In one of his letters, Paul used the terms "elder" and "overseer" interchangeably within adjoining sentences instructing Titus to appoint overseers in all of the cities of Crete, which in itself confirms the interchangeability of the terms "overseer" and "elder."[a] [184]

Another term used by the Apostles for overseer was *poimēn*, "pastor." It was derived from a Greek term that generally meant "shepherd," one who guards and guides livestock. In its contextual setting, Paul used the term "pastor" once to represent an "overseer" who was primarily concerned with training local church members in the ways of God in order to enable them to do the righteous works of God.[b] [185] In addition, there were Greek verb forms of the word "shepherd" used to show proper action by God's elders (overseers) who were commanded "to shepherd the flock" as they exercised oversight.[c]

The elder's primary responsibility was to take care of and encourage godly growth and ministry among the Christians of their respective cities. It appears that many of these overseers may have held local assemblies in large houses, synagogues, or other available structures. They had individual gatherings and/or collective gatherings at various times, but it is also clear from Scripture that they worked together *to transform their cities* for Christ. In a letter from Peter, we observe Peter, a fellow elder and an appointed apostle of Jesus Christ, encouraging the elders of various communities to take care of the sheep just as Jesus had personally encouraged him,[d]

> Therefore, I, a fellow elder and witness of the sufferings of the Christ and a partaker of (His) glory that is about to be revealed, exhort (encourage) the elders among you; shepherd the flock of God among you–not under compulsion but willingly according to God, ... And when the Chief Shepherd is manifested, you (pl) shall obtain an unfading crown of glory. 1 Peter 5:1–4

---

a: Titus 1:5–7.   b: Eph 4:11–12.   c: 1 Peter 5:2.   d: 1 Peter 1:1; John 21:15–17.

Deacons

Pastors, elders, and overseers represented the same level of leadership, so what about the *diakonos*, "deacon"?[186] What was the role of deacons? We find an abundance of usage of this term. Let us look at some people who were called "deacons" by either their title or by the performance of their duties.

From the standpoint of serving others, the following were deacons: Jesus Christ;[187] the Apostles; Paul; Barnabas; Mark; Timothy;[188] Apollos; Archippus; Epaphras; Erastus;[189] Onesimus (the slave); Phoebe (a sister in Christ);[190] Stephanas (entire household); and Tychicus.[191] Then stepping outside the Church, we observe Paul telling the church of Rome that all civil rulers are also God's deacons.[192] Even Satan has deacons (servants/ministers).[193]

We observe from Scripture that the term "deacon" was normally used to refer *to those who render service.* Jesus Christ serves humanity.[a] Jesus Christ's followers follow in His footsteps and serve humanity.[b] All who follow Jesus are deacons.

Yet, there is a special group of deacons discussed in Paul's first letter to Timothy. These deacons helped with the day-to-day administration of the church for each city. They were not required to preach the Gospel, teach, nor have the same level of administrative capabilities as the apostles or the elders who served on each of the city-councils. Although, the official duties of those holding the title of "deacon" were not explicitly stated, it is implied by the meaning drawn from the word "deacon" and from the stated requirements for this office that their primary function was to serve the overseers in whatever capacity that they were willing and capable.[c]

Men, Leadership, & City-Councils

The offices of "deacon," "overseer," and "apostle" were filled by godly men. A common requirement for both overseer (pastor) and deacon was that they were to be *mias gunaikos*

---

a: Matt 20:28.   b: Matt 20:25–27.   c: 1 Tim 3.

andres, "one-woman men (husbands)."[194] The phrase denotes husbands who have been married to one wife. Over the last couple millennia, that phrase has normally been interpreted by the vast majority of Christ's followers to mean that any man holding the office of overseer (pastor) should only have been married once. Through Paul, God adds that these leaders should have managed their own households well.[(a)]

Using similar phraseology in the *same* letter to Timothy,[(b)] Paul states that widows seeking long-term help must be at least sixty years of age and have been *henos andros gunē,* "a one-man woman (wife)."[195] With Paul using distinct terms to differentiate between men and women who have been married to only one spouse, it is clear in this context that overseers are to be men and not women, and that in general, God desires for men and women to have only one spouse. It is also clear that God desires His overseers to be *proven husbands* who have been married to the same woman *and* who have keep proper control of their own families.[(c)] In addition, overseers are to be above reproach, mature in Christ, able teachers, not addicted to alcohol nor drugs, not contentious but of a gentle nature, and have a good reputation in society.[(d)]

God has revealed Himself as "Father," and during the Creation of His eternal holy family, He has instructed *men* to be the head of their homes,[(e)] and for some who have been good husbands, fathers, and stewards of their own households, He also calls them to be heads of their local assemblies (churches). Keeping in mind the historical and literary context of Paul's letter to Timothy and supporting NT Scripture, it is clear that God's primary requirement for His Church leaders is that they are godly men who have demonstrated their leadership through proper leadership of their own families.

Although God appoints men to lead in the home and in the Church, on occasion, there are exceptions to this norm. During one period of Israel's rebellion during the Age of Judges,[(f)] we see God appointing a woman, Deborah, who was also a prophetess, to lead Israel (Judges 4 & 5).[(g)] Another exception noted in Scripture can be seen in the fact that Paul taught that women should not have authority over men nor teach them,[(h)] but Scripture shows that God

---

a: 1 Tim 3:4–5, 12; Titus 1:6. b: 1 Tim 5:9. c: 1 Tim 3:4–5; cf. Titus 1:6. d: 1 Tim 3:2–7. e: Eph 5:22–33; Col 3:18–19. f: Judges 2:16, 18. g: Judges 4 & 5. h: 1 Tim 2:11–12.

made an exception by using Priscilla and her husband, Aquila, to teach a notable preacher, Apollos, more fully in the Word.[a] God makes exceptions to the norm as He sees fit. I believe that in general God calls women into leadership roles within the Church when men fail to follow Christ and refuse their assigned duties.

Although Paul said that women are not to have authority over men, he praises women for serving. In one example, Paul praises Phoebe in his letter to the Romans. He speaks highly of Phoebe and her services that she had rendered to him and others.[b] Here, Paul is writing a recommendation for a fellow Saint who has served well, a woman.

Throughout the New Testament, we observe Jesus appointing elders through His apostles and then helping them develop so that they could lead their respective communities.[196] We observe four levels of organization:

(1) Jesus Christ was and still is the active leader of the Church establishing Church doctrine initially through Christ's followers at Jerusalem;

(2) through Jesus Christ and the Holy Spirit's guidance, the apostles were responsible for evangelizing and firmly establishing overseers as needed and councils of elders for individual communities;[197]

(3) the overseers/pastors/elders were responsible for managing the day-to-day activities of their local churches and working together through city-councils to transform their respective communities for Christ; and

(4) the deacons were to assist the elders using their God-given talents (gifts).

Today, Jesus Christ continues to guide His Body, the Church, through the leading of the Holy Spirit. The Church through the teaching of the Holy Spirit is to look into the written Word of God instead of seeking out Jesus' first disciples to understand Christ's teachings. The same Holy Spirit who inspired the authors of Scripture helps Christ's followers today correctly interpret that same Scripture.[198] Jesus Christ set up the "council-of-elders" as the fundamental form of collective leadership for communities. Overseeing elders working together within local

---

a: Acts 18:24–28.   b: Rom 16:1–2.

city-councils is still the biblical way for our local churches to transform our cities for Christ.

*Jesus has **not** given His Church a new commandment to change this form of leadership, nor has He changed the importance of community-wide ministries.* He wants to guide His followers on community-wide levels around the world. When a community does not have a **like minded council of elders** working together, it suffers from a lack of strong Christian cooperation.[199]

Without Church leadership *working together* in their respective communities, Jesus is not exalted nor proclaimed as clearly nor effectively as God desires.[200] We know that Jesus desires all of His followers to put some of their time in community-wide ministry. Jesus' followers need to stay focused on their *identity* and overall *mission*. God's love should compel Christ's followers to learn to work together and serve their respective communities and beyond.

When we come together to minister more effectively on community-wide levels, we will have to learn to put aside some of our denominational differences. If we do not allow Satan to tempt us into using our diversities to build dividing walls among ourselves, Jesus will use our diversities to strengthen our collective ministries.[201] Working under the lordship of Jesus, our unity in light of our different denominational, racial, socioeconomic, and generational backgrounds will help a fallen world see God's capacity to bring peace and joy in the midst of worldly chaos. In addition, as Christ's followers live out biblical principals and work together under Jesus' leadership, their joint-efforts *will* clearly proclaim and demonstrate Jesus' lordship and God's love for all. Through the leadership of the Holy Spirit, effective joint ministries will transform our hurting communities into communities that have experienced God's love at work, which in turn will bring hope and salvation to many. Through Christ's ongoing leadership, we will be able to turn our communities right-side up and see godly transformation of our cities.

Through deception, Satan will continue to try to divide Christ's leaders, which he can only do if we are not **paying close attention to God's Word and Jesus' leadership**. Being like-minded starts as we subject our personal desires under our Heavenly Father's. *As **we** submit* to our Father's appointed leader,

Jesus Christ, we will be empowered by Him to go beyond earthly cooperation and work; together, we will be empowered through the Holy Spirit to accomplish God's good purposes. Without Jesus Christ's ongoing leadership, we will not be able to minister according to God collectively and effectively in our communities. In addition, all of the Bible must be the common written foundational platform from which all serve Christ. Anyone not accepting *all* of the Bible as the inspired Word of God profitable for teaching, for reproof, for correction, and for training in righteousness[a] should *not* be sitting on any church councils.

If we allow God to guide us, He will teach us to minister on all levels including the highly effective community-wide councils of churches employed by first-century Church leaders. God's children are to love and help their neighbors. The people of our communities are truly our closest neighbors. God's developing love within our hearts should compel us to strive hard to minister individually *and* collectively in our communities as well as around the world. As local churches submit to Jesus' lordship and willingly sacrifice and suffer in order to bring as many as will listen into God's eternal close-knit holy family, the Church will experience more and more of Jesus' great joy.

For the next two chapters, we will look at our individual commitments to follow Jesus Christ. Without a genuine commitment to follow Christ, there is no spiritual rebirth and corresponding new or renewed creation and character. If there are only a few people saved in a local church, it is hard for that church to effectively witness to its community. The greater the number of individuals working to make God known, the more likely that it will be that many more will come to know Christ.

As you read the next two chapters, either allow God to encourage and strengthen you in your faithful service to Him or allow Him to show you that you need to make a sincere commitment to follow Christ out of a growing awareness of your need for a savior. God is worthy of our faithful service, and there is nothing anywhere that will give us more satisfaction, joy, and inner peace than following Jesus as He works with us to bring as many as will listen into His Father's Kingdom and our collective eternal close-knit family.

---

a: 2 Tim 3:16–17; cf. 2:15.

8

Coming to Our Senses

Right now, take a moment, close your eyes, and consider the following scenario. Imagine yourself on the northeast shore of Japan at Honshu on Friday in the early evening of March 11, 2011 when a nine point earthquake struck the region, the largest recorded in history. Just minutes after the quake settled, the coastal area was hit by a thirty foot tsunami wave. You have been on vacation sitting on the beach contemplating life when all of a sudden the earth started shaking violently and all of the buildings around you disintegrate before your very eyes. Before you can get over the shock from the effect of the earthquake itself and the screaming and moaning, you hear a great roaring sound, turn back toward the sea, and see a thirty foot wave descending on you. What do you say to God at that moment? With imminent danger, would you be resigned to any outcome with a sense of inner peace, knowing that if you died, you would immediately leave your physical body and meet God face-to-face, or would you be overcome with a sense of hopelessness?

Have you ever had a dream in which everything happening within the dream felt so real that you were surprised when you awoke and realized that it had all been a dream? In a very similar way, when anyone starts listening to God, he or she starts realizing that there is more to the world around them than meets the eye. God does not allow us to interact directly with the spiritual world that is directly interconnected to our physical world, but He gives us awareness. Within our physical world, God teaches all about godly social interaction and asks all to consider choosing life with Him for eternity.[a]

Although we are not given the ability to interact directly with the spiritual world around us, those who listen to God are taught to understand that many of the battles that we personally experience are spiritually based and can be won *only* through His

---

a: Rev 3:20; 21:1–4; 22:1–5.

assistance.[a] [202] The physical world is affected by the spiritual and visa-versa. In the present, we affect the spiritual world through our actions and through our prayers as God acts on our behalf. For those who listen to God, the reality of a future spiritual world–divided into two isolated regions called Heaven and Hell–becomes the main focus even as we live out our physical lives in the here-and-now.[b] *Our world is temporary and the future sinless Heaven and sinful Hell are permanent.*[203]

From the beginning of the Creation, God has asked everyone to make choices. Being born into sin causes us to experience both good and evil. We learn from both and then must choose to obey or disobey, to do good or bad. It has been part of God's creative design to give all a fairly large amount of free-will in order to allow each person to decide if he or she desires to join Him and others in holy living. God does not stand over His creation as a hovering parent forcing everyone to do what is right. Through the Holy Spirit's teaching, God works with our individual consciences and shows us the advantages of living holy lives with Him in peace and joy. But, *for many, it is difficult to submit to His lordship.*[204]

His gracious work in our lives runs counter to our sinful nature and many openly rebel against Him and His holy way of life.[c] But God is persistent not wanting any to perish but all to come to repentance, a change in life away from self-centeredness to following Him and acquiring His concern for all.[d] We learn from the good and evil around us, and God keeps asking us to turn away from the bad and submit to Him and become part of His eternal close-knit holy family. Everyone should willingly submit to God's authority because of His great love for all, but many choose their own lordship over His with the loss of long term inner peace and joy and loss of a future life in Heaven with Him.

Today, some think that God loves us so much that He will not allow anyone to reject Him and go to Hell or that going to Hell will be temporary and just feel like an eternity. *This is wrong!* Without submission to God, people will be confined in the future to a place called Hell with no contact with God and His righteous followers forever. *Everyone's choice matters including yours!*

a: Eph 6:10–18.   b: 1 Peter 1:3–9; 2:9–10. Phil 3:17–4:1.   c: Rom 5:8–10.   d: 2 Peter 3:9.

God created everyone free to make choices that have eternal consequences and will not force His way of life on any. It is clear from Scripture that God would like everyone to learn to trust Him and choose to live with Him for eternity,[a] [205] but He knows that many will not.[b] He consistently encourages everyone to look beyond themselves and choose a life of peace and joy with Him and others who want the same thing.[206] God does not allow those, who will not allow Him to mold and shape their lives into godly social beings, to come into His eternal Heaven and make life miserable for those who do.[c]

Others think that God does not really allow anyone to make such a significant choice as to either accept or reject Him eternally, but He does. His acceptance of individuals into His kingdom and eternal family is based on how each person responds to Him and His way of life. He is longsuffering toward all as He works with each individual encouraging everyone to turn from his or her self-centered way of life to His monarchial fatherly rule.[207]

God is *not* bound by time as we are. This is hard to comprehend, but it is clear from God's Word that He is not bound by our restriction of time. God's Creation has never been at the mercy of Satan or any other evil force. Prior to the physical creation, God already knew what was going to happen every second of the Creation with every single individual.[d] His creation is based on foreknowledge, knowing in advance what will happen.[e] A simplified analogy to His spiritual ability can be seen through what we can do in our physical world. God has given us the ability to design projects such as cars, houses, bridges, etc. knowing in advance how our designs will turn out. God has given humanity this basic mental ability. On a much grander scale, God has the capability to design a universe knowing in advance how His Creation with intelligent beings will turn out. God knew in advance who would become part of His eternal close-knit holy family and who would not.[f] [208]

God knew who would be born, and when, and how each person in His creation would live out his or her life. God also knew in advance how He was going to work with each person encouraging them to turn from evil and self-centeredness to Him for guidance and leadership. Based on His knowledge of what each

---

a: John 3:16, 19–20. b: Matt 7:13–14. c: Rev 22:14–15. d: Eph 1:4.
e: 1 Peter 1:1–2; cf. Rom 8:28–30. f: 1 Peter 1:1–2.

person of the Creation would do, He decided prior to physically creating the universe who would be allowed to be part of His eternal Kingdom and Family and who would not. He uses everyone's final decision whether to receive or reject Him to determine where each will spend eternity.[a]

  In reality, God calls all, but only a few are chosen depending on their response to His call. Jesus told one parable that clearly helps us understand all Scripture regarding this matter. God is filling His Kingdom and eternal family by calling all, but *if one wishes to enter His Kingdom, they must follow God's will and become like Christ.*[b] If they do not, they will be turned away.[c] This is why Jesus warns all that if they are not willing to listen to Him and do His will, they are *not able* to be His followers.[d] Everyone who desires to be a member of God's family must put God first and do according to His leadership.[e] [209]

  In reality, our choices matter! God's teachings are consistent in both the Old and New Testament. What people decide during their earthly life matters. The writer of Hebrews said that it is appointed for each of us to *die once* and then *a judgement* will follow.[f] There is *no reincarnation!* All people live this physical portion of their eternal life *only one time*, and all will be judged according to the way that they responded to God during this short portion of eternity.[g] [210] Everyone who learns to trust and obey God because of His great love for all will become part of His eternal close-knit holy family and given assignments.[h]

  Although we do not reach perfection prior to God's redeeming work after physical death, He still holds everyone accountable for their decisions.[i] [211] God has told us that our present sins affect our children and children's children into the third and fourth generations so we should take any sin in our lives seriously.[j] But, even more importantly, our present decisions regarding God and His way of life *affect our eternal life.*[k] [212] God wants us to choose life right now over death for a better life now and a better eternal life. For those who listen to God, their lives become better and better in the present world and perfect in the world to come.[l] God only allows individuals who have been perfected (completed) by Him to enter into His eternal presence.[m]

---

a: Jer 20:12; Luke 8:17; 16:15; 2 Thess 2:10. b: Matt 7:21; Gal 3:26–27. c: Matt 22:1–14. d: Luke 14:26–33; cf. Matt 10:38. e: Luke 14:26. f: Heb 9:27; Rev 20:11–15. g: 1 Peter 1:17. h: e.g. Jer 1:5; Gal 1:15–16. i: Rom 2:11–13; 1 Peter 1:17. j: Ex 20:5–6. k: Acts 2:37–40. l: Rom 6:22. m: Rom 6:23; 8:28–30; 1 John 3:1–2.

When we consider God's actions toward all, His love is the key guiding principal for His actions.[a] When God asks all to walk in His ways because He is holy, it is because He wants the best for all. "Holy" is a term used to describe His nature,[b] a nature based on love expressed through grace and truth, which is often demonstrated through His actions of "loving-kindness."[c] As you examine the reports throughout the Old Testament regarding God and His work with all humanity, a pattern emerges. God blesses those who listen to His guidance and walk in His righteous ways, and He dispenses judgement in many forms and fashions to those who do not.[d] [213]

God teaches us through His Word that any acts that are contrary to His instructions (His laws and decrees) are evil. They are bad. Disobedience is sin, and sin hurts others. Sin is undesirable and should not be a normal way of life for anyone listening to Him.[e] God gives all of His creation a fair amount of freedom but places limits on that freedom based on the rights of all. Love rejoices with righteousness.[f] When you look at Habakkuk 2:4 and Hebrews 11, you see that each individual's righteousness starts with a developing trust in God and His very nature.[214] God is worthy of our trust. If we allow God to work in our lives, He teaches us how much He cares about everyone and His ability to bring about good for all who place their faith (trust) in Him.

When we examine Israel's past, a nation that agreed to be *God's light* on a hill to the whole world,[g] we see a nation that prospered when it was obedient to God and suffered judgment, which included its scattering among the other nations, when it went the same way as the rest of the world. God made it clear to Israel and all–through His response to Solomon's prayer– that if people groups and/or individuals who were ignoring Him would return to Him with a humble heart seeking His will and living morally upright, He would forgive them of their sin and in the case of societies, He would heal their land.[h]

Believe it or not, the hardest part of life for most people is *just waking up* to the reality of the spiritual world around them. If we do not let God teach us, *our own personal desires are like little children's and cloud our reasoning* blinding us to what is really

---

a: 1 John 4:16. b: Lev 19:2. c: Ex 34:6–7. d: Deut 30:15–20.
e: 1 John 3:4, 9. f: 1 Cor 13:6. g: Ex 19:7–8. h: 2 Chron 7:14.

going on. In addition, Satan's deceptive work continually bombards us with all types of diversions and busyness.

Our self-centered desires combined with Satan's deceptions and busyness combine to produce a mental and spiritual smokescreen keeping many from coming to know reality. At times, God is able to get through that smokescreen and reveal Himself. *Through His revelation,* we come to realize how empty our lives are without a close relationship with Him and that He has many faithful followers working worldwide to bring as many as will listen into His eternal presence.[215]

Although Satan is busy in our world trying to keep as many as possible away from God so that they will not realize how good He really is, God is always at work in everyone's life either trying to get their attention, or after getting their attention, revealing reality to those who will listen. God brings bits of reality into all people's lives through evangelists, preachers, teachers, family members, friends, associates, and even strangers, who utilize all types of media including pamphlets, magazines, books, phones, computers, i-Pods, i-Pads, radio, TV, and other forms. He asks all to read His Word, the Bible, in order to dispel the darkness around them allowing them to see reality, which in turn frees them from their own sinful bondage.[a]

Billy Graham once wrote about a young lady who had written him a letter and told him how totally miserable she had been in her former free-spirited life. She had been pursuing the sensual pleasures of this world but found neither inner peace nor lasting joy from them. Through God's guidance, she decided to go to a Bible study and stump everyone with her cynicism. Instead, God used that time to build an interest in her to read His Word. She began studying a Bible on a regular basis and several months later God brought her to a point where she realized that God really loved her and had a much better plan for her life than she had for herself.[b] At that point, she submitted her life to her loving Creator. She said in her letter that after committing to follow Christ, she experienced a special happiness that she did not know existed. She stated that all those sensual pleasures were traps that had led her to confusion, unhappiness, guilt, and near-suicide. Now she was truly free as she followed Christ.[216]

---

a: John 8:31b–32f.   b: John 3:16.

God Is at Work

God is always at work helping all to understand the reality of the spiritual world as well as the physical. *Everyone senses both* through what they see in the physical world,[a] but it is only through their willingness to listen to the Creator that anyone is able to start to understand the spiritual.[b] Through that understanding, one is also able to understand more fully the physical world. It is sad that for most, God allows bad things to happen in order to get their attention.[217] It seems that when things are going well according to our way of thinking, we do not have the time nor desire to listen to God even when we are not experiencing the type of full life that God desires for us.[c]

Job is a good example of this type of thought. Job was a righteous man respecting God,[d] but did not know God well. In addition, although he was an upright man before God, he–like the rest of creation–fell short of doing God's will perfectly.[e] God allowed Satan to torment Job through trial after trial.[f] When the time was right and Job had commended his own righteousness long enough,[218] God introduced Himself in a very personal way and brought Job to the point of acknowledging his own sinfulness. Like Isaiah,[g] when Job realized his sinful nature, he repented by willingly turning from his own life style and committed to following God's.[h] In many ways, although our trials are not normally as severe as Job's, our life struggles are similar and God uses them to build our character just as he did Job's–if we listen.[i]

Although the spiritual forces at work around us cannot be observed through our physical senses alone, they are discernable through God's illumination to our conscience in our inner spiritual being.[j] If we do not allow God to work with us and illuminate the reality of the co-existing physical and spiritual worlds, we remain ignorant of the spiritual battles raging around us over the souls of each person. It is critically important for all to submit whole-heartedly to the lordship of the Creator. This gives Him permission

---

a: Rom 1:18–22; 2:11–16; John 3:19–20. b: John 3:21; Acts 22:14a; 1 Cor 2:10, 16. c: Rev 3:17–18. d: Job 1:1, 8. e: Rom 3:23. f: Job 30:25–31. g: Isa 6:1–7. h: Job 38:1–40:4–42:6. i: Rom 5:3–5. j: Rom 1:16–20; 2:11–16.

to train and empower them to be part of the creative process bringing as many as possible into His glorious eternal presence.

The greatest spiritual battle that every individual has to face is whether he or she will allow God to awaken him or her from the dreamlike state in which he or she lives. In reality, it normally feels safer and more comfortable to stay in this dreamlike state than to wake up. This state is somewhat like an altered state of consciousness wherein each individual has found a familiar place to hide from the unknown whether good or bad. It could be compared to a heroin addict who escapes from reality into a world where his or her sense of being has been altered to the point that they are not able to function anywhere near their unaltered state. Once someone has been on heroin for a long time, he or she becomes so immersed in that life that awakening to a world without heroin is very uncomfortable mentally and somewhat painful physically as the body has to adjust back to feeling normal pain from everyday living without constant numbing.

Our awakening to the reality of the existing spiritual world that permeates and influences our physical world can be just as discomforting as getting off drugs. God consistently works through our conscience and spirit to awaken us to an eternal world view and the consequences of our ongoing decisions. In our physical world, various forms of busyness are the worst barriers to understanding God and the spiritual world in which we live. King Solomon is a good case in point. As a king, he was very intelligent from the world's perspective and did well: he built up his cities and armies in order to protect himself and his people from the world around them,[a] but he failed to build up his personal and national spiritual strength.[b] At the end of his life, he realized that his busyness in the physical world was not very important when considered in light of eternity. He came to realize very late in life that the most important part of anyone's life was to respect God and allow Him to develop and lead all who listen to a place of hating evil and loving Him.[c] [219]

God invites those who listen to join Him in helping as many as possible enter into Heaven and become part of His eternal close-knit holy family. For those who respond positively to God and His love, they will be fighting in both worlds. They will be

a: 1 Kings 4:20–28; 10:14–29; Eccl 2:1–10. b: 1 Kings 11:1–13.
c: Eccl 3:14; 12:13–14.

introducing as many as will listen to God and His glorious nature
helping to complete God's Creation. Jesus is the Light of the
World, the express image of God, so that all who saw Jesus in His
perfect humanity clearly saw the very nature of God the Father.[a]
Jesus' disciples are being renewed from their fallen nature and are
becoming more and more like Jesus;[b] they are God's light for the
world during Jesus' Messianic reign.[c] Jesus' followers are an
important part of God's great creative rescue operation as they
show and demonstrate God's love to a fallen world.

For those who listen to God, He starts them on a path
within a much bigger world than first imagined. Those who allow
God to awaken them start realizing a need to reevaluate past
presuppositions and make appropriate adjustments in order to
realize a proper relationship with God and others. Their
consciousness of the true world starts shifting from one that had
been very self-centered to one that becomes more and more in tune
with God, His standards, and His Creation. God is bringing as
many as possible into alignment with His holy nature–producing
an eternal life for those who listen, that is full of love, joy, inner
peace, and excitement.

For all who allow God to awaken them from their personal,
self-centered, and delusional worlds and start learning and
obediently trusting the Creator of the universe, they eventually
come to the point of realizing that:

> (1) life is truly eternal for all with good or bad eternal
> consequences depending on choices made during this part
> of eternity;
> (2) those, who obediently listen to God during this part of
> eternity, will be transformed into perfected sinless
> individuals in Christ's image; and
> (3) those who obediently listen to God will live with Him
> and other perfected children forever in Heaven in His
> eternal close-knit holy family experiencing godly love, joy,
> and inner peace.

---

a: John 14:9; 8:12; Col 2:9; Heb 1:3. b: Col 1:9–12; 3:9–10. c: Matt
5:14–16.

Born To Die Once

> Just as it is determined (appointed) for men to die
> once, but after this judgement . . . . Heb 9:27

A long time ago, there was a king who wanted God to help him remember that he had a limited time to live out his physical life. It would help him stay focused on what was important in life.[a] [220] Like all of us, King David had a limited time to live out this part of eternity. He wanted to keep a proper perspective regarding time in order to live out this part in a way that was pleasing to his Creator.[b]

After fasting for 21 days along with continual prayer, God spoke to Daniel through one of His chief messengers (angels) about end times and the resurrection of the dead, some to eternal shame and others to eternal life.[c] Through the Apostle John, God has shown all of Christ's followers an end-time great white throne judgment. At the end of the Creation, Jesus will openly judge all who did not listen to God and exile them in a place called the eternal Lake of Fire (Hell).[d] God's Word is clear that everyone who was ever born physically will live forever either with Him or exiled in a place called Hell.

From the moment that anyone is physically conceived, he or she has an eternal existence. Then, God begins developing those who listen as eternal holy family members throughout this physical stage of their eternal life. The Creation is in process and will continue bringing people into God's eternal family until the last day of Jesus' thousand year reign. During this time, everyone has the ability to receive the gift of the Spirit and corresponding eternal life through submission to God. If individuals will walk in God's ways (holiness) and follow the leading of the Holy Spirit, they will be born a second time. This time they are born into God's eternal family through the eternal indwelling of the Holy Spirit.[e]

In Scripture, holy writers have used various terms such as God's "call, choice, or election" to denote those who have been born of God due to their submission to Him. God's love draws many to Him. God's Word also makes it clear that no one is

a: Ps 39:4–5. b: Ps 103:33–105:5. c: Dan 12:2. d: Rev 20:11–15.
e: John 3:1–8; Eph 1:13–14; 1 John 4:7.

allowed to bring character witnesses before Jesus to speak on their behalf at His great White Throne Judgement. He has perfect knowledge of everyone's inner motives and completed actions and exposes everything to the whole Creation.[a] [221]

Born into Sin on the Wide Road Leading to Destruction

As we consider God's Creation, we can make a few observations:

> (1) everyone was created as an eternal being without having a say in the matter;
> (2) everyone other than Adam and Eve was born into a world corrupted by sin, which marred their character; and
> (3) everyone who wants to live with God as part of His eternal close-knit holy family must submit to His lordship.

So, how marred are we, and why would anyone want to submit to God's lordship?

God tells us not to love the fallen corrupted world nor the various ways of the world because they are not of Him,[b] and they will not last.[c] He describes the ways of the world as based on a self-centeredness vs. a God-centered love for all.[222] God's Word is clear: a self-centered life style leads to eternal pain and suffering,[223] but for those who *willingly* live according to God's will and ways,[224] there is eternal life with God and inner peace and joy that starts immediately.[d] [225]

Let's take a deeper look at the prodigal son. As we look at Christ's teaching about a loving father and *two* self-centered sons,[e] we note a couple important points:

> (1) the loving father worked hard to provide for his family and workers. He did not live in the moment but instead lived his life based on genuine love in such a way as to bless others *over the long haul*;
> (2) the openly rebellious son was not concerned with others nor the future. When he became old enough to be on his

---

a: Luke 8:17; Rev 20:11–15; cf. 2 Thess 2:10. b: 1 John 2:15.
c: 2 Peter 3:7–13; Rev 22:1. d: Rom 6:22, e: Luke 15:1–2, 11–32.

own, he left home to live his life in such a way as to experience as much worldly pleasure as possible not considering how that would affect his future; and (3) *the second son,* who was also highlighted in Jesus' story, demonstrated a certain degree of faithfulness to his father by staying at home and helping to maintain their land, but *was just as distant from God as the younger son* because of his lack of genuine love for others especially his lost brother.

In reality, Jesus' story closes with two lost sons, who have experienced love from their biological father and had not yet allowed God to grow genuine love and concern in them. One son came home repenting because of what his father had to offer, and the other who stayed at home was living legally within his father's moral criteria but not from the heart.

When Jesus closed this story, He did not say whether either son had a genuine love for their father or others. It is possible that eventually both having experienced totally different circumstances would eventually come to the place of allowing God to teach them to love according to His standards. If they did not, neither would be allowed into God's eternal family. Allowing God to lead and teach each of us to love Him and others more and more is crucial to becoming part of His eternal holy family.[a]

When we consider Jesus' story, it is important to take note that Jesus is talking to Pharisees.[b] The Pharisees are known to be morally good and can be compared to many of our contemporary church members. Many church members today have good morals but are lacking a genuine concern for others. It is a good and noble thing to follow God's moral laws faithfully, but without genuine love and concern for others, one is missing what is most important.[c]

How many of us, who go to church regularly and try to follow God's general commandments, have no real compassion for the lost? In reality, both sons' lifestyles were ungodly, and those following either one have no place in God's eternal holy family. If we are still in either group, let's ask God to reveal Satan's deception and our own self-centered desires so that we might make a heart-felt decision to turn to God in order to learn to love more

---

a: Matt 5:43–48; 22:37–40; Luke 10:30–37.   b: Luke 15:1–2.
c: 1 Cor 13:1–8a.

fully. No one is truly a part of God's family unless he or she is allowing God to mold and shape his or her image into one similar to His.[a] 226

God's way of life and standards are high but rewarding. The only way to realize any true godly love, which produces inner peace and joy, is to live out our lives listening to God and living according to His standards. He is worthy of our submission as lord due to His great love and concern for us. God wants us to realize a good life and helps all who listen to Him learn to love as He loves.[b]

Unrest Is the Result of Disobedience Toward God

God has created each of us to have a loving concerned relationship with Him and one another. When Adam and Eve disobeyed God, they broke that caring relationship bringing unrest, anxiety, and a general sense of loss. Until individuals start listening to God and following His ways, they experience the same unrest, anxiety, and loss that Adam and Eve experienced. Many are covering up these troubling feelings with entertainment, excessive social networking, excessive work, drugs, and other forms of busyness, but deep down everyone not listening to God has lucid moments of despair.

God invites *all* to be reconciled with Him so that He may mend their broken relationships with Him and one another.[c] It is only through God's healing of their broken nature that they may be restored into whole beings created in His image according to His likeness.[d] Being whole and walking with God is the only thing that will bring any of us to a place of experiencing great inner peace and joy.[e] 227

Our selfishness and self-centeredness cause us to favor ourselves over others during our initial development. In addition, our selfishness and corresponding disobedience to God distorts reality.[f] Our disobedience against God's will has even distorted our collective sense of right and wrong throughout the various levels of our societies throughout all ages. Much of the early twenty-first-century Western Civilization has turned its back on

---

a: Matt 5:3–12; Gal 5:22–23. b: John 13:34; 15:10–13. c: 2 Cor 5:18–19; 2 Peter 3:9. d: Gen 1:26–27; cf. James 3:9. e: John 15:10–11. f: John 3:19–21.

God's social order and His leadership. Collectively, many have come to an extreme position against God to include condoning the killing of our youngest children (abortion) and casting aside God's family values. In addition to many sanctioning the murder of their youngest children, they have also begun to sanction same-sex marriages and have come to accept the daily exploitation of children and women through various forms of media, including advertisements, pornographic materials, and in extreme cases, human trafficking.

Jesus makes us vividly aware that the ability to know good and to do good comes only from our Heavenly Father.[a] He is the One who is good and all goodness flows from Him. Therefore, we need the Creator to help us evaluate our motives for everything that we do. Anytime that we consciously or subconsciously place ourselves, our families, or other organizations above others, we no longer see the world as God intended.[228]

There Are No Free Passes into Heaven!

If we would be honest with one another, most of us would admit that we want things our way and want everything to be as easy as possible. From what I see from God's Word, it takes commitment and effort in order for anything to advance, whether good or evil. From the side of evil, Scripture is clear that Satan has been and will continue to work hard to overthrow God and His children until he is permanently confined in Hell after Christ's thousand year reign. He will not win, but he is putting as much effort into bringing as many of God's children with him as possible. From the side of good, Scripture is clear that God has been longsuffering and working hard on humanity's behalf from the very beginning. The Son of God, Jesus Christ, working with His Father even died both physically and spiritually in order to provide a way for good to triumph eternally. Through Jesus' spiritual death on our behalf, He was separated from His intimate relationship with His Heavenly Father *for the first time* in order that those who were trusting God would never experience spiritual death even for one second.[b] [229] Jesus provided a way to undo

---

a: Matt 19:17; Luke 18:19; John 20:17.   b: John 11:25–26; Eph 4:8–10; Heb 2:9–11.

wrong and gives those who submit to God a righteousness like His own. [a] [230] Any real advancement, whether good or evil, takes commitment and effort.

If all advancement takes commitment and effort, why do so many think that God, who is fighting on our behalf, wants His children to sit on the sidelines and do nothing? Everything in Scripture teaches that God's children are to be fully involved in living holy lives and allowing God to lead them in righteous works overcoming evil with good. Yet there are many people who claim to be Christians (Christ-like), who do not live according to God's holiness nor try to follow the leading of the Holy Spirit. These same people will tell you that *they are confident that they are going to Heaven when they die*. This way of thinking is totally contrary to what God's Word teaches. *Here is another of Satan's lies*, which is being taught by many within our churches today.

All who listen to God are commissioned by Him to represent Him as they become engaged in the spiritual battles going on all over the world for the eternal placement of each person.[b] [231] God's children are not to sit on the sidelines. In fact, Jesus said that nobody is able to be one of His followers unless he or she is willing to deny self, pick up his or her cross daily, and follow Him into whatever battles He leads.[c] [232] *Nowhere in Scripture does God teach that someone can come to Him, pick up a pass into Heaven, ignore the battles going on around them, die physically, and have Jesus escort his or her spirit into Heaven.*

So *why* do so many people today make some sort of profession of faith–saying that they trust God and either were baptized as an infant or after professing Christ as savior–and never experience the new creation "in Christ"?[d] In reality, without a genuine commitment *to follow* Jesus Christ, there will be no spiritual birth into God's family nor corresponding new creation.

Satan has sold the world one of His biggest lies since the beginning of the Creation. Many believe that salvation is nothing more than obtaining a pass into heaven for when one dies. This lie causes people to think that they have to wait until they get to Heaven for anything to be better. *What a lie!* Sanctification, being

---

a: Gal 3:13–14; 2 Cor 5:21. b: Matt 5:13–10; 1 Peter 5:6–10. c: Luke 14:26–27. Obedience: John 3:36; 14:23; 15:14. d: 2 Cor 5:17.

molded and shaped by God, and good works starts immediately *for all who truly start following Jesus.*[(a)] [233]

As you consider God's Word, consider the fact that within a short time after God finished the initial part of the Creation, Satan lied to Eve telling her that she would not die if she ate from the Tree of Knowledge of Good and Evil.[(b)] God had already emphatically said that if man ate from that tree, he would surely die. She and Adam both ate, and mankind died. Humanity and the entire Creation were corrupted, and accordingly, humanity was removed from God's presence. Satan has been lying about the reality of death ever since working to keep people separated from God.

Today, Satan's latest major lie, which is being spread by many, **is as bad as** *the one that he perpetuated in the Middle Ages that caused a major reformation among Christians.* At that time, Satan had perpetuated a lie within a part of the Church originating from a misunderstanding of Scripture such as Matt 16:17–19. Satan's lie deceived many into thinking that they could pay church officials for forgiveness of sins for themselves and/or loved ones including the deceased, thereby giving them passes out of purgatory (Sheol) and into Heaven.[234]

This **new lie,** *which is being propagated by many proclaiming that* **everyone can pick up a pass into heaven** *by confessing their sins and claiming Jesus as their savior* **without following Him as lord,** is hindering many from considering a genuine commitment to follow Jesus Christ. It is only through a turning from self and following Jesus (repentance) that one is saved from judgment as a sinner and spiritually born into God's family. **Spiritual renewal only comes from God according to His will and His rules**.[(c)] Through spiritual birth into God's family comes the removal of sin and growth in God's righteousness. God's Word is clear, *if individuals do not make true commitments to follow Jesus,* **they cannot be His disciples**.[(d)] Without making a true commitment to follow Jesus, there is no spiritual birth into God's eternal holy family. Heaven is only open to God's children, His faithful angels, and His heavenly beings.[(e)]

Satan's contemporary lie is worst than His first to Eve in the sense that her decision did not condemn her and the rest of the world *eternally,* but Satan's current lie has eternal consequences

---

a: Rom 6:22. b: Gen 3:1–6. c: John 1:13; 2 Peter 3:9. d: Luke 14:26–27; Matt 10:38. e: Rev 21:7–8, 27.

for those who listen to him instead of God. Satan's latest distortion of truth has given many *a false sense of eternal security*, and thereby many who are even regular church attendees are living like the rest of the world and not actively following Christ.

When those who do not attend church on a regular basis look at many of our contemporary churches, they do not see a holy witness where godly love is at work among God's people. Therefore, we are suffering from a double blow from Satan's present lie:

> (1) many going to church are *neither being saved nor growing spiritually;* and
> (2) many outside the local churches have no desire to know about God because Christianity appears to be a social club where people placate one another through association but are no more concerned for one another or them than anyone else.

This ungodly activity is breaking God's heart! It is a terrible witness against God from many who are claiming Christ as their savior. Satan's great lie is being perpetuated more and more in our contemporary world giving many a false hope that everyone is going to Heaven.

Today, many are claiming Christ as savior but are not allowing Him to be lord, and consequently they are not being light to the World. *These are corrupting God's Gospel Message in such a way that does not encourage people to find an off ramp from the wide-road leading to destruction.* It is causing many to live out their lives in an empty state instead of being born of the Spirit and joining God in His ongoing Creation. This lack of spiritual rebirth causes many to continue living without a personal relationship with God and miss out on a life filled with godly love, joy, and inner peace. It is only when one confesses disobedience toward God and changes his or her direction in life from a self-centered life to God and His way of life (repentance) that one starts to experience the great joy of being part of God's family and working together with God to bring others into His eternal family.

Jesus' followers are being transformed,[a] and they are learning to love others as God loves all.[b] When they die physically, *they do not need a pass* into Heaven from anyone

---

a: 2 Cor 5:17; Gal 5:22–23.   b: 1 John 3:14; 4:16–19.

including church leaders because they are God's children. Heaven belongs to God *and* all of His children.[a] Jesus will meet them as they leave their physical bodies and escort them into the presence of their eternal Father.[b]

Choose Life!

Approximately thirty five hundred years ago, God told Israel, a people who had agreed to follow Him, that He had put before them life and good things and death and bad things depending on how they lived. He went on to tell them that if they would return His love and walk in His ways–obeying His commands, statutes, and judgments, He would bless them in the land that He had given them; they and their descendants would live an abundant life.[c] 235 Approximately fifteen hundred years later, God's Sent Son, Jesus Christ, told Israel and the rest of the World that everyone needed to beware and consider that those taking the easy road in life would not be entering Heaven.[d] He explained to Thomas that those who wanted to live with God and others who were holy would need to follow Him and His way of life.[e] 236

Our Heavenly Father gives us free-will and asks us to *seek* Him for cleansing from the past and development for the future.[f] 237 In demonstrating His incredible love for us through His *redeeming and reconciling work* on the Cross, God has given us proof of His sincere desire for a mature relationship with us. Because of His righteous nature and great love for us, we should subordinate our will to His and allow Him to develop us *into perfectly compatible members* of His family. God wants to shape us into His moral image so that we can live together in perfect harmony forever. In his book *Christ's Call to Discipleship*, James Boice reminds us that happiness only comes when we allow God to reorientate our lives to His standards.[238] In order for God to transform our lives, we must die to self and live for Him.

To teach this important concept of subordination, some of God's prophets used the metaphorical image of God being the

---

a: John 14:1–3; 17:24; 20:17; Rom 8:17.   b: John 14:3; 1 John 3:1–2; Rev 21:3.   c: Deut 30:15–19.   d: Matt 7:13–14.   e: John 14:6.   f: Matt 6:33; 7:7–8, 14; Luke 11:9–10.

potter and His children being the clay. This image helps us to understand the importance of allowing God to shape our lives into what He has planned from the beginning of the Creation (Isa 64:8; Jer 18:1–6). Good pottery is useful and a delight to all; marred pottery is discarded. He warns everyone that in reality there are only two paths in life. If we follow the broad path, which is the sum of all paths other than His holy path, we will ultimately lose the eternal joy and peace that God desires for us. The collection of these destructive paths make up a collective wide and easy path to follow especially for those who have good friends traveling it. Doing wrong with friends does not seem as bad as doing wrong alone.

Although this destructive wide path has its momentary spurts of pleasure, a person pays a terrible price by losing opportunities to join God in His good work for all during this present time and eventually his or her place in Heaven. This type of continual . . . continual . . . continual . . . self-centered, selfish action hurts everyone and causes tension between us and our Heavenly Father, who desires to shape us into the perfect moral likeness of His first son, Jesus Christ.

God Will Not Be Mocked

Beware, God will not be mocked![a] Each one of us will end up being judged according to our decisions and actions during this short mortal portion of our eternal life.[b] [239] Those who listen to God and learn to follow Christ and His teachings become part of His intimate family.[c] *Those who do not will perish.* They will be separated from God, His immediate family, and all of His Holy Heavenly Host for eternity.[d]

Jesus teaches us that loving God with all our heart, soul, and mind along with loving our neighbors as ourselves fulfills the intent of the Law–God's instruction for living,[e] which stands throughout the Church Age. In fact, Jesus says that He came to fulfill the Law and that nothing of the Law will be removed right up to the time of the final Consummation of the Creation.[f] Paul

---

a: Gal 6:7; cf. Luke 8:17; 16:15.　b: Rom 2:11–16; 1 Peter 1:17.　c: Ps 90:12; John 14:21, 23.　d: 2 Peter 3:7–10.　e: Matt 22:37–40.　f: Matt 5:17–19.

taught the Christians of Rome the same thing when he told them that Jesus was the *telos* of the Law, which means that Jesus is the fulfillment of God's law leading all who are trusting God into righteousness.[a] [240]

Although the Law pointed out sin and testified to the coming redeeming work of the Messiah,[b] it in and of itself did not keep anyone from sinning.[c] In fact because of our *rebellious* corrupted nature, it causes many to get even more hostile toward God and sin even more.[d] But, by God's grace, eternal life was made possible through God's righteous loving action.[e] Paul says it this way,

> But, when the fullness of time came, God sent forth His Son, born of a woman, born under the Law in order that those who are under the Law may be redeemed, in order that we may receive sonship. And because you are sons, God has sent forth the Spirit from His Son into our hearts crying "Abba, our Father."   Gal 4:4–6

When God the Father sent Jesus Christ into our world to be born of a woman and to live under His righteous standards, which are clearly shown through His Law, His plan was to redeem those who would obediently follow Jesus' lead. Those who listen are joyously welcomed into His eternal close-knit holy family. Nothing has changed in God's plan of salvation!

Through individuals such as Paul, God has taught that He is not partial in His love and guidance for all. Whether one sins and has heard the instruction of God physically or not, all sin has consequences. Paul proclaimed that only those who were doing what God taught would be justified, made righteous.[f] The Law was given by God's grace in order to expose sin and lead as many as would listen to Christ.[g] Does God's grace annul the Law? Paul says emphatically, "*no!*" God's true children establish the Law, God's instructions for daily living.[h] [241]

The Good News for those who are being led by the Spirit is that whenever anyone fails to fulfill the Law, Jesus' death on the Cross provides removal of sin, which allows Christ's true followers to enter into God's presence with a righteousness received from Him.[i] [242] Although the Law was never intended to

a: Rom 10:4. b: Rom 3:19–20; Gal 3:19, 24. c: Rom 3:21, 23; 6:23; Gal 3:21. d: Rom 5:20. e: Rom 1:16–17. f: Rom 2:11–13. g: John 1:16–17; Gal 3:19, 24. h: Rom 3:28–31. i: Rom 8:14–17; 10:1–4.

stop nor remove sin, it reveals God's holy nature with righteous and good commandments.[a]

Allowing God To Lead

Those who truly seek God and His will for their lives will find the narrow path to eternal life through Jesus. Jesus is the path to eternal life with God. He is the *only* Way to the Father–indeed He is the "door" to the Father's presence,[b] [243] and all other so-called paths to God are part of the Broad Path of Destruction. The author of Hebrews tells us that Christ, the eternal High Priest, offered Himself as an atoning sacrifice, once for all people of all time.[c]

We will never have inner peace while we are so blatantly violating the very reason that God created us, which was to have a pure, caring relationship with Him and one another. If we continue to ignore God's love and authority living only for ourselves, our own families, or any other group(s), our hearts will eventually become so hardened that *we will separate ourselves* from God for eternity.[d] [244]

Because God desires a *free-willed* multi-personal relationship with all, *He does not force anyone to join Him* just as a loving spouse would not force nor coerce their mate to stay with them. God warns us that living in selfishness and its corresponding disobedience and sin leads to eternal separation from Him (second death).[245] We must learn to listen to God and do what He asks of us or our separation will become so complete that we will feel extreme emotional pain that is hard to comprehend.[e] [246]

Turning Off the Wide Road That Leads to Destruction

Jesus taught, "Enter in through the narrow gate because wide is the gate and *spacious/easy is the way* that is leading into destruction, and many are entering in through it because narrow is the gate

---

a: Rom 7:9–12. b: John 10:7; 14:6. c: Heb 4:16–5:10; 10:10–14; cf. 1 Peter 3:18. d: Rom 1:18–24–28–32. e: Luke 13:24–28.

and *troubling/difficult* is the way that is leading into
life and few are finding it." Matt 7:13–14

Wow! What a difficult teaching. What makes walking in
God's ways so hard compared to living like most people, and why
does God make living with Him so difficult if that is what He
desires for His Creation? The bottom line is that God is perfectly
holy. His nature is pure love,[a] and He wants all to become holy
like Him.

Those who do not want to accept God's lordship, will be
allowed to remain immature, ungodly, and self-centered, but they
will not be allowed to trouble those who want to live with God in
peace. *Many do not want to believe that a loving God would create
a place called Hell*, and they become blind to the reality of Hell's
existence and importance. Those who reject God's authority will
be confined for eternity in Hell, which is also called "the Second
Death." Hell confines those who do not want to submit to God's
authority so that they are not able to disturb the lives of those who
do.[b] [247] See chapter 3 for more information on Hell.

The Righteousness of God

But now apart from law, the righteousness of God has been
manifested being witnessed by the Law and the prophets.
The righteousness of God is (realized) through faith in
Jesus Christ—for all who are trusting, because there is no
distinction for all have sinned and are falling short of the
glory of God—being made righteous (justified) freely by
His grace through the redemption which is in Christ Jesus.
Rom 3:21–24

The Consequence of Sin

God teaches us through Paul that the Law was weak on
account of the flesh, our fallen self-centered nature.[c] In other
words, our selfish desires are at times able to override the holy
spiritual desires that God implants into our hearts resulting in sin

a: 1 John 4:16.   b: Rev 20:11–15.   c: Rom 8:3.

and consequential death. Scripture teaches us clearly that the actual penalty for any sin, any act that disobeys God's instructions for life, is death, separation from God and His eternal close-knit family.[a] [248] We have been created to be part of God's eternal intimate family, but because of sin, we are separated from that very family.

During Moses' day, God taught those who would follow Him that they had to live holy lives: lives that were distinct and separate from those who were not walking in His ways. Israel agreed to follow God and was commanded to be a holy nation manifesting God's true caring nature to the entire world.[b] [249] They were to be a light to the world just as Christ's followers are today. God does not allow sin to disrupt His holy way of life. Therefore, He does not allow sin to exist in those who choose to live in His eternal presence. God with His righteous nature does not allow the co-existence of good and evil in His immediate presence. That is why Scripture teaches us over and over again that God is holy and demands that we, His created children, strive for holiness.[c]

All Are Sinning

Because our Heavenly Father is holy and will not allow sin to exist in close proximity to Him, Paul declared emphatically that "the wages of sin is death!"[250] By the time that he had encountered the Risen Lord and walked under the leading of the Holy Spirit for several years, Paul also stated emphatically that "all have sinned and are falling short of the Glory of God."[251] This was a change of thinking for Paul, who in his earlier years believed along with many of his countryman that they could live their lives zealously following the guidelines of the Law and be saved without the atoning work of the suffering Messiah.[d] The author of Hebrews made the bold statement that the blood of bulls and goats had been pointing to what God's Son was going to do and that sin had not been removed by their sacrifices; it was removed through Christ's.[e]

After his encounter with the risen Lord, Paul came to understand that he and his zealous countrymen had not really

---

a: Rom 6:23. b: Ex 19:5–6. c: Lev 19:1–2; 1 Peter 1:14–19. d: Isa 52:13–53:12; Rom 9:30–10:4. e: Heb 9:23–10:14.

understood the necessity of God performing a costly miracle stemming from His righteousness to remove sin from their lives.[a] [252] In God's economy, sin had to be removed, not covered. When we begin to understand how righteous God really is and how sinful we really are, we can make this personal by joining Isaiah and saying with him, "my eyes have seen the King, YHWH (leader) of the Hosts."[b] [253]

A Real Problem

Well, as we begin to understand that God does not allow anyone with any sin in His immediate presence, we begin to understand that we have a real problem. Sin causes separation from God.[c] We begin to understand that God is holy and that He will not allow *any* individuals who are sinning to enter into His immediate presence because *sin is not acceptable. It is like cancer.* If unchecked it will bring death to godly relationships starting with our relationship with God. Yet, we know that God has created us to be with Him in close proximity as close-knit family members for eternity. In addition, we realize that although God gave us the written Law through Moses as one of His many acts of grace, neither the Law nor our obedience to the Law has saved anyone because of *our failure* to live out the requirements of the Law perfectly.

To live in God's immediate presence, there must be *no* sin with its resulting destruction to perfect relationships. Sin is not acceptable to God. *We come face-to-face with the reality that without God's help, we would all face the second death spoken of in Revelation 20:11–15.*[d] Without God's intervention, we would all be separated from God for eternity. Without His help, no one would be allowed to live with Him as an eternal, intimate family member. There would be no eternal peace for anyone.

Justification: Becoming Holy Like God

As we reflect on God's supreme righteous act of love on our behalf, the death of Christ, we come to realize that although

a: Rom 1:16–17; Phil 3:4–11; 2 Cor 5:21. b: Isa 6:5. c: Isa 59:1–8; Rom 6:23. d: Gal 3:24.

the Father suffered great agony over His Son's rejection and death, both knew that they were making *the only way possible* for us to be reconciled to them forever due to their holy way of life.[a] [254] Their decision is based on godly justice, grace, and truth, which in God's economy meant that the penalty for transgressing others had to be satisfied in such a way that sin is removed and eternally eradicated. If any of God's creation was going to live with Him, *justification was required; it was not optional.*[b] We know that this is true through the world around us, God's Word, and the confirming consistent work of the Holy Spirit in everyone's life.[c] God's demonstration of genuine love and persistent encouragement should draw us to Him.

When someone starts to become aware of God's holiness and his or her own sinfulness, there is a personal desire to clean up one's life prior to submitting to God. The problem is that without God's help, no one is able through his or her own sin corrupted strength to achieve perfect holiness. That is why our Heavenly Father took matters into His own hands and provided a way through His Son's death to remove our sins and renew our character according to His holy likeness. It is God's righteous work,[d] not our own that ultimately has the ability to transform us into holy beings suitable to live with Him and one another in His Heavenly Kingdom. Through the miracle of Jesus' death on the Cross, His followers have *all sin removed and are given God's righteousness in exchange.*[e] [255]

I have personally seen many over the years continually reject God's invitation into His family, because they wanted to wait until they had their lives more in tune with His holiness. I know that no one is able to straighten out his or her life enough to approach God without repentance. The Good News is that no one has to. God just wants us to desire to live holy lives and make a commitment to follow Him and His ways. He does the rest. *It is God who shapes and empowers us so that we may start living godly lives witnessing to all.*[f] [256]

If we allow God to direct our lives, He cleanses us from our sins and draws us into His good works. The Apostle Paul stated that only the doers of God's instructions would be justified.[g] This

a: John 3:14–15. b: John 3:14–17; 2 Cor 5:21. c: Rom 1:20–22; 2:11–16; John 16:7–11. d: Rom 1:16–17. e: 2 Cor 5:17; 1 Peter 2:24. f: Acts 1:8; Rom 8:14; Gal 5:22–23. g: Rom 2:13.

becomes a critical point that we will discuss in more detail later in this chapter. God requires participation in His creation on two fronts: holy living and following the leading of the Holy Spirit.

With this in mind, let us grasp anew the meaning of reconciled sonship as described in Romans 8:28–30. Our Heavenly Father is telling us that *if* we learn to love Him because of His great love for us:

> (1) we are *called* (chosen) because of our responding love, and in that calling, God will help us to mature more and more into the likeness of Jesus with His pure level of grace and righteousness;[a]
>
> (2) we are *justified:* our sins are removed through a great miraculous work of God, who accepted our sins as His sins, and in exchange for our sins, He has given us His righteousness;[b] and
>
> (3) we are *glorified*, given full-sonship and eventual perfect moral character matching Jesus' sonship and character.[c]

As we learn to obey Jesus, we begin to stand upon our Father's promises. As we walk with God, we start to develop a trust for His perfect plan for a godly family and corresponding peace and begin looking forward to the day that we will be in Heaven with Him.[d] As we join God in His Great Work and allow Him to continually develop us, we come to realize that we will not reach perfection during this portion of our eternal life, but *we trust God to complete our transformation*.[e] He continually softens our hearts, and we become more and more compassionate toward others. We take great comfort in knowing that in the not-so-distant future, we will have our sins totally removed, we will be conformed perfectly into Christ's moral image,[f] and we will enter God's immediate presence where there will be no more pain nor sorrow.[g]

---

a: cf. James 1:12. b: cf. Rom 3:21–28; Gal 3:13; 2 Cor 5:17–21.
c: cf. John 17:23, 26; Rom 8:14–17; 1 John 3:1–2. d: Phil 3:20–21; 2 Peter 3:13. e: Phil 1:6. f: Rom 8:29; 1 John 3:1–2. g: Rev 21:1–7.

Awakening

> . . . there was a great famine . . . and he desired to
> eat his fill . . . and coming to himself (his senses)
> . . . and arising, he went to his father.
>
> Luke 15:14–20

Have you ever sensed that God had been or presently is saying to you, "Arise my love"? God is constantly asking people and nations to wake up, understand the consequences of sin, and begin living holy lives with Him.[a] [257] In Jesus' day as in every era, most people stay busy building their own relationships and estates, but too much busyness is counterproductive in developing relationships with the Creator and other people. As we discussed earlier, whether it is technological distractions, general entertainment, perversions, perverted relationships, work, or just busyness in general, one should not allow busyness to sidetrack them from listening to God. God uses His faithful people of every generation to awaken those who are spiritually slumbering through personal contact and all types of media including pamphlets, magazines, books, radio, TV, E-mail, i-Pods, i-Pads, and the list goes on and on and on. He also uses personal crises and other events in the life of each person to either draw people to Him or strengthen those who are already committed to following Him.

Initially, most people do not listen to what God is saying. They only ask God for help in fulfilling their self-centered desires. Not really understanding God, they consider God as a genie who has the capacity to fulfill their every desire. It is through God's work with all that He is able to eventually bring some to a place where they actually start to care about God and their neighbors.[b]

Although people constantly ask God for favors, many do not really start to listen to the Creator unless something bad is going on in their lives just as it was for the wayward son quoted above in Luke 15:14–20. Normally, people do not initially turn to God unless there is a special need in their lives. God takes these opportunities to reveal Himself and teach the importance of caring about others. While He has peoples' attention during difficult

---

a: Isa 60:1–3.   b: Matt 22:37–40.

times, He works in their lives showing them a genuine need for His help beyond their present circumstances. He shows them how much they need help in becoming caring members of an eternal society, the need for removal of sin, and how through His great love, He has provided a way through Jesus Christ for each person to become perfect and part of His holy family.[a]

For those who start to listen beyond their immediate concerns, God starts guiding them off the wide-road leading to destruction and onto their individual narrow roads with Him. These narrow roads have been assigned not only to lead Christ's followers into eternal life but to guide them into helping others to know Him as well. He consistently stays at their side asking them to allow Him to be more fully involved in their lives.[b]

Here is the crux of the matter. *Due to Adam and Eve's sin, everyone starts out self-centered desiring things for themselves without much concern for their neighbors.* Everyone starts out like a child with blinders on not fully seeing the bad consequences of their actions. During these moments of awakening and its corresponding lucidity, everyone must decide whether he or she will return to a familiar but lesser life satisfying personal desires or start obeying God's Word and His leading.

During those lucid moments, everyone has to go through an inner struggle deciding whether or not they are willing to give up their temporary worldly pleasures. It is during these lucid moments that individuals realize that God has a better life for them if they are willing to become part of His holy family instead of insisting on having things their own way. If individuals stay focused on themselves, they will soon revert back to the familiar lesser satisfying life of self-absorption and soon forget the better life that God has shown them.[c]

God will continually work with people throughout their lives confirming or condemning every action bringing those who will obey Him into a place of understanding the reality of His creation and mandatory standards for eternal life.[d] [258] In addition to what God teaches us about Himself through His creation,[e] He will ask all who are willing–whether committed to Him yet or not–to learn more about Him through the reading of His Word.[f]

---

a: John 17:23; 20:17; Eph 4:1–6; Rev 21:3. b: Rev 3:20. c: James 1:23–24; Rev 3:15–20. d: Rom 2:11–16. e: Rom 1:18–32. f: Deut 4:1; 30:15–16; Ps 103:17–18; 119:5–12.

God has inspired each of the writers of His Word and it profits all who listen.[a] Through God's Word, *those who have a genuine desire to do what God desires,* will eventually come to know the reality of Jesus Christ and His saving work.[b]

If you have a desire to know more about God or have made a commitment to follow Christ, you should be reading God's Word on a regular basis and allowing Him to teach you reality, which if followed sets one free from self-centeredness and corresponding sin. Jesus promises that those who "remain" in His Word will know reality and be set free from sin in doing so.[c] "Remaining," which is a present tense active participle in the Greek text, is translated from the Greek root *meno.* It indicates both a *reading* and a *living out* what God is teaching through His Word.

If God has been working in your life teaching you His ways, remember to *allow Him to teach you from His Word instead of reading into His Word what you want it to say* to fit your existing life style. Many, who do not really want to live holy lives and follow God either consciously or subconsciously, *read into* the Bible what they want it to say, *ignore* parts that cannot be made to fit into their desires for life, and in general *do not allow* God's Word to shape their lives.

Who Do You Say That I Am?

After teaching His disciples and having them observe Him and participate with Him in ministering to thousands, Jesus asked them who people thought that He was. The general consensus was that most thought that Jesus was a great prophet.[d] Then Jesus asked them, "But you, *what* are you saying that I am?"[e] Simon Peter responded that Jesus was the long awaited Messiah, the Anointed One of God, but he did not stop there. He went on to say that Jesus, the Messiah, was also "the Son of the Living God."[f] These are the most important truths that all must consider. Who and what is Jesus?

God gives everyone multiple times in his or her life to make a commitment to follow Jesus and His holy way of life. If you have not personally made a commitment to follow the Messiah

---

a: 2 Tim 3:16–17.   b: John 7:17.   c: John 8:31b–36.   d: Matt 16:14.
e: Matt 16:15.   f: Matt 16:16.

(Christ), God's Anointed One, as both lord and savior of your life, you will have another opportunity as you read further. We never know how much time that we have prior to our physical death. Therefore, Scripture is clear that we should not put off a genuine commitment to follow Christ; it should be done sooner than later.[a]

You know that God loves you, created you to be part of His eternal family, personally died for you, and gave you free-will to think about good, evil, and His love for you. He wants you to decide for yourself whether or not you would like to be part of His family. So, the first question that you need to ask yourself is this: is Jesus Christ really the Son of God, who created everything that is visible in our physical universe and saves all who call upon Him from the consequences of their sins? After walking with Jesus for three years and seeing Him die for the sins of the world,[b] [259] buried in a new tomb,[260] and raised after being physically dead for three days,[261] *all* of His closest disciples started proclaiming Jesus as the saving Son of God.

Even prior to Jesus' death, God revealed Jesus' identity and upcoming sacrifice to Matthew.[c] Satan and his demons knew all along the true identity of Jesus Christ, but they did **not** know about the Father's plan of redemption through His death.[d] [262] Do not let Satan and his helpers keep you so preoccupied with *less important* things in life, that you do not at least come to realize that God loves you more than you can presently comprehend. Our Heavenly Father sent Jesus, the Messiah, into our world to die for your sins providing you with the one and only way to live with Him forever.[e]

Once you know through God's Word and any historical research that you may want to do in order to know that Jesus truly lived, died, and was raised from the dead for all,[263] you are ready to reconsider following Christ. If you have not done so already, *will you submit to God and His ways and pledge allegiance to Christ as your lord and savior*? If you ask God to help soften your heart, He will. If you have not allowed God to speak to your heart and received Jesus as lord as well as savior, you need God's help now. Everyone needs God's help in changing from his or her self-centered hearts to a heart more like His.[f] [264]

---

a: Acts 2:40–41; 3:19–20; Heb 3:7–4:13. b: John 1:29. c: Matt 16:16–23. d: Mark 1:34. e: John 14:6; Eph 2:11–16. f: Matt 13:14–16.

What I have observed over the last thirty years as a minister of Christ is that allowing Jesus as lord is very difficult for many. Many come to the point of realizing the validity of Jesus' claim to be the Son of God and savior of the world, but only some have understood that without total submission to Christ's lordship, God does not give spiritual birth into His family. Even with this understanding, many who did understand would not commit to following Jesus because they did not want to give up some of the things that they were currently doing. It was not so much that there was major sin in their lives, but whatever they were doing took precedent over accepting God's invitation into His family. If you fall in this category, I want to stress the fact that Satan works hard to keep as many as possible from understanding how pure God's love is. But, when one truly turns his or her life over to Him, God begins a transforming process that produces inner peace and joy that surpasses present understanding.[a] God liberates, but sin clouds reality and corrupts our closest relationships restricting our development.

God is worthy of our submission and loyalty and so is Jesus Christ.[b] As adults, I believe that total submission to our Creator is the hardest act of the will that anyone has to face, if they had not turned their lives over to God as children. To submit your will to God's and not know the details of what lies ahead is hard to accept until you come to realize how much God loves you and how great His ability is to bring everything into compliance with His will. Christ's followers will be brought into God's eternal presence totally transformed into Christ's image.[c] For those who listen to God, it is His love and ability that finally allows them to subject themselves to God's authority *even when they do not know most of the details.*[265]

If you are convinced that Jesus is the Son of God but have not submitted to His lordship, pray that God will show you His heart and worthiness as you read the next chapter. If you pray for God's guidance, He will reveal Himself to you. You will come to see that He is worthy of your love and obedience, and from there God will encourage you to solidify a genuine commitment to follow Jesus wherever He leads regardless of the consequences.

---

a: 1 Cor 13:9–13; Eph 1:18–20.   b: Rev 4:11; 5:8–10.   c: 1 John 3:1–2.

9

Discipleship Starts with Commitment

Jesus taught that *everyone's understanding of God* and His atoning work on everyone's behalf *was limited unless they had a desire to do His will.*[(a) 266] As you consider our Heavenly Father's love, do you have a genuine desire to follow Him? Jesus does. Jesus said that doing the will of His Father is what sustained Him even more than food.[(b)] *Without sin* in His life, Jesus focused on pleasing His Heavenly Father.[(c)] We should do likewise. If we allow God to expose sin in our lives and confess it before Him, He will cleanse us from sin allowing us to return His love and grow in our love for our neighbors.[(d)] Like Jesus, if sin is removed from our lives, we will gladly obey God and love one another.[(e) 267]

Our relationship with our Heavenly Father and Jesus depends on our level of desire to do His will.[(f)] Both the Father and Son through the Holy Spirit are constantly working with all manifesting Themselves at opportune times in order to draw as many as possible close to Them.[(g) 268] *Our response makes all the difference.* Do we call on God only when we have personal needs, or do we listen to God during good times also and stay in touch with Him in continuous communication desiring to do His will out of a growing love for Him? Although many sense that God loves them beyond their ability to comprehend, few give Him the respect and love that is due. Many times, like most, we are mainly concerned with our own welfare and do not see the eternal big picture. In a state of self-centeredness, it is hard to give up the little control that we each have and allow God to have His way in our lives.

*If we will just turn to God with an open mind and heart and start **studying and acting** on His Word,*[(h)] *we will start to see His loving glorious nature through the life and ministry of Jesus Christ.* Jesus is the ideal representation of love and as such is full

---

a: John 7:17. b: John 4:34. c: John 4:34; 8:29; cf. Isa 6:1–8.
d: 1 John 1:9. e: 1 John 3:23; 4:7–19; 5:3. f: Matt 12:49b–50 et al.
g: Rev 3:20; John 16:7–1. h: John 8:31b–32.

of grace and truth.[a] [269] We will come to realize that sin is very harmful for all and not acceptable in God's eternal holy family. God will not allow sin in Heaven because it corrupts every relationship, and therefore, everyone who wishes to be part of His holy family must allow God to transform them in holiness bringing peace and joy out of chaos.

As people come to a place in their lives of wanting something better beyond experiencing both good and evil and turn to God for help as *both lord and savior*, God begets them spiritually into His holy family and starts His work of molding and shaping them into His image.[b] In the Bible, this process is called sanctification. Our English word is translated from the Hebrew of the Old Testament, *qadosh*, and the Greek of the New Testament, *hagios*.[270] The primary idea behind both words is that one is living a life that is *set apart* from the ways of this world, *dedicated* to God, and *emulating* God's life. Those who want to live a godly life start by emulating the life of Christ who perfectly represented our Heavenly Father's life.[c]

Sanctification, living a godly life separate from the ways of the world, *starts* when one willingly steps out trusting and obeying God because of His glorious nature. It is a biblical fact that God only accepts people into His eternal family who are willing and committed to allow Him to shape them into the moral and obedient image of His son, Jesus Christ. God asks everyone who wants to be part of His eternal family to give up personal ambitions and submit to His leading. There is no room for lukewarm followers.[d]

Jesus is our perfect example and leader. Jesus takes pleasure in doing and saying those things that His Heavenly Father desires.[e] [271] Like the Father, Jesus loves all people dearly. ***Jesus came to serve, not to be served***.[f] He consistently spent His time and energy teaching as He healed the sick and removed demons. His main teaching to all was "go and sin no more."[g] There were many nights that Jesus just dropped where He had been ministering without an adequate or comfortable place to sleep.[h] There were many times when He could have used some rest but pushed on bringing light to as many as possible during His short

---

a: Col 1:13–20; Heb 1:1–3. b: Eph 1:13–14; Rom 6:22. c: John 14:9; Heb 1:1–3. d: Rev 3:16. e: John 4:34; 8:26–29. f: Matt 20:28; Mark 10:45. g: Matt 3:2; 4:17; 11:20–24; cf. John 5:14; 8:11. h: Matt 8:20; Luke 9:58.

stay on earth. All of this culminated with many asking for His death and the release of a known criminal.[272] Jesus does not ask for anyone's sympathy, but He does ask for our love and obedient service to others in response to His obedient service and suffering for all.[273]

Although many start out wanting a savior but not a lord, every individual must eventually choose whether he or she wishes to follow God and His caring way of life or follow the current leader of evil in our world, Satan, and his destructively anti-God ways.[a] When individuals follow Christ, through the leading of the Holy Spirit, God transforms their mind to care as Christ's and empowers them to follow His leading instead of Satan's.[274] If one continues to follow Satan knowingly or unknowingly, he or she stays on that wide easy road that leads to eternal separation from God. They end up in Hell with its eternal state of shame and suffering.

Denying Self

The first point that Jesus made for all who were interested in following Him is that they must allow God to lead and in so doing must die to self. They must lay aside personal ambitions and follow Jesus. This does not mean that God wants everyone to be a full-time minister, but it does mean that *all of Christ's followers will minister on some level* and that all who follow Jesus will live out their lives under Jesus' lordship and not their own. In his book *Christ's Call to Discipleship*, James Boice stated that earlier followers of Christ would never understand how people today could profess to follow Christ and ignore self-denial, which is the very essence of being one of Jesus' disciples.[275]

Those who follow Jesus will not be working out success according to the world's standards but instead according to God's leadership. God asks all of Christ's followers to give of their resources, which include talent, time, and money. The good news for those who make a genuine commitment to follow Christ is that when they become part of God's eternal holy family, they also become part owner of everything. Although it is not apparent

---

a: John 3:36; 8:43–46; 14:23; 1 John 3:7–10; cf. Deut 30:15–16; et al.

presently, in reality not only do Christ's followers share in Jesus' glory, they are also fellow heirs with Him.[a]

But, what we own with God is nothing compared to our developing relationship with God and other Saints that brings great inner peace and joy. What we give up in personal success and possible material possessions during this present age to serve God, we gain back more than our minds can possibly imagine both in this present world and in Heaven.[276] In reality, it is the turning away from a self-centered, selfish way of life to God's way of life, that brings great joy and inner peace.

Worldly Pleasures & Personal Ambitions

*In a kind of seductive and deceptive way, Satan deceives many into believing that if they start listening to God, **they will have to give up much more than they will receive in return.*** Many people fail to follow Christ when they are young for this very reason. I have personally seen many who came to understand God's love in some limited way, but failed to grasp the severity of the consequences of not following God's ways and leading for their lives. Just as the Laodiceans, they did not realize how much more God had for them, if they would just turn to Him.[b]

Most of us know that God is asking us to follow His lead and give up some of our personal time and resources in order to help others physically and spiritually, but we do not want to do so. The concept of helping others other than our own immediate family is foreign to much of the world. The idea of denying self makes no sense to those who do not trust a loving Creator to look out for their best interests.

Jesus taught that those who desire to follow Him must start by "denying" themselves.[277] They must let go of their personal desires of the flesh including success and obediently follow Him out of genuine love for all.[c] For many, Jesus was and still is asking too much. It is amazing how much time can be wasted on being entertained, entertaining, engaging in sports, social networking, doing hobbies, using technology, or just spending

---

a: John 20:17; Rom 8:17, 28–30. b: Rev 3:15–18. c: 1 John 2:15–17; 3:23.

extra time with family or friends at the expense of becoming involved with God.

In reality, it is all about willingness. Are we willing to help others, both spiritually and physically? Years ago, I went into a local jail about once a week and meet with some men and taught about God's love to as many as would listen. One day a chaplain who worked with the men and women on a daily basis told me that an inmate had challenged his level of concern for them. The inmate asked this particular chaplain if he really cared about them. He wanted to know if he was genuinely concerned about them on a godly level. Was their chaplain agonizing over their present spiritual state and doing what he could to help as many as possible know and follow God? This is what it is all about. Does the world see God working in Christ's followers agonizing over their lost state?

Over time, I have seen some who initially would not follow Christ eventually start following Him and consequently learn to care more about others. *When they began to finally realize that God gives much more than He asks of anyone, it was easier to give up control and let God lead.* One such individual, whom I had not heard from for many years, called me just a few months before he died. He was suffering from a liver ailment brought about by his personal life style. I went to meet with Him knowing through the Holy Spirit's leading that he had never started following Christ. We spoke for a couple hours and he finally realized at the end of his life that it would be an honor and privilege to follow Jesus.

He repented and asked God's forgiveness because of his worldly life style and committed to follow Christ for the rest of his life knowing that God probably would not heal him physically. God did heal him spiritually and gave him a peace and joy that was supernatural. Over the next few months, his body slowly shut down. As I watched his final decline, he noticed that I was feeling sad about his physical state, and he told me not to be sad because he was the happiest he had ever been in his life. He had become a child of God and witnessed accordingly to his family and friends before he died. I was reminded again of God' grace and the truth of Scripture, which said that those who receive the living water of

God will never thirst again and *that the Living Water residing in them, the Holy Spirit, would become a living spring* for others.[a]

Repentance: the Final Frontier

The idea of repentance is translated from various forms of the Old Testament Hebrew words *shuv* and *naḥam* and the New Testament Greek words *epistrephō* and *metanoeō*. Within biblical meaning, it indicates a change of heart, a change of one's life and life style, a turning from self and sin to God's righteous way of life.[278] It is a change of the heart that triggers action. There is a true commitment to stop living for self and start living for God. In reality, God knows everyone's heart and true repentance brings about conversion, being spiritually born into God's holy family, which is the work of God and God alone.[b] We learn from Scripture that repentance is the last hurdle to overcome. It is the last frontier as individuals come to the place of asking God for forgiveness of sins and "turn" from their personal self-centered lifestyles to Him and His way of life. ***It is necessary!***[c]

The Septuagint–an early Greek translation of the Hebrew Old Testament (mid third century B.C.)–translates various Hebrew verb forms of *shuv* into Greek forms of the verb *epistrephō*.[279] In 2 Chron 30:9 and Neh 1:9 it is written that if Israel "turned back" to God after serving other gods and being expelled from their land, God would give them grace through their captors and allow them to return to their land. In Jer 18:8, God said that if any nation turned away from doing wickedness, He would relent of their up-coming judgment. God's response to repentance, individually and corporately, has always been the same. If an individual repents or God's people as a whole repent within nations, God will make both whole, individuals and/or nations.

In Acts 15:3, the Greek noun *epistrophē* is presently translated as "conversion" by many–it would have been better translated as the "turning" of the Gentiles (toward God). Luke used this word to describe a change of lordship and lifestyle for those Gentiles who had given up their pagan lifestyles to follow Christ. In addition, we see Luke using various verb forms of this noun to describe a "turning" to God by both Jew and Gentile. In Luke 1:16,

a: John 4:14. b: John 1:12–13. c. Matt 3:2; 4:17; Acts 2:38; 20:21.

we see a prophecy given about Jesus, the Christ: He will "turn" many of the Sons of Israel *back* to the Lord, their God. In Acts 11:21, Luke speaks of a connection between believing (trusting) and "turning to" the Lord Jesus. In Acts 14:15, he reports that Paul proclaimed the Good News to all in Lystra in order "to turn them away" from empty-vain things and "turn them to" the Living God.

In Acts 26:19–20, Luke speaks of repentance being part of the process of "turning to" God. He recalled Paul telling King Agrippa that he, Paul, had been obedient to God's revelation to him, and therefore, he was proclaiming the Good News to many including the Gentiles telling them "to repent and turn to the (one true) God" *doing works* worthy of repentance.[280]

God speaks to all people of all ages about good and evil.[a] ***Biblical conversion occurs through God's action after one "turns to Him" giving up their own way of life and submitting to Him and His ways.*** A genuine conversion is completed by God when an individual desiring to do God's will "turns" from his way of life to follow God and His way.[b]

When one listens to God and starts to follow Him based on a developing love for Him, trust in God grows through *experiencing* His trustworthiness.[c] All who commit to follow God and His way of life experience a fuller and fuller life here-and-now through sanctification[d] [281] and are made perfect upon physical death.[e] [282] They are completed in their final form when they receive their resurrected bodies.[f] All who have learned to trust and obey God over the ages become part of His close-knit holy family and kingdom forever.[283]

We all are born into sin and begin our lives rebelling against God.[g] So as we learn about God and His desire for us to join Him forever, what might hinder us from submitting to His lordship and receiving Him into our lives?

(1) Our second President Bush said that his *ego* had been an obstacle. President Bush finally came to a place in his life where he realized that God with His unbiased love

---

a: Rom 1:18–2:16. b: John 7:17; 1 John 2:17. c: Gal 5:6. d: Rom 6:22. e: 1 John 3:1–2. f: Phil 3:20–21. g: Rom 5:8–10.

toward all offered a better way of life than he was living
and surrendered his life to Him;[284]
(2) there are others who have simply grown up *wanting
everything their own way* making it hard to submit to
someone else's authority even a loving Creator;
(3) there are some who are *jealous* of those who are
listening to God and being blessed by Him. Jealousy
hardens one's heart against God and man;[285] and
(4) there are many other reasons that others will not submit
to God, but in reality, until one starts listening to God, they
will not really get to know Him well enough to submit to
Him and His way of life.

When looking at biblical repentance, the key to "turning"
to God is ***His love***.[a] [286] There are quite a few who will respond
positively to God's love,[b] [287] if they would just slow down and
listen to Him above all of the competing voices, of which many are
satanic distractions. When one turns to God, repentance is
manifested through an obvious developing trust and obedience
toward God.[c] God's people learn through Christ's leading to do
less and less harm toward others, because God is developing godly
love in them and love does no harm.[d]

The New Testament is clear regarding the spiritual impact
of turning to God. One must turn from self to God in order for God
to give spiritual birth into His family. And many, like the Prodigal
Son, have to experience some difficult event or series of events
before they will slow down and allow God to help them come to
their senses. There are others that during moments of quiet, God is
able to speak to them and eventually reveal Himself and His way
of life. In either case, ***there must be a turning to God prior to
being spiritually born into His family***.

In the context of the writings of the New Testament, it is
taught that those who repent of their wickedness and commit to
following Christ start to experience life changes:

(1) they immediately *become new creations* "in Christ"[e]
through spiritual birth into God's eternal close-knit holy
family;[f] [288]

---

a: 1 John 4:16. b: 1 John 4:19. c: Gal 5:6; John 14:21, 23. d: 1 Cor
13:4–8; Gal 5:13. e: 2 Cor 5:17. f: Eph 1:13–14.

(2) they immediately *start experiencing the sanctifying work of the Holy Spirit*;[a] those who have been born of God sin less and less and less due to the Holy Spirit living in them;[b]

(3) they are *immediately justified* before God [c] although their justification is not realized until they experience God face-to-face.[d] In reality, with spiritual birth into God's family comes a miracle through which God removes their sins having placed their sins in Christ on the Cross and makes them righteous before Him through His righteousness;[e] [289] and

(4) as they follow Jesus *empowered by the Holy Spirit, they tell others about God's goodness,*[f] deny self, and pick up and carry their individual crosses each day.[g] [290]

Carrying One's Cross

In order to be saved and born of the Holy Spirit, God asks us to commit to carrying our own personal crosses, individually giving, and willingly suffering on behalf of others. This is not easy, but worthwhile in every aspect. Kyle Idleman, a pastor of one of the US's largest churches, eventually realized that he had been trying to bring people to God through messages that were appealing, comfortable, and convenient.[291] Then, he came to the realization that *Jesus did no such thing*. Jesus emphasized repentance, surrender, and brokenness more than forgiveness, salvation, and happiness.[292] Jesus taught that His followers were to deny self, pick up their crosses daily, and follow Him.[h] Idleman realized that a cross best expressed Jesus' life and ministry and His invitation for others to join Him in humility, suffering, and death.[293]

Although Jesus was eternal like His Father and had physically created the universe and all that is in it, He did not think it beneath Him to humble Himself and die for His creation giving life to all who obediently respond. *Jesus is an example of godly love in action!*[i] [294] Jesus' ministry did not stop with His death and

---

a: Rom 6:22. b: 1 John 3:9. c: Rom 5:1. d: 1 John 3:2. e: Rom 1:16–17; 2 Cor 5:21; 1 Peter 2:24. f: Rom 8:14; Acts 1:8. g: Luke 9:23; 14:26–27. h: Luke 9:23. i: Phil 2:5–8.

resurrection but is ongoing from His place in Heaven at the right hand of the Father.[295]

God does not tell us in advance what each of our individual crosses on behalf of others will be, yet He has specific duties for each of Jesus' followers to help bring His Creation to completion.[a] There are no surprises for God. He knows what He is doing. He asks that *we make a commitment to follow Him* based on His character and ability. He tells all that those who follow Jesus **will suffer, <u>but</u> they will also experience great joy** as they join Him in rescuing people from eternal pain and suffering. Are we willing to give up our personal aspirations as we learn to trust Him with our physical and spiritual lives?

Sometimes, we make half-hearted commitments that end up leaving us without fulfillment due to our lack of faith. God is looking for genuine trust in *His character and ability.* He is looking for true commitment, sacrifice, and allegiance in the face of whatever circumstances that He allows in our lives. In all cases for those following God and His ways, **He uses His people out of ever tribe and nation to represent Him to the world.**[296] *Those who follow Him are His priests and light for all.*[b]

After God showed His love to Israel as a nation and rescued them from slavery in Egypt, the whole nation, agreed to follow Him not fully understanding His holiness nor priestly demands.[c] Many who said that they would follow God had not made a long-term commitment and thus continued to sin and rebel against God. They did not make it into the good land that God had set aside for them because they would not undergo the trials that He set before them, which made all who listened stronger.[d] God has a better way of life for us now, but it also includes trials and tribulations.

The Mind of Christ

Paul said that Christ's followers have the mind of Christ.[e] If we continue to take time to *study* and *act* on God's Word, Jesus Christ and our Heavenly Father teach us to know the reality of both the physical and spiritual world that surrounds us. If we continually read and act in obedience to God's Word and the

a: Eph 2:10; Phil 2:13. b: Matt 5:14–16; 1 Peter 2:9–10. c: Ex 19:4–6. d: Num 14:20–35. e: 1 Cor 2:16.

leading of the Holy Spirit, we learn to hear God more fully as He speaks to each of us. He starts maturing us in order that we may live in a closer relationship with Him. Our character will eventually become totally transformed to be like Jesus' resulting in a very close mature relationship after mortal death.[297]

Knowing about Jesus' Joy

What did it cost God to redeem those who learn to trust Him over the ages? From Scripture, we find that *it is mandatory that all sin be removed* from those who want to come into God's eternal presence. Sin cannot be just covered over with a bandage. The wound has to be totally healed to the point that there is no trace that a wound ever existed. The Psalmist David once said that due to God's loving kindness, He has removed the transgressions of those who love and respect Him as far as the east is separated from the west.[a]

So how did God remove our sins from us allowing us to be with Him for eternity? Paul uses three basic thoughts to express how God removed the sins from those who learn to trust and obey Him out of love:

(1) in Galatians 3:13–14, Paul stated that Christ became a *curse* for those who are trusting in God so that those who are "in Christ" might receive the blessings of Abraham, which includes the indwelling of God through the Holy Spirit. From the Old Testament, it is clear that when someone violates God's law (His teachings), he or she is cursed in the sense that judgement for sin is coming because of doing what was wrong. The penalty for sin (doing wrong) is death, separation from God and His community. From Scripture, we know that our lord and savior, Jesus Christ, became a curse on our behalf, was judged guilty, crucified on our behalf, and spent three days in Sheol separated from God the Father and His holy community on our behalf;

(2) in Colossians 2:13–14, Paul stated that when we were dead, separated from God, because of our transgressions,

---

a: Ps 103:11–12.

Christ's atoning work on the Cross allowed God to take the master list with our names and corresponding charges and *nail it to Christ's cross condemning Him and cancelling out the charges against us;* and

(3) Paul explicitly stated in 2 Corinthians 5:21 that when Jesus Christ died on a cross on our behalf, God the Father *transferred our sin to Him* who had been sinless up to that moment. Peter said the same thing.[a]

In this same Scripture, we discover that in exchange for our sin, God has placed His righteousness in us so that when we stand before Him, we are one hundred percent righteous, holy. ***This is a miracle of gigantic proportion.***

It is easy to consider God's saving miracle on our behalf, thank Him for dying in our place, and go on with life as usual. But, this is where we need to really *pause and consider* what God has done for us, and what He wants in return. ***At great cost to Himself through suffering, pain, and death, God took on the sins of all who learn to trust Him.*** In exchange, God asks all to trust Him enough to allow Him to apply the miracle of the Cross to their personal lives. If people consider carefully what God has done, I believe that many will be more considerate about following Jesus.

When the Apostle Paul finally came to realize who Jesus was and realized immediately how God had fulfilled His prophesied grace through Him, he turned immediately to Jesus of Nazareth, the real messiah, and started following Him.[b] Later, he taught others that they needed to allow God to develop in them the same attitude that was in Christ. He had humbled Himself and *become obedient unto death* on humanity's behalf.[c] This is the same Jesus who put the physical universe together.[d] This is the same Son of God who became more complete by obediently *experiencing* death for His brothers and sisters under the direction of our Heavenly Father.[e] 298

Jesus knew that dying on a cross and dying spiritually was going to produce ***terrible pain and suffering*** both physically and emotionally. Just before He was arrested to go to His death on a cross, He asked the Father one last time if there was another way to take care of our sin. In reality, He already knew the answer to

a: 1 Peter 2:21–24. b: Gal 1:11–24. c: Phil 2:5–8. d: John 1:1–3.
e: Heb 2:9–11; 5:8–10.

His question and had submitted to His Father's will.[299] This same
Jesus who willingly endured the shame and suffering of death on a
cross as a criminal on our behalf *simultaneously experienced
great joy* because He was providing salvation for all who desire a
righteous life with God.[a] *This is godly love! What are you willing
to do for your friends?*

If we consider both the *suffering and joy* of Christ, we will
start to understand the mind of God, which is also the mind of
Christ.[b] *Because God so loves all*, the Father sent the Son to
suffer and die on the whole creation's behalf.[c]

It is hard to imagine what the Father went through
emotionally when He saw His Son being rejected by His own
people.[d] Think of the emotional pain of both the Father and Son
when the very people whom Jesus had ministered to for three years
turned against Him and asked for Barabbas, a known criminal, to
be set free.[e] Imagine the Father's emotional pain when Jesus was
humiliated, scourged, and died physically a cruel physical death on
a cross. Then imagine the most painful part of all: because Jesus
took on the sins of those who learn to trust God, the Father had to
turn His back on His obedient faithful Son for three days while He
was undergoing ex-communication from Him on our behalf. This
is Jesus' spiritual death, separation from His Father with whom He
had had perfect unity up to this point in time.[f]

Consider Jesus' abandonment by the Father when our sins
were placed on Him. As Jesus was dying, He cried out loudly, "My
God, my God, for what reason have you abandoned me?"[g] [300]
Jesus knew why His Heavenly Father was abandoning Him. That
proclamation was to remind us of the great cost that He and the
Father were paying for our redemption.

We know from Jesus' discussion with one of the thieves
that Jesus and that particular thief would be in upper Sheol
(Paradise) that very day,[h] and we know from multiple places in
Scripture that Jesus would be in Sheol (Hades) for three days
preaching the Good News of how God the Father and He had
arranged to remove sin.[i] As He ascended to the Father after
spending time in Sheol on our behalf,[j] He was also freed of sin

a: John 15:10–13; 17:13; Heb 12:2. b: 1 Cor 2:16. c: John 3:16–17;
Rom 6:3–11; Heb 10:10–14; 1 Peter 3:18. d: John 1:11. e: John
18:39–40. f: Matt 27:46; John 2:18–22; Heb 2:9. g: Matt 27:46.
h: Luke 23:43. i: Isa 53; Gal 3:13–14; 1 Peter 2:24; Eph 4:7–12.
j: Acts 2:31.

and set free all those in upper Sheol. Those who were trusting God prior to the Cross were finally able to be made perfectly righteous through His death allowing them to be in God's immediate presence after Christ finished His atoning work. Jesus' death on humanity's behalf removed all sin from all who submit to the loving Creator for all time. *The major spiritual battle that was critical for a saving opportunity for all mankind had been won.*[a] This battle was won through Christ's obedient and sacrificial life and death through which He suffered greatly on humanity's behalf. *This is true love in action!*

Your Personal Cross

Jesus said that *if we are not willing* to carry our individual crosses and follow Him, *we are not able to be His disciples.*[b] [301] So, is God worthy of our turning from self to Him? *Of course He is worthy!* If you do not feel a sense of awe and reverence toward God, you are still too focused on yourself. When we come to realize what God has done for everyone, the normal response should be to return God's love by asking Him into our lives.

Think of it his way. If you have not yet come to understand *why you should joyfully follow Jesus and stop looking for personal gain*, you are still being deceived by Satan. If you have any real understanding on what is going on around you spiritually, you would want to do your part in building God's eternal close-knit holy family. Consider this: what would you personally be willing to do to save someone whom you love dearly from a terrible fate such as dying in a fire, a drowning, or auto accident? Most of us would do whatever it takes including possibly giving our own lives to save those whom we love.

Rescuing others from an eternal painful state and helping them to improve their lives right now is what God is asking us to join Him in doing, which fulfills the purpose of God's creation. Jesus gave His life that we may live life abundantly.[c] *Jesus is asking us to join Him in suffering* and to pick up our individual crosses and suffer for others because of what He has done *and* our

---

a: John 19:30; Rev 5:9–10; 11:15. b: Luke 14:27; cf. Matt 10:38.
c: John 10:10–11; 1 John 3:16.

growing love for all.[a] If we have not yet allowed God to teach us to truly care about those around us, we will not be willing to suffer on their behalf.[b] It is that simple.

Consider what Paul said about his own suffering for others. In a letter to the Saints living at Colossae, Paul said,

> Now, I am *rejoicing* in those things suffered on
> your behalf and I am supplying the needs of the
> afflictions of Christ in my body on behalf of His
> Body, which is the Church, of which I have become
> a minister according to the (my) stewardship
> (management) from God, . . .   Col 1:24–25[302]

Paul wanted Christ's followers at Colossae to understand that his suffering was not something that destroyed his joy but instead built it due to the advancement of the Gospel, which brought many out of the bondage of darkness into the Kingdom of His Son.[c] Paul was working under Christ and was being empowered by Him to present as many as possible before God at the Judgment Day *complete* in Christ.[d]

In a similar way, Paul told the Corinthians that they were sharing in the ongoing afflictions due to spiritual warfare with Satan as they proclaimed the Gospel.[e] [303] He went on to tell the Saints residing at Corinth that the Macedonian Saints, who were also being afflicted for their trust in God as they followed Jesus, were experiencing great joy through their generous behavior towards others.[f] Paul also encouraged the Thessalonians to continue to do God's work in spite of the afflictions that they were suffering as they followed Christ. Paul and the others who were helping him were rejoicing because the Saints at Thessalonica were continuing to grow in their faith.[g] [304]

God's children rejoice in godly advancement for all. *The critical issue for all people is whether or not they are truly following Christ.* If they follow Him, God will be teaching them to love others and rejoice in their spiritual success. If they are not, they are not born again nor truly loving others enough to be willing to suffer on their behalf.

---

a: John 15:20; cf. Matt 10:25. b: 1 John 3:17; 4:11–16. c: Col 1:13–14. d: Col 2:28–29. e: 2 Cor 1:3–11; 4:7–10. f: 2 Cor 8:1–4. g: 1 Thess 2:14–3:13.

Following Jesus: Daily Apprenticeship

> Jesus said, "Behold, I am standing at the door (of
> each person's life) and knocking. If anyone hears
> my sound (from knocking) and opens the door, I
> shall come in onto Him and I will fellowship with
> him and he with me." Rev 3:20[305]

OK, as we contemplate Jesus' requirements for those who
consider following Him, we come again face-to-face with *the one
critical decision* that has to be answered in the affirmative by
everyone prior to death or it becomes an eternal "no." *Everyone
has to decide prior to death whether or not they will submit to the
lordship of a gracious and loving God who is definitely worthy of
everyone's love and loyalty.*
    Many are so caught up in their own aspirations and desires
that they never give serious consideration to eternal good and evil
and God with His open invitation into His eternal close-knit holy
family. Jesus taught an important parable regarding people in His
day and their personal busyness. He taught how such busyness lost
many a place in God's eternal Kingdom. This parable applies to all
ages because there are always those who are just too busy
accomplishing personal ambitions or fulfilling personal desires
that they do not have time to listen and accept God's invitation into
His eternal family and Kingdom.[a] Jesus' parable has two
important points:

> (1) do not put off responding in the affirmative to God's
> invitation into His eternal holy family because there may
> come a point in your life where you do not hear God's
> invitation any further; and
> (2) if you accept His invitation to follow Jesus, God is also
> asking you *to accept the conditions of that invitation* which
> include denying self, picking up your cross daily, and
> submitting to His lordship.

Just as in the parable, God expects you to act appropriately if you
accepted His invitation into His family. If you do not accept the
conditions of the invitation, which are clearly stated at multiple

---

a: Matt 22:1–14.

places in Scripture–just as in this parable–you will end up being separated eternally from His holy family and sent away to live in Hell.

In Jesus' day, when individuals became disciples (students) of a particular teacher, they would normally live in a close relationship with their teacher emulating both the teacher's teachings and the teacher's way of life. In modern terms, His followers are close *apprentices.* Jesus expects His disciples to emulate Him. He asks all to submit to the Father's teaching, His leading, and allow Them to teach godly love to the point that His followers acquire a godly concern for others. He even asks His disciples to be willing to lay down their lives for one another.[a] All disciples are expected to suffer according to God's will in order to be part of His great rescue operation.[b]

Following Jesus is not easy, in fact, at times it is difficult and requires hard work, but the rewards are much greater than anything else that we will ever do on earth. If you are willing and make a genuine commitment to be an active part of God's family and follow Jesus' leadership in this grand rescue operation, you will begin to experience great joy as you help save those whom you personally have come to love through God.[306] *Love is the key!* Love never fails,[c] because God's nature is grounded in genuine love for all.[d] God is able to bring all who follow Him to eventual completion in Christ.[e]

OK, let's go back and reconsider the critical question of acceptance. Are *you* willing to receive God's invitation into His family knowing that all members of His family are committed to help one another and help those who have not yet received Him into their lives? God's children have agreed to sacrifice personal ambition in order to know Him more fully and help Him bring as many as will listen into His eternal holy family. No one accepts God's invitation into His family fully understanding His love or demands. But, they receive God into their lives because He is a loving and trustworthy sustainer and they want to be part of His eternal close-knit holy family that experiences love, joy, and peace. It is a privilege and great opportunity to live together with God and others *without sin* in an environment of pure love.

---

a: John 13:34; 15:12–13. b: John 3:16–17; 2 Peter 3:9; cf. 1 Tim 2:4.
c: 1 Cor 13:8a. d: 1 John 4:16; John 3:16. e: Phil 1:6, 9–11; 3:20–21.

Stepping Out & Experiencing Jesus' Joy

Jesus said to him (a potential disciple), "No one setting his hand upon a plow and then looking at things behind him is suitable for the Kingdom of Heaven." Luke 9:62

If you have made a genuine commitment to follow Jesus at some time in your life, you will see fruit.[a] The Holy Spirit will be working in you developing your character and helping you to lead others to the Father through Christ.[b] ***If there has been no fruit, no leading anyone to Christ, let's consider a new commitment.***

In Luke 9:57–62, Jesus teaches the importance of following through one's commitment for those who are either following Him or considering following Him. No one can be truly loyal to two or more masters.[c] *A genuine commitment to follow Christ means that you must let go of your personal aspirations and become a team player of Christ's.* Wherever He leads each of us who are committed to following Him, we should go without thinking about what it might be like going some other route.

Let's talk further about trusting God. Hebrews, chapter 11, gives us great insight to the importance of individual faith in God. Faith is trust. Do we trust God to do what He says in Scripture for others and us personally? Is He trustworthy and capable? God asks all of us to step out in faith and to follow Him not knowing where He will lead.[307] Hebrews 11 gives us a list of individuals, who despite what was going on around them, trusted and followed God.

When the writing of Heb 11 is matched with the accounts recorded in the Old Testament, we note that each of these individuals *grew* in their faith over time. Each one grew to a place of faith, a place of trust in God and His ability, that even when God asked them to do something very difficult, they did it:

(1) consider Abraham, who was willing to give back his and Sarah's only biological son to God after waiting many many years for him;[d]

a: Matt 28:18–20; John 15:1–5. b: Gal 5:22–24. c: Matt 6:24–34.
d: Heb 11:17–19.

(2) consider Noah, who built a very large ship to house hundreds if not thousands of animals on dry ground waiting for a massive world wide flood;[a]

(3) consider Elijah, who went up on Mount Carmel to confront Baal's false prophets in front of Israel knowing from his faith in God that God would not let him nor Israel down;[b] and

(4) then, consider Jesus, who came into His world incarnate as a new born baby living out His life among sinful hostile people who would eventually crucify Him for doing good and speaking truth. He took on their sin and trusted the Father to remove it and raise Him from the dead defeating death for as many as would receive Him.[c]

I have witnessed God's goodness and saving work in many lives over the last 30 years. The biggest obstacle that I have observed for those who slowed down long enough from their busyness to listen to God is that they were still enjoying life on the wide road that leads to destruction too much to submit to Him and His way of life. *Without submission to God, there is no spiritual birth into God's eternal family!*[d] God does not allow any chaos in His Kingdom, and in order to keep total peace, He demands that all who become part of His eternal holy family submit to His lordship. Every kingdom has a king; God rules the Kingdom of Heaven.

Billy Graham tells us in his autobiography, *Just As I Am*, that at just the right time for him, an evangelist, Dr. Mordecai Ham, got through to him as he preached revival services in his area. Billy Graham was spell bound as the Holy Spirit spoke through this evangelist and taught him about Heaven and Hell.[308] *Billy realized through Ham's teaching that he did not have a personal relationship with Christ and could not depend on his relationship with his parents nor his local church to save him from sin.*[309] After struggling over submission, one night Billy Graham went forward and turned his life over to the rule of God.[310] With that decision to submit his life to God's authority, he came to a place of feeling both peace and joy.[311]

Years later, Billy Graham spoke with George W. Bush, who would become our forty-third president. God used that

---

a: Heb 11:7. b: 1 Kings 18:16–39. c: Receive: John 1:12; Rev 3:20. Defeating Death: John 1:29; Phil 2:5–11; Rev 11:15; 12:11; 1 John 2:1–2; 3:5. d: Exod 20:1–7; Deut 30:15–16; John 3:36; 14:23; 15:14.

opportunity to help George Bush realize that although the Bible provided good self-improvement tips, that was not the real message of the Bible. The center of life had to shift from self to Christ, who had to become lord of one's life.[312] President Bush said that prior to surrendering his life to God, religion had always been part of his life, but he had not been a Believer.[313]

I know from personal experience, that surrendering to God is serious. I accepted God into my life as a child of eight. It was God's love that drew me to Him at that time. When I was baptized that same school year at the age of nine, God gave me a special gift: he allowed me to feel a little of His love for everyone in the room that day. That blessing helped me later through some of my own personal trials and helped me to become a more understanding minister. But, although I was saved by God's grace at an early age, God still forced me to consider total submission as an adult. Twenty years later at the age of twenty eight on a Sunday evening at church, after wrestling with the idea of *total* submission to God's lordship for months, I came to the place in my life that my trust in God allowed me to totally submit to His lordship. I prayed telling God that I was now ready to follow Jesus without reserve–to the best of my ability–anywhere He desired me to go.

Life has been exciting ever since I submitted to Christ's lordship as an adult. God has had me serving others in many capacities. He has been patiently teaching me to give up control as I learn to follow Jesus more fully. I try to live each day serving God with an open mind to His leading helping people along the way. What a rewarding life! As I serve others through Christ's leading, I experience godly inner peace and joy.

The Apostle Peter encouraged those in his day to follow Christ no matter how difficult the journey became. This also applies to us. Peter encouraged all in his day to deny self, pick up their individual crosses daily, and follow Jesus rejoicing in their suffering with Christ as they brought light into a darkened world.[a] [314] Spiritually, nothing has changed over time. We should all follow Jesus as fully as possible and watch Him working through and in us to bring many out of darkness into His marvelous light.

---

a: 1 Peter 4:12–13.

What Do You Say?

From what you have already read, you know that you have been created by God to be part of His eternal close-knit holy family. This is your primary purpose for existence! God wants you to voluntarily join Him and His family. When you willingly turn your life over to Him for justification and development, God works in your life building a character that comes closer and closer to matching that of Jesus Christ's. At death, God completes His work in you,[a] and when you stand before Him entering your assigned place in eternity within His family, you will be morally like Christ standing before God clothed in His righteousness without any sin.[b]

God asks all *to respond to His great love through repentance, obedience to His Written Word, and obedience to His leading through the Holy Spirit.*[315] Prior to making a commitment to follow Jesus, no one can clean themselves up righteously enough to be presentable in his or her own righteousness,[c] but the good news is that *God receives you just as you are.* If we have a desire to do God's will and come to Him committed to follow Jesus as our lord and savior, *it is God who cleanses us* of our sins.[d] As we start a committed life with God, we learn to obey Him more and more because of His great love for us, and our trust in God continues to grow. *As we experience obedient discipleship following Jesus,* we continue to grow in love, trust, and obedience through His trustworthiness.[e] It is true. As Christ's followers are more obedient to God and grow in their relationship with Him, they also learn to love others more fully.[f]

For some who have been listening to God through the work of the Holy Spirit,[316] it only takes one exposure to the proclaimed Word of God and they repent of their wrongdoing and submit to God. They immediately look forward to a better life with God and others now and in the future.[g] But for others, there is an ongoing spiritual growth process that continues for a season while they listen to God. Eventually, some realize *a need* for a savior for the purification of their soul. They come to realize that the way to inner peace and joy is through Jesus and His atoning death.

---

a: Rom 8:28–30; 1 John 3:1–2. b: 2 Cor 5:21. c: Rom 3:23.
d: 2 Cor 5:21; Col 2:13–14; 1 Peter 2:24. e: 1 John 4:16. f: John 13:34; 15:12; cf. John 1:7; 3:16; 4:7. g: Rom 6:22.

As you have been reading this book, it is my prayer, that you have become more biblically anchored in God's Word and realize more fully that He loves you dearly and wants you to receive Him into your life. If you have never submitted to God asking Him to be the *lord* and *savior* of your life, now is the time.

Let's Talk Commitment

Let's talk commitment:

(1) Are you at a place in your life where you know that Jesus Christ became incarnate as a babe, lived a serving life, died on a cross for the removal of your sin, was buried, and was raised from the dead three days later according to Scripture?;[a]
(2) do you understand that sin causes disharmony, hurt, and destruction and needs to be removed from your life in order that you may be reconciled to God and others?;[b] and
(3) do you know that everyone is a sinner and in need of a savior?[c]

Considering God's pure nature of love, which has been demonstrated by His actions for all and shown by His words as recorded in Scripture, have you come to a place where you trust Him enough to submit your life to Him?[d] Once you have turned to God and have submitted to His lordship (repentance), He will never lose nor forsake you.[e]

Jesus asks all who are considering submission to His lordship to consider what He is asking prior to submitting.[f] [317] He tells all who wish to be part of God's family that if they are not willing to join Him in building His Father's eternal holy family, the Father will not allow them to be part of His family.[g] [318] Jesus' marching orders for all family members have one common point, "As you are going (living your lives), *make disciples*."[h] Without being willing to follow God's leadership in helping to reconcile a lost world unto Himself,[i] individuals will not be empowered by

---

a: John 1:29; 3:14–17; Luke 1:26–35; 1 Cor 15:4.   b: Rom 6:17–23; 2 Cor 5:17–21.   c: Rom 3:21–26; 6:23; Gal 3:13–14, 24.   d: 1 John 4:16; cf. 1:3; Rom 10:9–13.   e: John 10:9–17, 27–30.   f: Luke 14:26–33. g: John 15:1–2.   h: Matt 28:19.   i: Matt 7:21; cf. John 7:17.

the Holy Spirit *enabling* them to be disciples of Christ.[a] [319]

As we presently come to a place of commitment, I am reminded that we all need Jesus as both lord and savior in every aspect of our lives. I know that God will lead all who listen to Him out of an unfulfilled life into one filled with inner peace, joy, and great expectation. In addition, I know that as individuals start listening to God, their lives change for the better *immediately* and *forever.*[b] *Within a relatively short period of time*, their family and friends will be blessed right along with them. There is no greater gift for a parent, spouse, or child than for a loved one to start following Jesus.

Knowing that whenever someone submits to our Creator, their life starts changing immediately for the best encourages Christ's followers to stay off the bleachers and sidelines and get in the game whenever God opens a door to help others know Him more fully. *There is nothing more important* that any of us can do *than to witness about God* and His glorious nature to those who are living out their lives on that wide road leading to destruction.

Ok, *now* is the time. If you have *not* already turned to God, you should do so. It's time to make a commitment to follow Jesus. Remember that Jesus does not accept lukewarm followers.[c] With a firm commitment to follow Jesus, *God will come immediately into your life through the indwelling of the Holy Spirit and start developing you so that you are able to walk in godly love and righteousness blessing many.*[d] If you try to wait until you become righteous enough to approach God, you will be waiting forever. Everyone needs God's help in becoming righteous.[320] *So let's pray to God asking forgiveness of our wrongdoing and committing to follow Jesus.* Pray this prayer or one similar to it to our Heavenly Father, who knows your heart, *and trust Him to start His redemptive and transforming work in you immediately:*

> Heavenly Father, thank you for sending Jesus
> Christ, who put the physical universe together, to
> die on everyone's behalf. I know that you love me
> beyond my comprehension. Through your Son
> Jesus Christ's death, you have provided the one and

---

a: Luke 14:27, 33; Acts 1:7–8. b: Rom 6:22. c: Rev 3:15–16.
d: Rom 6:22; John 14:23; Eph 1:13–14.

only way to remove all my sin and replace it with your righteousness. I ask for your forgiveness of my sins and pledge my allegiance and loyalty to you forever. I know that sin has kept me from having a close personal relationship with you, and that by submitting to your lordship, you will remove my sin and make me righteous forever. Please help me to walk in your holy ways and follow your leading. In return, I commit to follow Christ as faithfully as I know how. I trust you and your ability to enable me to do your will, walk in your ways, and ultimately bring me into your eternal presence. As you raised Jesus from the dead and placed Him eternally at your right hand, I know that you will raise and place me into your eternal presence as a member of your close-knit holy eternal family. Father, thank you for creating me and patiently waiting for my submission. You are worthy! I pray that from now on, my life will bring honor and glory to you as people see my life becoming more and more like Jesus' life. Amen.

Putting Aside Worldly Thinking

OK, now you have done it! If you have prayed that prayer or one similar to it now or in the past, the angels in heaven are celebrating with God.[a] God starts your reconciled life with Him by saying to the rest of the Church, *"loose (unbind) him and let him go his way."*[b] Just as Lazarus needed to be loosed from his burial wrappings, each of Christ's new followers need the help of the Body to remove the wrappings of this world that bind them from godly living.

God expects you to connect–if you are not already connected–to a local church, and He expects the members of that church to have a genuine interest in freeing you from your worldly thinking and actions through proper assimilation of His Word, which comes from sound study, proper application of His Word, and a submissive heart to His leading.

a: Luke 15:7, 10, 22–24.   b: John 11:43–44.

Now that you have turned from your sins and current way of life to follow Jesus (repentance), *life is going to become exciting.* You are now officially a child of God, a king and priest, who takes orders from Jesus Christ, the King over all kings. It is important that you, just as all of God's children, stay closely connected to God through the reading and proper application of His Word. Jesus said that His disciples will know reality if they remain in His Word:

> If you remain in my word, you are truly my
> disciples, and you shall know the truth (reality),
> and the truth shall set you free. John 8:31–32[a]

By obediently serving God and reading and applying His Word, God teaches Jesus' followers reality setting them freer and freer from the diminishing sin within them. As they stay in His Word and follow His leading, He continues to bring their thinking into close alignment with His.[b] [321]

The Father's Work & Your Development

In reality, the Father is the One who ultimately does the final shaping and trimming in *everyone's* life,[c] and He uses the Holy Spirit to help all of Christ's followers know what is good and what is evil from everything that they see and hear.[d] It gives Christ's followers great comfort to know that they are important enough to the Father that He does not give this responsibility to another. God the Father takes primary responsibility for everyone's development and controls events to the point that Christ's followers are developed properly.

As the Father gives His obedient children a proper world-view,[e] He develops their patience, kindness, righteousness, faithfulness, gentleness, and self control through the leading of the Holy Spirit.[f] In addition to everyone witnessing,[g] [322] God uses Christ's more mature followers *to develop the less mature building up the entire Body of Christ.*[h] [323]

---

a: cf. Ps 1:1–3; 119:1–12. b: Rom 12:1–2; 1 Cor 2:16. c: John 15:1–2. d: 1 John 2:27. e: Rom 12:1–2; cf John 8:31b–32. f: Gal 5:22–23. g: John 15:1–5; 1 Peter 2:9. h: Matt 28:18–20; Eph 4:11–16.

In the next chapter, we will look at your potential role in the Body of Christ. It is a great honor and privilege to serve Christ together. God helps each of us find our specific place within His family and work together following Christ's lead. When we work together under the lordship of Jesus and our assigned leaders on earth, we experience the joy of using our God-given talents to help rescue the lost from eternal pain and suffering as well as helping one another become complete "in Christ."

10

Doing the Father's Will

Jesus said that only those who had a desire *to do the will of the Father* would come to know Him.[a] He also said that there would be some who called Him "lord" who would not be with Him in Heaven because *they had not done the Father's will.*[b] If someone wants to know God, he or she must be willing to follow His lead. God does not weigh people's good and bad activities throughout their lives to see if they have done enough good to enter Heaven. *Perfection is required* and no one other than Christ has lived a perfect life.[c] In reality, God only accepts people into His eternal family who are willing to allow Him to shape them into Jesus Christ's moral image and obediently follow Him. *There is no place in God's eternal holy family for lukewarm followers of Christ.*[d] *God requires commitment with corresponding action!*

One day while He was talking to a group, Jesus asked them "why are you calling me 'lord, lord' and *not doing* what I am saying?"[e] Jesus went on to say that those who *did* what He was instructing were similar to individuals who built their homes on firm foundations. When floods come, the rushing waters could not destroy their homes. But, for those who *do not* listen to the Son of God, they are similar to those who built their houses without sound foundations. When floods come, the rushing waters will immediately destroy their homes.[f]

When the eternal Jesus Christ lived on earth among people, He experienced joy as He suffered for others, because He was providing a way into God's eternal family for all who would learn to trust and obey God.[g] What a joy to help those you love! When it was time for Jesus to make the ultimate sacrifice on everyone's behalf, He prayed that those who followed Him would experience that same type of great joy that He was experiencing.[h] *Learning*

---

a: John 7:17; 8:39–47; cf. Matt 25:31–46; Rom 2:13. b: Matt 7:21.
c: Rom 3:23; 2 Cor 5:21. d: Rev 3:16. e: Luke 6:46. f: Luke
6:47–49. g: John 1:11–12; Rom 5:8–10. h: John 17:13; Heb 12:2.

to love like God is the key to inner peace and great joy. Because Christ's followers love all, they experience great joy from being family members of God *and* by seeing loved ones rescued from imminent harm and eternal pain and suffering.

Just as in Malachi's time, God wants us to trust Him enough to do our part in supporting His Kingdom. It is one thing to know about something, *it is something else to love others enough to get involved.* God asks all to step out in faith and seek to do His will.[324] Our Creator is seeking out and working with all who *honor Him through their* **actions** as well as their words.[a] [325] Are you willing to advance and solidify God's will for your life more fully? This chapter should help all who desire to know more fully their special place in the Body of Christ. It is important to remember that God works with those who listen to Him of all ages to build His eternal family and kingdom. If you are a follower of Christ, God will put you to work doing your part. *Everyone is important and everyone has a place of service in God's family.* All who listen to God realize that everyone is just traveling through this part of eternity either headed for the new Heaven or headed for Hell. Presently, we are all sojourners.

Sojourning

> . . . And the land shall not ever be sold because the land belongs to me, (and) because you are temporary dwellers and sojourners with me; . . .
>
> Lev 25:23

> For *our place of citizenship exists in (the) heavens* out of which we are awaiting a savior, the Lord Jesus Christ . . . . Phil 3:20

> Blessed is the God and Father of our lord, Jesus Christ, who according to His rich mercy has caused us to be born again into a living hope through the resurrection of Jesus Christ from the dead—into an inheritance (that is) eternal, pure, and unfading,

---
a: Luke 6:46; Rev 22:12.

which has been kept in the heavens for us, who
through the ability of God are being guarded
through faith for a prepared salvation that shall be
revealed at the end of time . . . . 1 Peter 1:3–5

We are just traveling through! We are sojourning with
God as we join Him in rescuing as many as possible bringing them
into His eternal close-knit holy family. Our journeying with God is
fulfilling His purpose in the Creation.[a] [326] When we accept God's
love through Jesus Christ, we become fully reconciled children
beginning our role as His priests, His representatives on earth.[b]
God's obedient children have been born a second time through
God's imperishable Seed, the Holy Spirit, into His eternal holy
family.[c] [327]

As God's representatives, we are to proclaim the reality of
God's Creation and act as mediators between God and man. We
are *not* to settle down and become satisfied using our personal
talents and blessings from God solely for ourselves and our
families. We have come to recognize that our physical life is only a
small portion of our eternal life, and that we have been called to be
co-laborers with God.[d] We have been fully reconciled to God with
all the emotional and legal rights of direct descendants. *We have
an **eternal** home with God* awaiting us, and we know that in a short
time the trials and challenges of this age shall be over.[e]

Christ's followers are not just waiting to go home and
presently acing as spectators watching God's performance from
the sidelines! ***Christ's followers are full-time co-laborers with the
Creator.***[f] [328] They have *the privilege and honor of representing
God on earth* to those living out their lives under the deceptions
and leadership of Satan. It brings Christ's followers **great joy** to
see as many as possible **rescued** from present harm and future
eternal pain and suffering as they receive God into their lives.

---

a: Eph 2:10; 2 Tim 1:8–9. b: Ex 19:5–6; 1 Peter 2:9–10. c: 1 John
3:1–11. d: 1 Cor 3:9; 2 Cor 5:17–6:1. e: Phil 3:20; Titus 2:11–14;
Rev 21:1–7. f: John 5:19; 15:5; 1 Cor 3:9.

Sojourning & The Great Commission

Prior to His ascension to rule Heaven and Earth from the right hand of His Father, Jesus said to His immediate and all future disciples,

> All authority in Heaven and on Earth has been
> given to me. Therefore, while living out your lives,
> *make disciples* of all nations, baptizing them in the
> name of the Father, the Son, and the Holy Spirit,
> teaching them to keep all that I commanded you.
> And behold! I am with you all every day until the
> completion of the Age. Matt 28:18–20[329]

During this Age of Grace, the Messianic Age, Jesus commands all of His followers to make disciples from *all* nations of the world.[330] *This is the one overarching command given to all who follow Him.*

As Christ's followers live out their daily lives, they are to proclaim the Gospel Message and develop disciples from all who listen to God through their *actions as well as their words*. The Gospel message has the power to make all people whole.[a] All of Christ's followers are to tell others about God's love for all and His desire for them to accept His leadership.

Although God tells Christ's followers to love all, He also warns against falling in love with our fallen world and its ways because they are contrary to His way of life. He describes the ways of the world as primarily being grounded in self-centered desire instead of genuine love for all.[b] [331]

Each of Christ's followers have the honor of participating with God in His ongoing Creation inviting all who will receive Him into His eternal close-knit holy family. It is through Jesus Christ that each of His followers exits off that wide-road, which leads to eternal shame and suffering, and walks on God's assigned narrower road that leads Home.[332] Jesus' followers come to understand that their permanent place of residence is not on Earth; it is in Heaven.[c] [333] *Trusting the Creator*, Jesus' followers join God in building His eternal holy family. *In that transforming*

---

a: Matt 5:16.   b: 1 John 2:15–17.   c: 2 Peter 3:13–14; Rev 21:1–8.

*process, Christ's followers are also experiencing **untold joy** as they help rescue family, friends, associates, and strangers from an eternal life of pain and suffering.*[a]

God gives Christ's followers an eternal world-view of service because He loves and ministers to *all* people.[334] Without listening to God's leadership and receiving His empowerment for their lives, Christ's followers would not be able to join God effectively in His world-wide ministry that starts at home. ***Without empowerment from God, none of His followers have the ability to do anything within the spiritual realm*** to overcome Satan and rescue people from his temptations and deceptions.[b] [335]

Being "in Christ"

Being "in Christ," having a close obedient relationship with Christ, is critical. It is our obedient close association with Christ that gives us access to the Father and enables us to ask Him for empowerment to overcome evil as we lead others to Him. Without Christ, we cannot know the will of the Father. With Christ, we have the mind of Christ.[c] Being "in Christ" is the only way that anyone finds true peace. Jesus brings true inner peace to all of His followers.[d] The Holy Spirit works in all of Jesus' followers producing great love, joy, and inner peace.[e] Through the work of the Holy Spirit, God rearranges Christ's followers' priorities and they rejoice in being part of His great rescue operation.

Christ's disciples are being shaped daily by God to be more and more like Jesus.[f] [336] Christ's true followers understand the importance of following Jesus' commandments including the one that directs them to go out and make disciples out of every people group of the world.[g] ***Making disciples means more than introducing people to God, it means taking the time to train those who decide to follow Jesus.*** Teaching the ways of God to those who do not know Him well takes time and effort.

---

a: John 15:11; 17:13.   b: John 15:1–5; Acts 1:8.   c: 1 Cor 2:16.
d: Eph 2:13–19.   e: Gal 5:22–24.   f: Rom 8:28–29; Eph 4:11–14.
g: Matt 28:18–20.

The Body of Christ

Those who are "in Christ" are also part of the Body of Christ. Christ is the head of the Body, the Church.[a] The phrase "Body of Christ" appears in the New Testament in various forms to represent Christ's literal body or figuratively to represent His followers working together as *His bodily representative* throughout the Messianic Age.[337]

Some New Testament writers used imagery of a human body to represent the collective work of Christ's followers as they *submit to His leadership* in order to carry out His ongoing saving work. From this metaphorical imagery, two critical attributes of Christ's followers are highlighted:

(1) godly unity; and
(2) the synergistic ability and strength that is gained through utilization of combined individual talents for the good of all.

Regarding the latter, Jesus' "Parable of the Talents" is important for all who wish to follow Him because it reminds His followers that God expects and demands that they use their individual talents to help others as they join Him in building His eternal family.[338]

In his metaphorical imagery of the Body of Christ, Paul wants all of Christ's followers to understand the importance of each member. *Everyone is important and has work to do.* When considering any physical living body, each member–whether foot, hand, ear, eye, heart, lungs, kidneys, and the list goes on–has an important contributing function to the overall ability and well being of that body.[b]

Considering how the various members of a living physical body work together for the good of the whole, Paul stressed the importance of *unity* among the various members of the Body of Christ.[c] Christ's followers are to live out their lives *radically different* from the practices of the surrounding world. *They are to unite under the lordship of Jesus Christ making disciples of all people.*[339]

When Paul used a metaphorical image of "the Body" of Christ in his first letter to the Corinthians, he was asking the

---

a: Col 1:18. b: 1 Cor 12:12–25. c: 1 Cor 12:26–27.

Corinthians to unite under the teaching and leadership of Christ and follow their local teachers and leaders such as himself as individuals who were secondary to Christ. There should be *no divisions* in any of the local churches over anything including the teachings of their local leaders such as Paul, Peter (Cephas), and Apollos. Christ's followers were to stay **united** under *the lordship* of Jesus Christ.[a] [340]

Although Jesus shares His glory (His sonship and personality) with His followers in order that they may experience godly unity,[b] it was and still is a real problem for Christ's followers. Due to existing sin and ongoing self-centeredness, even Jesus' followers will not fully realize godly unity until they physically die and stand in God's presence.[c] But, just because they have not reached perfection yet *does not* give any of Christ's followers permission to sin nor live without godly unity as they follow Him.[d] In Ephesians 4:3–4, Paul exhorts Christ's followers **to strive for godly unity** through their obedience to the leading of the Holy Spirit. Just as there is only one God, there is also only "one Body."[e] To help Israel with its unity prior to the Cross, there was only one recognized Temple, the House of God. This reminded Israel that they were all serving the *same* god.

Earlier in this same letter, Paul had emphasized the importance for Gentile and Jewish Christians to treat each other as *equal family members* disregarding the prejudices that they had both learned through their different religious, cultural, and social ways of life.[f] He began his teaching by using two metaphorical images to help Christians understand godly unity:

(1) Paul used the idea that the Jew and Gentile Christians should be living out their lives as members of a **single** family. In his metaphorical imagery, he stated that Christ had destroyed "the dividing middle-wall" that divided them through His death on a cross.[g] [341] In this metaphorical image, Paul brought to mind a common way of living in the first-century Mediterranean world through which families living in cities often lived in large buildings subdivided into family living areas by "middle-walls." These "middle-walls" were solid without doors and windows providing

a: 1 Cor 1:10–15; 3:1–8. b: John 17:20–23. c: Phil 1:6; 1 John 3:1–2.
d: Phil 3:12; Rom 6:1–2. e: Eph 4:6. f: Eph 2:11–22. g: Eph 2:14.

separation for families and businesses, one from another.[342] Paul was not advocating that all of Christ's followers live together, but he was telling his audience that they now belonged to the *same* family, the Family of God; and (2) Paul went on to use a second metaphorical image stating that through Christ's redeeming work, they were reconciled into "one body."[(a)]

Paul went on to explicitly state that both Jew and Gentile *Christians* were members of the same family, God's household, which made them family members and fellow citizens of His eternal kingdom.[(b)] He closed this important teaching on Christian unity by using one last metaphorical image. Christ's followers could consider themselves as individual parts of a great House of God, which is continually under construction until the last person is added to God's holy family. The foundation consists of prophets and apostles with Jesus Christ Himself being the Temple's cornerstone.[(c)]

The Church

The Greek word *ekklēsia*,[343] which was understood in the first century as "assembly," is being translated today by many as "church." First century "assemblies" normally referred to called meetings whether religious, political, or general. Paul taught his various local assemblies that met in homes, synagogues, and other structures,[(d)] **that the risen Lord Jesus was still the active lord of the world-wide Church**.[(e)] He told Christ's followers at Corinth, "You are the Body of Christ, indeed *a member of a part of the whole*."[(f) 344] The followers at Corinth were a part of their region, which was a part of the entire world-wide Body, the Church.[(g)]

After Jesus died on the Cross for all humanity and ascended to rule from His Father's right hand in Heaven, we see a major shift from God's people, the national Israel, to God's people, the new Israel, consisting of all who became faithful followers of Christ.[(h) 345] Initially, all of God's people came out of the nation

---

a: Eph 2:16. b: Eph 2:19. c: Eph 2:20–22. d: Heb 10:23–25. e: Col 1:18. f: 1 Cor 12:27. g: 1 Cor 12:28. h: Gal 6:16; Phil 3:3.

Israel, but within the first 20 years after Jesus' ascension, many Gentiles had begun following Christ.[a] Within 30 years, Paul said that the Gospel had been made known to all nations.[b] Many Gentiles of various nations had decided to follow Jesus.

With Christ's ascension to sit at the right hand of the Father,[c] He became known as the King of Peace and Eternal High Priest.[d] When the Creation is consummated, everyone–saved and unsaved–will bend the knee before Christ, who will in turn hand everything over to the Father that the Father may be all to all.[e]

During Jesus' present reign over the Heavens and Earth, the Church, His Body, is doing His physical and some spiritual work on Earth. The Church is no longer obligated to keep the nation Israel's ordinances that regulated cultural activities[f] nor the sacrificial laws, which were fulfilled in Christ.[g] This allows the Church to follow the moral lifestyle of God within all cultures as long as those cultural practices do not violate God's moral standards.[h] Wherever God's people live, they are expected to live according to God's moral standards caring for all.[i]

Denominational, racial, generational, socio-economical, and political walls have all been constructed through Satan's prompting as humanity has struggled against God's will. Christ's followers should be dismantling these walls as they live out their lives.[346] Therefore, Christ's followers should allow God to teach their hearts to love as He loves and live together as members of the same family. The Church is the part of God's eternal holy family that is living on Earth. It needs to act accordingly.

The Church's Greatest Mission

The Father's greatest mission is also His family's greatest mission. The Father's greatest mission is to bring as many of His creation into His eternal close-knit holy family as will listen.[j] The Father desires that all come to a place of turning from their individual desires and aspirations to Him and His way of life.[k]

---

a: Acts 15:3. b: Rom 16:26. c: Eph 1:20–21. d: Heb 7:1–8:6.
e: 1 Cor 15:28; cf. 11:3; Eph 5:23. f: Acts 15:4–21; Eph 2:13–16; Col 2:9–23. g: Heb 7:26–27; 8:13; 10:4, 10–14. h: Rom 3:31; 6:1–2; 7:12. i: Eph 4:1–6; 1 Peter 1:17–19. j: John 3:16–17; 2 Peter 3:9.
k: Matt 11:28–30; Luke 9:23.

Those who listen become part of His loving eternal family. Christ gave His life to help fulfill the Father's greatest mission.

Jesus' followers die daily to self and are a great witness as they join God in His life transforming work.[347] As Jesus' disciples learn to hear and obey His voice more fully, they have a closer and closer fellowship with God and one another and become much more effective in witnessing and making disciples. Our families, local churches, and local communities are our *daily* mission fields. One of Max Lucado's new books, *Out Live Your Life: You Were Made To Make a Difference*, offers some sound reflection with practical examples on how Christ's followers should be helping those around them.[348]

When Jesus died on the Cross for humanity to remove sin, He provided peace for all who follow Him removing all barriers.[a] *Within the Church*, Jesus effectively removes all walls that Satan has encouraged the fallen world to build, if His followers listen.[349]

Walking With Others in Our Local Churches

The Church first and foremost is the Family of God! Local churches make up small units of God's family within specific geographical areas. Through Christ, all churches are interconnected as part of the same family whether they recognize it or not. *Jesus is lord as well as savior for all within His Body, the Church; without His leadership, congregations will fail.*

Whether or not Christ's followers are part of the same local church does not make them any less a close-knit family member of God's eternal family. They are part of the same Kingdom and have the same Sustainer living in them.[b] Christ's followers worldwide and locally must allow Jesus to teach them more fully about God's family "oneness (godly unity)," which became reality through His death as the world's sacrificial lamb.[c]

Let's consider Christ's local assemblies. Members of each local church everywhere in the world should be so caring for one another that they are able to bear their innermost thoughts with one

a: Eph 2:11–22.   b: Eph 4:1–6.   c: John 1:29; 17:20–23.

another without worrying about sensitive information being used later to cause additional hurt. Church members should love one another as God loves them making it possible to live in transparency with one another. That type of living brings joy.

Within each local church, Jesus should be producing inner peace and joy in the hearts of all members because:

> (1) its members are family members of God, who is transforming each life to be more and more like Christ. Consider the difference of living in a disfunctional family where you would be constantly guarding against injustice vs. living in a family where everyone is living righteously, which includes taking care of one another. Shouldn't there be *a special joy for those who are members of God's family*?; and
> (2) its members are joining God as He builds love in their hearts for all. Whenever they are able to help one another and especially *when they are able to help someone turn to God and become a family member, a great joy is experienced over each one's rescue.*[350]

If there is little joy in your local church, you and your fellow members need to fast and pray seeking God's help in removing sin and walking more closely with Him until God gives you a breakthrough. Members of congregations that are walking closely with God *will* experience great joy as people are saved.

Being Social Beings

John the Apostle proclaimed that God is light, and in Him there is no darkness at all.[a] He went on to say,

> If we are walking (living) in the Light as He (God) is in the Light, we have *koinōnia*,[351] "close commonality (fellowship)," with one another and the blood of Jesus, His Son, cleanses us from every sin. 1 John 1:7

---

a: 1 John 3:5.

This scriptural passage clearly states that *if someone does not have close fellowship with other followers of Christ, he or she is not walking with God.* In reality, individuals who are following Christ should feel closely connected to the rest of Christ's followers.

In addition to God being Light, He is pure Love and the one who does not love those whom he or she comes in contact with especially those who have been born into God's eternal kingdom, does not love God whom he or she cannot see physically.[a] *It is God* who helps Christ's followers learn to love one another to the point that their love overrides Satan's divisive schemes.[352] Satan loves to use fear and other deceptions to isolate one from another.

As godly social beings, we should be doing *our part* within the Family of God. When members of the family are all doing their part, they will all experience more joy. Consider living at home for a moment. Think of the importance of parents teaching their children to do their part. If children do not learn to help with the basic work around the house and yard, they grow up with a handicap in managing and taking care of their own families in the future. It is important for the sake of the family health that each member does his or her part, or the entire family suffers. If some are not socially responsible, others have to do more than they should taking away from other areas of their lives. This is contrary to God's desire for our personal families, His local church families, and even His World-wide Family. May God help us work together as His family on Earth. *It is only through Christ that we can learn to work together in a godly fashion.*

Knowing & Employing My Talents

It is God who is working in you-all to desire and to work according to His good purpose. Phil 2:13

We are His doing, having been created in Christ Jesus for good works, which God has prepared ahead of time in order that we may live out our lives accordingly. Eph 2:10

---

a: 1 John 4:8, 16, 20.

It is God who gives each person his or her assignments,[a]
and it is God who places a desire in each person's heart to do
*those assignments. In addition, it is God who gives each person
the ability* to carry out their assignments.[b] Each person in God's
family has assignments to help our local families and our
international family function more smoothly. God has gifted each
person with special skills so that when Christ's followers utilize
their diversity properly, the Family of God operates in a
synergistic fashion:[c] the combined output of everyone is greater
than the sum of all individual work (synergism). This is true on
local church levels and on our combined international level.

Each of Christ's disciples should be *seeking God's perfect
will* for their lives so that they may grow into effective, loving co-
members of their respective local churches. Each follower should
be striving to find his or her place within their local assemblies so
that their local churches may be working at peak performance in its
local, regional, national, and world-wide ministries. *It all starts by
submitting to Christ and picking up one's cross*. With Christ as
the head, local churches comprising the Church, utilize their great
diversity to help one another and witness with power to the world.

After submitting to Christ, **knowing God's will is
developed by studying His Word while staying open to His
leadership through prayer.** It is important when you study God's
Word that you do not misread God's Word by reshaping it through
your current beliefs and life style. It is critical for all who want to
understand God's Word to allow God to teach them *what He is
saying* through those who wrote under the inspiration of the Holy
Spirit. It is much easier to read into God's Word what we want it to
say instead of allowing God to teach what He is actually saying.

As you study God's Word, you may wish to have a couple
good literal translations, such as a New American Standard Bible
(NASB) complimented by a New King James Version (NKJV),
and a good functionally equivalent translation, which rephrases the
original text into grammatical constructions that are more
commonly used today. Personally, I would avoid functional
equivalent translations such as the TNIV (Today's New
International Version) because of its gender bias, which
distorts God's prescribed order. The Living translations,

---

a: Eph 2:10; individual crosses: Luke 9:23.   b: Phil 2:13.   c: 1 Cor
12:12–27.

sometimes called paraphrased translations, are useful for gaining
overall perspective, but I do not recommend them for in-depth
understanding due to their loss of detail from God's original text.
Keep in mind that *the Holy Spirit is the final guide to proper
understanding as you seek truth.*[a]

In addition to using a couple good translations, there are
many good biblical study aids available such as Bible dictionaries,
concordances, and commentaries that are very helpful in grasping
biblical ideas that span several thousand years. Some aids can help
individuals understand the various literary forms (genres) along
with historical and literary contextual fundamentals. One such
book is Gordon Fee & Douglas Stuart's *How To Read the Bible for
All Its Worth.*[353] It is a practical short guide to general biblical
interpretive principles, but it also contains some cultural bias.

So what about your gifts/talents from God. Many of you
have already figured out what you are good at and what you are
not. But, if you are still struggling with understanding your God-
given talents, there are many straight forward spiritual tests
available that show individuals their overall strengths and
weaknesses. But, do not let any test result become your automatic
guide to service within your local church and beyond. *Pray and
ask God to reveal His desire for your work.* **God will initiate** a
desire in your heart to do what He has designed you to accomplish.
It may not match your greatest apparent skills. In reality, skills are
important, but without Christ no one can do any work of spiritual
worth. The battles are much too great for humanity without God's
leading and empowerment.

Paul taught the Corinthians, that although everyone was not
a great evangelist, a great preacher, nor a great teacher, all had an
important part in Christ's Body.[b] Some will be carpenters, others
cooks, others accountants, and the list goes on. *All will witness.*
Every position is important. God has no favorites and all of His
children are loved just as He loves Jesus.[c] Therefore, enjoy
whatever God has appointed you to do. Remember, it is God who
has created you with unique talent, and it is God who gives you a
godly desire to fulfill your part of the Creation and the capability
to carry it out.[d] *Your journey with God starts with submission to
Christ and continues when you step out in faith and find your
place in the Body.*

a: 2 Tim 3:16–17; 1 John 2:27; cf. John 8:31b-32. b: 1 Cor 12:11–31.
c: John 17:23. d: Phil 2:13.

And finally, after submitting to Jesus and committing to live according to His Word, *the last major part of knowing God's will is established as you step out in faith (trust) and participate in His Creation.* Consider how you might bless your local church and others through God's calling on your life. If you somehow misunderstand God's calling and start on a path that does not work, God will help you move to a more appropriate place of service. It is a lot easier for God to help you find a closer match to His desire if you are serving in some capacity rather than doing nothing.

At all times, continue to listen, read, and live out God's Word. God speaks mightily to each of His children through His Word and leading helping them to understand reality in general and His desire for each one's life.[a] Listen to your preacher(s), join a Sunday School class, consider Bible studies as led by the Spirit, and most importantly, *do* what God tells you through His Word and direct leading. *Without a genuine commitment and corresponding action, you will not advance in your walk with Christ.*

Empowerment as Needed

In his book, *The Journey*, Billy Graham reminds all that when one submits to God's lordship they are not alone. When someone submits to Christ as lord and savior, *God gives them a whole new destiny with a new purpose and power.* Jesus' followers are given a *new life*. This new life includes a *new relationship* with Him and others as a member of His eternal holy family and citizenship in the Kingdom of Heaven.[354]

If we are following Jesus, God will empower us to carry out our assigned ministries. In reality, spiritual battles are beyond our capability without Jesus leading the way. Through Jesus Christ and the indwelling of the Holy Spirit, the Father supplies the appropriate authority, power, resources, talent, and frame of mind to each and every one of Christ's followers. *It is empowerment through Christ that enables His disciples to work effectively together joyfully helping all.*[b] It is the Holy Spirit, who enlightens

---

a: John 8:31b–32; Heb 4:12.   b: Acts 1:8; Eph 3:16, 20; Phil 4:13; 2 Tim 1:7.

and works in each of Christ's disciples as they bring a lost world to God through their actions and words.[a]

Stepping Out in Faith

God asks each of Christ's followers to help others on an individual, family, local-church, and community-wide level as part of their *daily* life. Although God is not asking all of Christ's followers to go into full-time ministry, He is asking all of them to step out in faith and become involved as He leads. As Christ's followers listen to God, they do their assigned parts helping their local church families proclaim the Gospel. Through prayer, seeking utilization of godly talent, and ministering under Christ and His appointed local overseers, God helps all of Jesus' followers serve others individually and collectively.

Once an individual has made a genuine commitment to follow Jesus Christ, there is only one thing left to do: *do it!* We are justified and empowered only when we *trust and obey* the Sent Son. We join God in His saving work because we are justified and empowered by Christ through the Holy Spirit.[355] Therefore, let us *joyfully do* our assigned works, not out of resentment and fear but out of a great love for God as He develops our hearts.

It is critical for Christ's followers to actually *step out in faith and follow Him. Implementing your commitment matters.* Consider this potential personal scenario:

> (1) you see a vegetable stand on the side of the road selling incredibly good fresh local grown vegetables at 80% off local pricing;
> (2) you seize the opportunity and purchase some fresh vegetables for the rest of the week thinking about how good fresh salads and steamed vegetables will be for your health;
> (3) you take your fresh vegetable home and put them away planning on using them starting tomorrow; and
> (4) you never take the time to make the first salad nor steam the first pan of vegetables and they all spoil.

---

a: Rom 8:14; 1 Cor 2:13; Eph 1:13; 2 Tim 1:14.

What type of benefit did you get from buying those fresh vegetables? Do you see the problem? Desiring something and even investing in something does not mean that you will benefit from your planning and investing. How many of you have all sorts of good plans and investments such as exercise machines and self help books collecting dust? *If you do not follow through and implement your plans and investments, they will never do you any good!*

This is the same phenomena that is continually occurring in our contemporary local churches. Many are meeting on a regular basis with others and making plans to get serious about their walk with Christ. But, through Satan's deceptions and personal desires, most do not make a solid commitment and implement it by stepping out in faith and truly following Him. In their book, *Beyond Belief to Convictions*, Josh McDowell and Bob Hostetler state that if individuals do not follow through on something that inspires them within hours after inspiration, many forget and move on as if nothing had occurred.[356] When you are inspired by God and become convicted about a change that you should make in your life, make a commitment, step out in faith, and live accordingly.

Many people go to church, read their Bibles, go to Bible studies, make good plans to follow Christ, but never make a solid commitment to follow Christ. *Many in our churches today have never actually stepped out in faith and started following Christ.*

Prayerfully, you are one of the ones who has made a genuine commitment or would like to (see the preceding chapter). If you would like to be part of God's eternal family and have not done so yet, this is what is required: *commit to follow Jesus, step out in faith, and start following!* What God said to His people through his prophet Malachi about trust and obedience regarding the tithe is applicable to everyone's life in all areas of our relationship with God and fellow Christians. *Test God!* Step out in faith as the Holy Spirit leads and see how God will use and bless you.[a]

---

a: Mal 3:10.

Experiencing Joy as I Sojourn

While Christ's followers live out this short part of eternity, they are reminded to keep their focus on Jesus Christ. Jesus' followers are **radically different** than the world. They live with godly love growing in their heart, which in turn radically alters their outlook on others. While Jesus' followers follow Christ, *the world begins to understand the nature of God* through their individual and collective good works for all people.[a]

Christ's followers are growing daily in their **love for all** (1 John 4:16), and through their ongoing growing love, they are more and more willing to suffer and sacrifice on behalf of others having great inner peace and joy as they do.[b] This presents a paradox to those who are not following Christ, but it makes perfect sense to those who are.

How can someone who has experienced hostile actions and pain by someone actually have a desire to help that same individual at great personal cost and additional suffering? Even more so, how can that person who has been treated with hostility or deception experience inner peace and joy in the process of helping a perpetrator? Suffering and joy can only occur simultaneously under similar conditions when one really loves the one whom he or she is helping. Let me repeat this important concept. *One can only experience inner peace and joy while suffering and sacrificing for others, if that individual really has a genuine love for those being helped.*

If God is teaching you to love others, consider the following? Do you know people who are hurting others? Take them to Jesus because He can teach them to care. Do you know people who have just given up on life? Take them to Jesus because He can restore and strengthen them. Do you know people who look out only for themselves and their families? Take them to Jesus because He can teach them how to love as He loves. Do you have any personal needs that need special attention? Take them to Jesus because He loves you and will help.

For us just as for Jesus, it starts with a genuine love for all people. *Without love, we will not truly be concerned for others,*

---

a: Matt 5:16; Col 3:10.   b: John 15:8–11; Heb 12:2.

and therefore, we will not be willing to suffer and sacrifice on their behalf.[a] Jesus expects His followers to meet the physical needs of people,[b] but even more importantly, He expects those who are able to help others become and grow as disciples.[c] In order to do this, Jesus' disciples have to interact with the people around them teaching them about God and His holy ways and inviting them to turn from their self-centered ways and join Him. *Jesus' followers are commanded to engage their cultures and shed light through their actions as well as their words.*

Being Light

Jesus is the Light of the World: He exposes reality.[d] [357] Jesus only speaks what the Father tells Him.[e] The Father never lets Jesus minister by Himself.[f] After Jesus' ascension, His disciples, *the Church, became the light of the world*.[g] They do not minister alone. Jesus and the Father dwell in them providing guidance and empowerment as needed.[h] [358] If individuals reject Jesus' followers, they are in reality rejecting the Father and Son.[i] Jesus does not leave His followers alone. The Holy Spirit, the Comforter, guides them in all truth speaking to them the words of the Father.[j]

Jesus' earthly life was an exact representation of His Heavenly Father's nature.[k] Jesus' earthly life was a visible *image* of the invisible Father.[l] If you knew Jesus during His earthly life, you had seen the very nature of His Heavenly Father.[m] Prior to disobeying God and being corrupted by sin, Adam and Eve were created in the image of the Father and Son.[n] Jesus' followers, the Church, are being renewed into the *image* of Jesus and the Father.[o] If Jesus' followers act like Jesus, the World will know the nature of God. The Church led by Christ through the Holy Spirit is the Father's only representative on earth.[p] Are Christ's followers representing God well and being bright light in the World? Bright light reveals reality; dim light allows much to be hidden.

---

a: 1 John 3:16–18; Col 2:10; 3:10–17. b: Matt 25:34–40. c: Matt 28:18–20. d: John 8:12; 8:31b–32; 18:37. e: John 8:28. f: John 8:29. g: Matt 5:14. h: John 14:23; 1 John 3:9. i: Luke 10:16. j: John 16:7, 13. k: Heb 1:3; Col 2:9. l: Col 1:15. m: John 14:9. n: Gen 1:26. o: Col 3:10. p: Col 2:10; 2 Cor 5:17–21.

I heard a story one time about a blind lady who worked at an airport making a living there selling merchandise. One day a traveler in a great rush knocked over her stand with all its merchandise but was in too much of a hurry to go back and help her straighten her stand and pick up her stuff, which had been scattered everywhere. Everyone else seemed equally in a rush and the blind lady managed by herself to straighten up her stand and then started crawling about on the floor feeling for her merchandise. She was emotionally distraught as she tried to recover her merchandise in the midst of such hectic people. Finally, a traveler seeing her plight stopped and took the time to help her gather all of her merchandise so that she could place it back on her stand. She thanked him for helping and asked him a simple question prior to his departure, "are you Jesus?" How many opportunities do we all miss on a regular basis because we are so self absorbed and/or just busy that we do not take the time to show others the Jesus who lives in us?

Initially, Jesus' followers waited together for empowerment from God, which occurred on Pentecost, the Feast of First-fruits.[a] *After being empowered*, they ministered together with one heart and mind providing a great witness,

> All those who were trusting (God) were together
> and had all things common, and their possessions
> and property they were selling and dividing these
> things (giving) to each one according to whatever
> he or she had need; and throughout each day they
> were together of one mind in the Temple, and
> breaking bread from house to house, receiving
> (eating) food *with great joy* and humility of heart
> praising God and having grace toward all people.
> And the Lord was placing those who were being
> saved throughout each day together.   Acts 2:44–47

They did not sell *all* their possessions, *nor* was it mandatory to sell any of their possessions to be part of the Church.[b] In reality, Christ's first-century followers still had personal property including homes, yet they had relinquished

---

a: Acts 1:14; 2:1–47.   b: e.g. Acts 5:4.

personal ownership to God. They were striving to be good stewards of everything under their personal authority.[359]

We observe that as Christ's followers were filled with the Holy Spirit (born from above, born of the Spirit), they were more willing *to share* their possessions with others. A proper relationship with God, which is built on love, taught them to be genuinely concerned for people who were not part of their immediate biological families. Jesus gave–and still gives–His disciples a desire to become close with God and one another. Many of Christ's early followers lived out a close-knit unity with one heart and mind.[a] They followed Jesus' desire for their oneness within His family.[b]

As Jesus' disciples proclaimed God's love, they also proclaimed His holiness, His righteous standards for life, because they go hand-in-hand.[c] God's love for all establishes His standards of righteousness. *Love does no harm!*[d] All Scripture declares God's righteous standards, and all Scripture declares that the penalty for violating God's righteous standards results in judgment (wrath) concluding in death, separation from God.[e]

Therefore, in order to proclaim the Gospel, like Jesus' closest first-century disciples, *Jesus' twenty-first century disciples must declare God's holiness, as part of the Gospel Message.* The Gospel declares God's righteousness and work on everyone's behalf along with His desire for everyone to turn to Him in order to be saved from judgment.[f] Sin must be forsaken. The whole purpose of God's death is to provide a way for those wanting to live with God in His eternal family to experience a purification (justification) whereby sin is removed and each one's corrupted nature is restored to holiness.[g] Living in holiness (godly righteousness) is what provides eternal peace in Heaven. God's children will be perfected as God is perfect.[h]

Christ's followers should be engaging their cultures in order to teach God's holiness and plan of redemption to all who will listen. The New Testament is replete with historical occurrences where Jesus' followers helped as many as possible realize that their world views were incorrect as they shared the reality of God, His holy ways, and His plan of redemption.[360] Over

---

a: Acts 2:42f; 4:32f. b: John 17:11, 20–23. c: Matt 22:37–40; Gal 5:14. d: 1 Cor 13:4–8a. e: Rom 6:23. f: Rom 1:16–17; 6:1–7. g: 2 Cor 5:17–21. h: Lev 19:2; Rev 22:14–15.

172   Experiencing Jesus' Joy

the centuries, many have followed Christ and proclaimed God's righteousness and His work of redemption for all. ***Our generation must do the same!***

It is never easy to take a firm stand where you live or travel and proclaim God's righteousness to people who are enjoying sin for a season. But, as Paul taught, if Christ's followers do not proclaim the Gospel, how will those traveling on the Wide Road to Destruction understand what is really going on?[a] [361] Not only will Christ's followers be unpopular much of the time, there will be times when Satan will encourage those not following God to persecute those who are.

It takes courage and commitment to step out in faith and teach God's Word when it is unpopular, but God will help. A German, Dietrich Bonhoeffer, was a faithful follower of Jesus during the years leading up to WWII and was martyred in a concentration camp located at Flossenburg on April 9, 1945.[362] Bonhoeffer's life was one of engaging his culture and speaking out against the terrible things that Hitler was doing. Many of his own countrymen would not speak out against Hitler either because of fear or potential personal gain in following him. He called many of His countryman to task for not following Christ's teachings and wrote a book titled *The Cost of Discipleship* reminding people that following Jesus required commitment and action. After spending a couple years suffering in German prisons, Bonhoeffer came to the point in his own life that he realized that following Jesus depended on wholeheartedly turning one's life over to God. Christ's followers need to live life out as fully as possible trusting God in all circumstances *unreservedly*. He came to realize that repentance was a true turning to God, a throwing oneself in the arms of God. By turning to God and depending on Him fully, one became a true follower of Christ, *a renewed man of God*. He came to realize that God–no matter what the circumstances–would lead him and all of Christ's followers home to Himself.[363]

If we wish to live in God's will today, we must do as Jesus' followers of previous generations have done. Until Jesus returns, the Church is the only likeness of God's nature that the world will see. We must allow God to grow our concern for all. Our greatest witness will come as we come to realize who we are in Christ and

___
a: Rom 10:14.

act together as the reconciled children of God that we are. *Godly unity and corresponding peace will not come to individuals except through Jesus Christ.*[a]

Jesus did not come into the world to force world peace during this Age of Grace but instead to divide the world according to those who would and those who would not obey the Sent Son.[b] [364] Jesus' redeeming death and message of God's grace divides the world according to those who learn to trust and obey God and those who do not. Jesus makes it clear that when one does not follow God, that individual prefers to walk in darkness in order that his or her selfish and self-centered activities are not exposed to others.[c]

In order that we may work together effectively to help people spiritually and physically, we must learn to share God's love even with those who are rebelling actively against Him. In addition to ministering to the physical needs of all individuals, we must come to understand more fully that *eternal separation from God is the worst thing that can happen to anyone.*

God's Creative Work

Through Jesus Christ, God has fulfilled His promise to all by making it possible for everyone to be blessed through Abraham.[d] When Jesus carried out His mission by coming to us on our human level proclaiming God's great love and righteousness, He fulfilled our shortcomings of living perfectly according to the Law through His sinless life and redeeming death on the Cross.[e] He made God's perfect unity possible for all who receive Him.[f] Jesus has made the Father's perfect plan of reconciliation possible and is revealing it to all people through the Church.[g]

God's plan of rescuing *both* Jew and Gentile from the corruption and binding caused by sin with its consequential judgment had been hidden from all including Satan and his evil coworkers from the beginning of the Creation.[h] The Gospel Message states clearly that *all who freely receive the Father's Sent Son and submit to His lordship are fully reconciled to Him for eternity.* They are born spiritually into His eternal close-knit holy

a: Gal 3:26–28. b: Luke 12:49–53. c: John 3:18–21; 1 John 1:5–7.
d: Gen 12:1–3. e: Gal 3:13–14; Col 1:13–14; 2:13–14. f: John 17:20–23. g: Eph 3:9–11. h: Col 1:26–28.

family. They do not allow Satan to continually distract them from joining God as He carries out the greatest rescue mission of eternity.[a]

Jesus' followers know that what they do in the physical world affects both worlds, the spiritual as well as the physical. They continue in their forefathers' footsteps introducing as many as will listen to God and His glorious nature. This is how they do their part in joining God to complete His Creation. Yes, Jesus is the Light of the World, the express image of God. Now, during the Messianic Age, Jesus' disciples are being renewed from their fallen nature and are becoming more and more like Jesus. Jesus' disciples are God's light for the world helping the world to know Him and His glorious nature.

Moving Foward: Developing Disciples

> And Christ gave on the one hand apostles, but on the other prophets, evangelists, pastors, and teachers for the establishing of His Holy Ones (Saints) for the work of the Ministry for the building up of the Body of Christ, until we all come, to the unity of faith and knowledge of the Son of God, to a perfect (complete) man, to a measure of the maturity of the fulness of Christ.
>
> Eph 4:11–13

As we allow Jesus to lead us, He teaches us to do God's good works. A great part of that work is developing God's family so that Christ followers can collectively become a better and better witness. God wants those who are more mature in His family to help those who are less mature. After leading people to Christ, it is very important that the more mature teach the less mature how to live out all that Jesus commanded![b]

Jesus' command to make disciples is important! In his book, *The Journey*, Billy Graham reminds us that people who have recently turned to follow Christ are in reality like new born children regarding their understanding of spiritual things.[365] There may be barriers to spiritual growth such as continuing sin, ungodly

---

a: 1 Peter 5:8–9; 2 Cor 11:13–15.   b: Matt 28:18–20.

pressure from family members, friends, or associates, or uncertainty in what is expected.[366] Christ's more mature followers should be teaching and mentoring those who are less mature. It is the job of the more mature to help the less mature realize Christ's ultimate goal for them in becoming like Him.

It is Christ's more mature followers' *duty and honor* to help those who are less mature grow in their understanding and walk with Christ and others.[(a) 367] Christ's more mature followers should be providing regular times of collective worship, regular small group meetings, Bible studies, specialized discipleship classes, and actual times of active ministry to help the entire Body grow. If the mature members do not help new disciples grow *including their own children*, who will follow Jesus and witness of God's great ongoing love and rescue operation to our future generations?

It is important that all of Jesus' followers continually remain in God's Word reading and living it out.[(b)] If they do not, Satan will be slowly but surely reconditioning their minds toward accepting His lies and deceptions.[(c) 368] Knowing that Christ wants all of His followers to become more and more like Him should bring everyone to the place of reading God's Word daily and being in touch at all times with Him through ongoing open ended prayer. Prayer should be a two way street all of the time, one of listening as well as speaking.[(d)] *Staying in God's Word, praying without ceasing, and keeping an open, obedient mind to God's leading is critical for the success of all Christ's followers.*

---

a: Matt 28:20; Acts 2:42. b: John 8:31b–32; Rom 12:1–2. c: John 8:43–44; 2 Cor 11:13–15. d: 2 Thess 5:17.

11

—

Closing Thoughts

Most of us sense that life should be something more than a moment in eternity. That is because life is eternal. God the Creator, who is also eternal, created both the angels and humans as eternal beings. In addition, both are given free-will. Every angel and human has to decide to live with God for eternity or live isolated from Him.

When we consider the big picture, we want to thank God for His holy nature and creating us to be an intimate part of His life. The Father, the Son, and the Holy Spirit comprise a living "oneness," unity,[a] that is held together with perfect love without sin. There are no divisions within Their intimate holy relationship. We were created in God's image according to His likeness to be part of Their intimate holy family.[b] No one is being forced to join God, but He desires all to turn from a self-centered, selfish way of life to His, which is based on mutual equal love for all. God asks everyone from every generation to choose eternal life with Him instead of an eternal life of suffering and shame with Satan and those following in his rebellious footsteps.

Satan–rebelling against God before the Universe was created–has continued to rebel along with one third of God's angels.[c] He will fight against God and His developing family until he is placed in the Eternal Lake of Fire (Hell) *forever*.[d] Jesus said that Satan was a liar and murderer from the beginning, which has been and is repeatedly demonstrated through his actions starting when he deceived Adam and Eve. Immediately after creating humanity in a new and pure universe, Satan talked Eve into disobeying God. Adam followed in Eve's footsteps bringing sin and death into the lives of all humanity. Knowing God's requirement for a perfect world order where love prevailed, it looked as if God had lost His children shortly after the start of the

---

a: John 17:11, 20–23. b: Gen 1:26–27; cf. James 3:9. c: Rev 12:4, 7–9. d: Rev 20:10.

Creation. Adam, Eve, and all future generations were expelled from God's immediate presence.

But, God knowing all things in advance was not surprised and had already set a plan in place to save all who wanted to be with Him prior to creating the Universe.[a] He had given His children enough free-will to rebel knowing that His first children, Adam and Eve, would place all future generations in rebellion against Him.[b] He made a way to rescue those who wanted a better life style through His own death.[c] With Christ dying on the Cross as a common criminal to remove sin supernaturally from those who turned back to God,[d] the Father and Son both experienced the pain of death, separation, for three days, which for God might have seemed like three thousand years.[e]

God's desire for all is for everyone to choose good over evil (bad). In one sense, life is simpler than we imagine, because each individual's decision regarding living for self or community determines his or her eternal destiny. For those who choose to receive God as lord and savior, they are choosing good over evil. They are choosing what is good for self *and* for others. For those who choose self over others, they are choosing an empty life that brings about suffering and shame.

Along each of our life journeys, God reveals Himself in a multitude of ways wanting all to know Him. To personally know God helps one to submit to His will and confidently follow His lead. Until one knows God and His genuine love for all, it is easier to follow a self-centered path without submitting to Him. But, once an individual has started paying attention to God's revelation of His world and Word, many of Satan's deceptions and his/her own personal self-centered desires become apparent making it much easier to submit to Him. He is a loving holy Father and Sustainer.

*Is there **anything more glorious** than God and His eternal close-knit holy family?* I do not think so. What a privilege and honor to be invited into God's holy family to be loved as much as Jesus.[f] What a privilege and honor to be able to join God in the greatest rescue mission of all eternity helping lead people out of Satan's deceptions into God's marvelous presence and light.

---

a: 1 Peter 1:1–5; Rev 13:8. b: Rom 5:8–10. c: John 3:14–17.
d: Isa 53:4–6; Gal 3:13–14; Col 2:13–14; 2 Cor 5:21; 1 Peter 2:24.
e: 2 Peter 3:8. f: John 17:23.

Now, in our generation knowing what we know, how are we going to live out our lives? Are we going to live solely for ourselves and our families following Satan's rebellious ways, or are we going to turn to God and His way of life? If we follow the wide road to destruction,[a] which leads to eternal shame and suffering, we will miss all of the great opportunities that God has for us. But, if we listen to God and turn to Him, He will start transforming our lives immediately to be more and more like His.[b] We will have the honor and privilege of following Jesus Christ, the Son of the Most High. This Son of the Most High loves us dearly and died on our behalf calling us brothers and friends.[c]

In reality, God has suffered much on everyone's behalf. There have been no surprises for Him. The creation of His eternal close-knit holy family is moving forward according to His plan. If you are part of God's holy family, your life should be filled with love, excitement, joy, and great inner peace. God did not create any of His family to sit on the side-lines watching life slip by. During this part of eternity, He wants as many as will to follow Jesus and His way of life. Let's reverence Jesus and follow Him obediently helping many to know God and turn off that wide road that leads to eternal destruction. Let's follow Jesus and experience His joy[d] as we grow in our love for others and give of our lives to help others know God[e] and His good purposes.[f]

Making a genuine commitment to follow Jesus obediently and then stepping out in faith to do so is the answer to everyone's desire for lasting inner peace and joy. It sounds *so simple* and yet it is true. Godly love produces genuine concern for all, and genuine concern for all promotes action. Despite the shame and terrible pain suffered, *Jesus said that His joy had been made full at the Cross.* This is true because He was providing salvation for as many as would listen. In addition, *Jesus said that He wanted all of His followers to experience the fulness of His joy.*[g] The only way that Jesus' followers can experience the fulness of the joy that Jesus experienced at the Cross–and still does as He leads His Church–is to step out into the ongoing spiritual battle and *join God in the greatest rescue mission of eternity.* Out of a growing

a: Matt 7:13–14. b: Rom 6:22; Gal 5:22–25. c: John 15:12–14; 20:17. d: John 15:8–11; 17:13. e: John 17:3; Luke 9:23; 14:25–33. f: Eph 2:10; Phil 2:13. g: John 17:13; cf. 15:8–11; Heb 12:2.

genuine love for others, Christ's followers experience great godly joy by being part of God's family *and* helping rescue those whom they have come to love. ***There is no greater joy than helping to save loved ones from real disaster especially an eternal separation from God.***

It is my personal prayer that reading this book has helped you desire a closer relationship with God as a member of His growing eternal close-knit holy family. If you have not done so yet, it is now time for you to seek God's will in knowing and doing your part in building His eternal family. ***As you submit more fully to Christ's leadership and His appointed Church leaders, your level of inner peace and joy will continue to grow. As you lead others out of their spiritual darkness***—which has been created by self-centeredness, selfishness, and Satan's deceptions—***into the marvelous light of God's presence, your joy will become more and more like Christ's.*** Keep your eyes fixed on Jesus, the author and perfecter of our faith, who leads all who will follow Him into the joyous presence of our Eternal Father and Heavenly Family.[a]

If I do not personally meet you on this side of eternity, I want you to know that it is my prayer that you have an exciting and rich life "in Christ." May we continue to listen to our Heavenly Father as He leads and guides us in helping others to know the reality of His caring nature and His desire for all to join Him with Christ at that grand Passover banquet at the consummation of the Creation when all of God's close-knit holy eternal family will celebrate God's love together.[b] Let's all remember that when God's people obediently listen to Him and reveal His wondrous nature through their actions as well as their words, people are saved from eternal suffering and shame and our lands are blessed.[c]

Thank God for Jesus!

---

a: Heb 12:2; 1 Peter 2:9–11. b: Luke 22:15–18. c: 2 Chron 7:13–14; Matt 5:14–16; 28:18–20; John 15:8; 17:22–23.

Notes: Joy

1. God is in the rescuing business: Daniel was given revelation by an angel of God who was assigned to a portion of the eastern world. This angle let Daniel know that God would be rescuing His people at the appropriate time. God's people would be rescued by God (יִמָּלֵט ; *yimalit* ; Niphal passive; BDB, 572); their names had been written in the Book (of Life). At that time there would be a general resurrection from the dead, some entering into God's presence forever and some raising from Sheol into a state of eternal shame (Dan 12:1–2). In both Col 1:13 and 1Thess 1:10, we have statements telling us that Jesus is rescuing His followers from the present evil age and the wrath/judgment to come. They both use a form of the Greek word ῥύομαι (*rhuomai* BDAG, 907) meaning "to rescue" from real danger. In Matt 27:43, some of the chief priests and scribes were taunting Jesus as He hung on a cross saying ρυσάσθω νῦν, "let Him (God the Father) rescue (Jesus) now" since He claims to be the Son of God. Various forms of the same Greek root were used in all three verses to express the idea of someone "rescuing" a person or persons from a terrible outcome. Jesus' brother Judas (Jude), asking fellow Christians to contend earnestly for the faith (Jude 3), encourages them also on the one hand to have mercy on some who are doubting and on the other hand to pull some of the lost out of the fire of eternal Hell whenever the opportunity arises to save others (μὲν . . . οὓς δὲ σῴζετε: Jude 22–23). Note repeated from page 5: I have translated all Hebrew and Greek text into English used in direct quotes for this book.

2. Compare 1 Cor 9:22; 10:33; James 5:20; Jude 23.

3. Compare Exod 33:18–19; 34:6–7.

4. Compare Gal 3:13–14; 1 Peter 2:24.

Notes: The Creation

5. Eph 1:3–8; 1 Peter 1:1–2; Gal 4:4; Rev 13:8.

6. Gen 1:31; in the Hebrew Bible, it says: "God saw all that He had made, and behold it was טוֹב מְאֹד, "good exceedingly."

7. Gen 3; John 10:10; Eph 6:12; Heb 2:14.

8. 1 Peter 1:8–9; Rev 11:15; 21:1–4.

9. "In *our* image" is translated from the Hebrew word בְּצַלְמֵנוּ; "according to *our* likeness" is translated from the Hebrew word כִּדְמוּתֵנוּ: Both words show that the term "God" consists of more than one person/godly entity working together. Gen 3:22 makes this even clearer as we have a thought from God recorded saying that when Adam and Eve ate, Adam/man had become כְּאַחַד מִמֶּנּוּ, "as

'one' from among us" now knowing both good and evil. Until their disobedience, Adam and Eve had only known good, but God had allowed them to be tempted by Satan, who lied to them encouraging them to disobey their Creator. To put all of this in perspective, not only does this show God as a multi-person unity, but it shows that the Creator of mankind put the creation of His eternal family together in such a way that all would initially experience both good and evil. We understand from further revelation that God desires all to choose Him and His way of life, but it is a choice and many choose to go their own way away from God who loves them dearly.

10. Compare Gen 3:22; Col 3:10.

11. John 16:7–14; Acts 1:8.

12. Compare John 14:16, 23.

13. Gen 5:2: זכר ונקבה בראם ויברך אתם ויקרא את שמם אדם ביום הבראם:, "Male and female He created them, and He blessed them and called their name "Adam/man" in the day that He created them."

14. Compare Matt 7:13–14; 2 Peter 1:2–4; 3:9.

15. Compare Heb 2:9; 2 Cor 5:21; 1 Peter 2:24.

16. I have given my personal translations from the original Hebrew (*Biblia Hebraica Stuttgartensia*, 1987) and Greek (UBS 3d ed.) texts for this book. "And all of us are the work of your hand" is translated from the following Hebrew: ומעשה ידך כלנו.

17. Compare Jer 5:3; 8:4–12; 15:7; Ezek 18:32.

18. Hosea 2:14–23; John 3:16–17; Rom 1:16-17; 3:21–28; 10:9–13.

19. The range of meaning for the Greek word πίστις, *pistis*, "faith, trust," can be studied more fully in lexicons such as Liddell & Scott's *Greek-English Lexicon* and Bauer's *Greek-English Lexion of the New Testament.*

20. James 2:22. James teaches this principle clearly in his statement that by completing our good works, which comes from our obedience to God, our πίστις, *pistis*, "faith, trust in God," is made more complete, more mature; our faith is strengthened.

21. Regarding obedience derived from love, see John 14: 15, 21, 23–24. Regarding trusting God through love, see Rom 10:9–10; Gal 5:6. In Galatians, faith/trust originates out of God's love and an individual learning to return God's love because of God's trustworthy and loving nature.

22. In Rom 10:10, the wording καρδίᾳ πιστεύεται, "with the heart, he (man) is trusting" carries with the it the idea of emotion as well as thinking.

23. In the early Greek text, the Apostle John states that ὁ πιστεύων, "the one who is trusting," the Son will be saved, but that ὁ ἀπειθῶν, "the one who is disobeying" the Son shall not see eternal life because the judgment of God remains on him.

24. Compare Rom 8:28–30; Heb 1:3a.

Notes: Good, Evil, and Spiritual Warfare

25. In God's economy, He has created each individual with unique gifts to work together with others to accomplish good things not possible individually. When looking at the Creation as a whole, everyone who listens to God has a unique part to play in bringing others to a saving knowledge of God's love. When you look at the life of Jeremiah and Paul, they may seem to be the unusual, but in reality, they both had a zeal to do God's will. Just like Jeremiah and Paul, we have pre-ordained work to do if we are willing (Jer 1:5; Gal 1:15–16; Phil 2:13).

26. God's love for all (John 3:16–17; 1 John 4:16; 1 Tim 2:1–4; 2 Peter 3:9) draws many to Him as long as they will accept His benevolent lordship (John 14:21, 23; 15:12–14; Rom 10:9). When we begin to understand God's love and His resulting standards, we begin to realize how short we come to living up to His standards (Rom 3:23) and how much in need of a savior we really are in order to stand in righteousness before Him (Rom 6:22–23; Gal 3:13–14; 2 Cor 5:21; Titus 2:14; 1 Peter 2:24). Without being completed in perfection, God will not allow us to live with Him nor anyone else who wants to live in perfect peace and joy forever (Rev 21:1-4; 22:1–5, 14).

27. Compare Rom 1:18–2:16; Gal 6:7–8; Col 3:5–6; Rev 20:11–15.

28. We have come to translate the Greek word γέεννα, geenna, as "Gehenna or Hell." In Jesus' day, the city dump, which normally had fires burning in it most if not all of the time was called Gehenna by those living in the area. This burning dump was a good metaphorical image of the upcoming Eternal Lake of Fire, and therefore, the future place for those judged guilty of sin (disobedience) by God at the final judgment (Rev 19:20; 20:14–15). See books such as *The International Standard Bible Encyclopedia* for further information on Gehenna.

29. The text of Eph 6:10–12: From now on, ἐνδυναμοῦσθε ἐν κυρίῳ καὶ ἐν τῷ κράτει τῆς ἰσχύος αὐτοῦ, "be continually strengthened in the Lord in the strength of His might"; ἐνδύσασθε τὴν πανοπλίαν τοῦ θεοῦ πρὸς τὸ δύνασθαι ὑμᾶς στῆναι πρὸς τὰς μεθοδείας τοῦ διαβόλου, "put on all of the armor of God to enable yourselves to stand before the scheming of the Devil," ὅτι οὐκ ἔστιν ἡμῖν ἡ πάλη πρὸς αἷμα καὶ σάρκα, because

our battle is not against blood and flesh," ἀλλὰ πρὸς τὰς ἀρχάς, πρὸς τὰς ἐξουσίας, πρὸς τοὺς κοσμοκράτορας τοῦ σκότους τούτου, πρὸς τὰ πνευματικὰ τῆς πονηρίας ἐν τοῖς ἐπουρανίοις, "but instead against the leaders, the authorities, the cosmic powers of this darkness, the spirits of evil in the heavenly places."

30. Compare Phil 4:13.

31. Compare Matt 11:28–30; 13:23; Rom 8:14–17; 1 John 3:2.

32.Compare Matt 19:29; Mark 10:29–30; Rom 5:3–5.

33. Rev 20:2, 7, and 10 show explicitly that Σατανᾶς, "Satan," is also called the Διάβολος, "Devil."

Two Kingdoms at War

34. The Greek Text of Matt 11:12: ἀπὸ δὲ τῶν ἡμερῶν Ἰωάννου τοῦ βαπτιστοῦ ἕως ἄρτι ἡ βασιλεία τῶν οὐρανῶν βιάζεται, καὶ βιασταὶ ἁρπάζουσιν αὐτήν.

35. The Greek Text of Luke 16:16: Ὁ νόμος καὶ οἱ προφῆται μέχρι Ἰωάννου· ἀπὸ τότε ἡ βασιλεία τοῦ θεοῦ εὐαγγελίζεται καὶ πᾶς εἰς αὐτὴν βιάζεται.

36. Compare Luke 4:5–8.

37. Hell is a real eternal place of confinement for all who will not submit to the rule of a loving creator. If you have any doubts about a literal Hell, take a look at another contemporary book written by Francis Chan and Preston Sprinkle titled *Erasing Hell: What God Said about Eternity, and the Things That We Have Made Up* (Colorado Springs: David C Cook, 2011).

38. Compare Gal 3:13–14; 2 Tim 1:9; 1 Pet 1:19–20; Rev 13:8. In the Greek text of Rev 13:8, the relative clause, "who was slain from the foundation of the world," is grammatically associated with "the Lamb" showing that the Father and Son had worked out the timing of Jesus' crucifixion prior to physically putting the Creation into place. This thought is supported by the biblical idea that God is not bound by time but instead works with His creation *according to foreknowledge of everyone's choices*. Knowing everyone's motives and actions prior to putting the Creation together physically, He has decided what to do ahead of time in all circumstances.

39. Compare Heb 2:9; 10:10–14; 1 Peter 3:18.

40. Compare John 17:4; 19:28–30; 1 Cor 15:55–57.

41. In the Greek text, it is clear through the Apostle John's use of the Greek word δεῖ, *dei*, "it is necessary," in context saying that "it is necessary that the Son of Man" be lifted up as Moses lifted up the serpent in the wilderness in order that πᾶς ὁ πιστεύων ἐν αὐτῷ ἔχῃ ζωὴν αἰώνιον, "every one who is trusting in Him may have eternal life." By the Father's standards of justice, *it was necessary* that the penalty for sin was realized (cf. Rom 6:23). The Good News, the Gospel, is that God personally took on death for all who learn to trust and obey Him in order that His obedient children would not have to do so (John 11:26; Heb 2:9).

42. Josh McDowell, *A Ready Defense* (San Bernardino: Here's Life, 1990, reprint 1991).

43. Look at the opposite concept, knowing reality sets us free from the bondage of sin (John 8:31b–32).

44. Compare Matt 11:28–30; Rev 21:1–5.

45. Jesus taught that He was the light of the world while He walked on earth and that He is the light of the world through His followers after His resurrection (John 3:19; 8:12; 9:5; Matt 5:14–16).

46. Compare 2 Cor 5:21; 1 Peter 2:24.

47. Compare Matt 24:8 and Mark 13:8 regarding end-time birth pains.

48. Compare 1 Cor 15:51–57; Heb 2:14; Rev 11:15; 12:11.

49. Compare John 14:21, 23.

50. Compare Luke 9:23; Matt 16:24; Mark 8:34–35; Phil 2:13.

51. When we consider God's teaching through John, we know that we are to love even our enemies if we are going to be like God (Matt 5:44–48). In this text, we normally translate the Greek word μισῇ, *misēi*, as "hates" but *misēi* has a range of meaning which better translates in this context as "disregards." If we disregard those around us instead of genuinely being concerned for them, we do not have the love of God working in us.

52. Spiritual birth begins immediately after making a genuine commitment to submit to Jesus' lordship and follow Him (Eph 1:13–14).

53. Compare James 4:6–10.

54. C. Mark Corts, *The Truth about Spiritual Warfare: Your Place in the Battle Between God and Satan* (Nashville: Broadman & Holman, 2006).

55. Compare Gal 3:13–14; Col 2:13–15; Titus 2:14.

56. God is in the rescuing business and asks Christ's followers to join Him. See end note #2.

57. Compare Matt 16:24 & Mark 8:34–35.

58. Consider Scripture such as Job 2:4–6; 38:1–4; 40:1–8; 42:1–6; Luke 22:31–32 and others.

59. There are many examples in the NT of Christ's followers bringing many into God's presence (e.g. Acts 2:1f).

60. Bill Hybels and Mark Mittleburg, *Becoming a Contagious Christian* (Grand Rapids: Zondervan, 1994);
    Bill Hybels, *Just Walk Across the Room: Simple Steps Pointing People to Faith* (Grand Rapids: Zondervan, 2006);
    Dick Innes, *I Hate Witnessing: A Handbook for Effective Christian Communications.* rev. ed. (San Clemente: Acts Communications, 2003).

61. Compare John 8:31–32, 42–47; 1 Cor 10:21.

62. Compare Isa 14:11; 66:24.

63. Compare Matt 25:41; Rev 19:20; 20:10, 14–15. Starting in Isa 14:11, we see a תּוֹלֵעָה , *toleah*, "worm," (in the singular) being uses as a covering for those in Sheol. From other Scripture, this would take place in the lower depths of Sheol for the unfaithful. This term is translated into Greek in the Septuagint as σκώληξ, *skolēx*, "worm," also in the singular. The same words are used in the Hebrew and Greek in Isaiah 66:24 to represent the worm that shall not die for those being tormented forever. God uses the same imagery and wording in Mark 9:43–48 to help all who are listening understand the disgrace and pain of living in Gehenna, in the Kingdom of Hell. For a brief description of the Hebrew term תּוֹלֵעָה, see BDB, 1069; for a Greek description of σκώληξ, *skolēx*, see Liddell & Scott, 1618.

64. Matt 8:12; 13:42, 50; 22:13; 24:51; 25:30. The Greek wording was ὁ κλαυθμὸς καὶ ὁ Βρυγμὸς τῶν ὀδόντων, "weeping and gnashing of teeth."

65. Compare Eccl 12:13–14 and Daniel 12:2 whereby even 500 years before Christ came, God had made it known to His prophet Daniel that there would be a resurrection life for all, some to *everlasting life* with God and some to *everlasting disgrace/shame* and contempt. When he was considering some of the evil that individuals who were following Satan were doing, Paul stated that their end, judgment/sentence, would be according to their work (2 Cor 11:15).

66. Tartarus only shows up once in the Greek New Testament in 2 Peter 2:4; The Greek word, γέεννα, *geenna*, "Gehenna," which we normally translate as "Hell" was used in Matt 5:29–30; 10:28; 18:9; 23:15, 33; Mark 9:43–47; Luke

12:5; and James 3:6. *The International Standard Bible Encyclopedia* is a good source for general background on many biblical subjects to include Gehenna.

67. Acts 2:27 is a good Scripture to compare to Ps 16:10 in the Greek version of the Old Testament (Septuagint) and the Hebrew version of the Old Testament. Peter is quoting David here and so when we look at Greek and Hebrew versions, we see that those reading the Greek Bible in the first century would have seen the same Greek word that Peter used, ᾅδης, *haidēs*, "Hades," and those reading from the Hebrew Bible would have seen שְׁאוֹל, *Sheol*, which shows the equivalency of the two words.

68. Luke 23:43: in the Greek, ἐν τῷ παραδείσῳ, *en tō Paradeisō*, "in the paradise."

69. Compare Matt 8:11–12; 22:31–32.

70. Ignatius of Antioch, "To the Trallians," Long Version, Book 2, 2.9.4. This matches Scripture such as Acts 2:27, 31 and Eph 4:8–10.

71. In both Luke 23:43 and 2 Cor 12:4, the Greek word was a form of παράδεισος, *Paradeisos*, "paradise," which was normally considered a place of blessedness such as the Garden of Eden, which was a paradise (BDAG, 761).

72. One website shows some of our worlds tallest buildings with the highest in Dubai, UAE (United Arab Emirates) with a height of 2717 ft. finished in 2010, that is a little over one half mile tall (5280 ft./mi.) and the second tallest in Taipei, Taiwan with a height of 1670 ft. finished in 2004. URL: http://architecture.about.com/od/skyscrapers/ a/Worlds-Tallest-Buildings.htm (accessed 02/12/2011).

73. Phil 3:20–21: Jesus Christ, who μετασχηματίσει, *metaschēmatisei*, "shall transform," (BDAG, 641) our body of lowly nature σύμμορφον τῷ σώματι τῆς δόξης αὐτοῦ, "into a similar form to the body of His glory: BDAG, 958)," according to τὴν ἐνέργειαν τοῦ δύνασθαι αὐτὸν καὶ ὑποτάξαι αὐτῷ τὰ πάντα, "the effective working of His ability and the subjecting of all things to Him"; (two articular infinitives use similar to English gerunds: τοῦ δύνασθαι, ὑποτάξαι. When we compare Rom 8:29, we have similar phraseology when Paul stated that for those whom God knew would love Him, He predestined them: συμμόρφους τῆς εἰκόνος τοῦ υἱοῦ αὐτοῦ, "to have a form similar to the image/form (εἰκόνος) of His Son" εἰς τὸ εἶναι αὐτὸν πρωτότοκον ἐν πολλοῖς ἀδελφοῖς, "in order for Him to be the first (πρωτότοκον: BDAG, 894) with *many* brothers." Rom 5:10: we shall be saved by His life.

74. See Chapter 3, "God's Eternal Close-knit Holy Family," for more details.

75. Compare Rom 8:17, 29.

76. Compare John 17:9, 13.

77. Compare Rom 8:28–29 & Heb 5:8–9.

78. Compare 1 Cor 15:41–43; 2 Cor 3:18; Rom 8:17.

79. Save from corruption of sin (John 8:34–36 & others).

80. Billy Graham, *The Journey: How To Live by Faith in an Uncertain World* (Nashville: W Publishing, 2006), has a thought provoking chapter, "Can We Start Over?" Many people have been deceived by Satan into thinking that they cannot start over, but this is one of his many lies. God desires all to turn to Him and be saved (John 3:16; 2 Peter 3:9).

Notes: God's Eternal Close-knit Holy Family

81. When one studies John 17:20–23, one sees a little of God the Father's plan to expand Jesus' immediate family from a count of three, the Father, The Son, the Holy Spirit to however large God wishes to grow His family. Consider the parable of God filling heaven as a fisherman filling his dragnet; when the net is filled, the catch is complete (Matthew 13:47–50).

82. Compare Col 1:16.

83. Compare Matt 25:31–46.

84. Compare Isaiah 53; also consider Gal 3:13–14; Titus 2:14.

85. Compare Heb 12:3; 2 Peter 3:9; 1 John 4:10, 16.

86. Compare Mark 2:14–17; Luke 7:33–34; 15:1–2.

87. Compare 1 Cor 15:28 to Eph 4:6; cf. John 17:20–23 & 1 Peter 2:9–10 to Eph 2:19–22.

88. Compare Eph 2:18; Col 2:9; Rev 3:20.

89. Compare Eph 2:10; James 1:22; 2:20, 26; Titus 1:16.

90. Romans 3:21–26. The idea that sin causes death, separation from community, is not a new idea. When God taught Israel about sin through Moses and the Prophets, it became explicit that there were many types of sin that required immediate death or excommunication from the community of Israel. In God's economy, the wages of sin has always been death! In God's economy, we are not allowed to hurt one another. Consider Jesus' summary of all the Father's teachings (Matt 22:37–40) compared to Paul's teaching on love (1 Cor 13:1–8a).

91. Compare Rev 3:20.

92. In both Rom 8:15 and Gal 4:5, Paul uses the Greek root υἱοθεσία to denote "adoption as sons."

93. Paul use of the Greek term υἱοθεσίαν, "adoption," which would have been understood by those living in the first-century Mediterranean world as a legal term showing that an individual or individuals were considered legally the same as someone's biological children (BDAG, 1024).

94. Compare Rom 2:11–13; James 2:14–17.

95. James B. Joseph, "Unity and Obedient Discipleship in John 17" (MA thesis, Wake Forest University, 1993), 54–55.

96. Deut 6:4: שְׁמַע יִשְׂרָאֵל יהוה אֱלֹהֵינוּ יהוה אֶחָד: "Hear O' Israel, YHWH is our God; YHWH is one." Septuagint: Ἄκουε, Ἰσραήλ Κύριος ὁ Θεὸς ἡμῶν Κύριος εἷς ἐστι: "Hear O' Israel, the Lord is our God; the Lord is one." Mark 12:29: Ἄκουε, Ἰσραήλ κύριος ὁ θεὸς ἡμῶν κύριος εἷς ἐστιν: "Hear O' Israel, the Lord is our God; the Lord is one."

97. Gen 2:24b: וְדָבַק בְּאִשְׁתּוֹ וְהָיוּ לְבָשָׂר אֶחָד: "and he shall cling (stay attached) to his wife and they shall become 'one' flesh." Septuagint: καὶ ἔσονται οἱ δύο εἰς σάρκα μίαν: "and the two shall become 'one' flesh. Matt 19:5: καὶ ἔσονται οἱ δύο εἰς σάρκα μίαν: "and the two shall become 'one' flesh."

98. Judges 20:11: וַיֵּאָסֵף כָּל אִישׁ יִשְׂרָאֵל אֶל הָעִיר כְּאִישׁ אֶחָד חֲבֵרִים: "Every man of Israel gathered to the city uniting 'as one' man."; Septuagint: Καὶ συνήχθη πᾶς ἀνὴρ Ἰσραήλ εἰς τὴν πόλιν ὡς ἀνὴρ εἷς: "Every man of Israel gathered together into the city 'as one' man." Compare Judges 20:1, 8.

1 Sam 11:7: וַיִּפֹּל פַּחַד יהוה עַל הָעָם וַיֵּצְאוּ כְּאִישׁ אֶחָד: "And the dread/awe (BDB, 808) of YHWH fell upon the people and they came out 'as one man.'" Septuagint: ὡς ἀνὴρ εἷς: "as one man."

99. Compare Rom 5:10.

100. Compare Ps 138:2, 5–8.

101. The heavens declare God's glory: Psalm 19:1, 29; 96:11–13; 97:6; Isaiah 6:3. The creation glorifies God (1 Chronicles 16:23, 31–31) and is filled with knowledge of God's glory (Habakkuk 2:14). God's people are to declare His glory: 1 Chronicles 16:7–36; Psalm 96:3–10; 105:1–15. God's children are to ascribe to God the glory that is due Him: Psalm 29:1–2; 96:7–10.

102. In the original Hebrew, the ‏ל‎ marker is attached to the word ‏כבודי‎, "my glory." The natural translation for this complex word is "the glory, which belongs to me." In other words, God's glory can be seen through His creation especially through those who are called by His name whom He has created, shaped, and worked with. In the Greek Septuagint, God's Word says that ἐν τῇ δόξῃ μου, "in my glory," I have prepared, molded, and worked with him, the one who is called for my purposes. In Romans 11:36, God speaks through Paul saying "all things have come forth from Him and exist through Him and (therefore) belong to Him. Paul goes on to say αὐτῷ ἡ δόξα εἰς τοὺς αἰῶνας, "to Him is the glory for every," meaning that God's glory can be seen in everything that exists. We have a song that teaches this doctrine titled "To God Be the Glory." It starts with this thought, "To God be the glory—great things He has done! So loved He the world that He gave us His son."

103. The Song of Moses and Israel recorded in Exodus 15:1–19 depict God's strength, loving-kindness, and gracious salvation. Compare Psalm 63:2–3; Jeremiah 32:17–18. Regarding God's loving-kindness and truthfulness see Exodus 33:18–20; 34:6–7; Psalms 26:3;40:11; 89:14; 115:1; Jeremiah 9:24; Hosea 2:19–20.

104. Compare Ex 33:18–19; 34:6–7; Col 1:15; Heb 1:3.

105. God: Acts 10:34–35; Rom 2:11–12; Eph 6:9; 1 Peter 1:17. God's Desire For Humanity: Lev 19:15; Deut 1:17; 16:19; 2 Chron 19:7; James 2:1, 9. God's longsuffering 2 Peter 3:9.

106. Our obedience to Christ is also based on our love for Him: John 14:21, 23; 15:14.

107. Compare Rom 5:1; 8:1; Eph 1:13–14; 1 John 3:2.

108. Compare John 1:12–13; 1 Cor 2:12–16; Rev 21:8.

109. Jesus rebukes the Jewish leaders for not believing that the Father sent Him after He had performed many miracles of love giving proof that He was working with and being empowered by the One who sent Him. Then, Jesus told them that when they crucified Him, they would know that He was not doing anything on His own authority, but instead He only spoke as the Father instructed Him; the Father would raise Him from the dead and give Him and all who trusted God the ultimate *victory* over Satan and His evil followers. His Father was always with Him and pleased with His actions, because He was always doing His Father's will (John 8:28–29).

110. Compare Mark 1:10–11; Luke 3:22; John 1:32–34.

111. Constantine Scouteris, "The People of God–Its Unity and Its Glory: A Discussion of John 17:17–24 in the Light of Patristic Thought," *The Greek Orthodox Theological Review* 30, no. 4 (Winter 1985): 399–414.

112. Ibid., 401–01. "The People of God"

113. Ibid., 403. "The People of God"

114. The process of sanctification starts as soon as an individual steps out in faith and starts to follow Jesus (Rom 6:22).

115. Ibid., 405–06. "The People of God"

116. Ibid., 407. "The People of God"

117. Ibid., 411. "The People of God"

118. Ibid., 414. "The People of God"

119. C. H. Dodd, *The Interpretation of the Fourth Gospel* (New York: Cambridge University Press, 1953, reprint 1958), 187–200; cf. John 14:20.

120. Ibid., 196. *Interpretation of the Fourth Gospel*

121. Ibid., 197. *Interpretations of the Fourth Gospel*

122. Bruce Milne, *The Message of John*, The Bible Speaks Today (Downers Grove: Inter-Varsity Press, 1993), 247; cf. John 15:10.

123. Compare Rom 8:28–30; Phil 3:20–21.

124. John 5:18. The apostle John wrote πατέρα ἴδιον ἔλεγεν τὸν θεὸν ἴσον ἑαυτὸν ποιῶν τῷ θεῷ, "He (Jesus) was saying that His father is God (thereby) making Himself equal to God."

125. Compare Gen 1:26–27. John 10:34–36; 20:17. This was God's plan from the beginning for those who allow Him to teach them to love, trust, and obey Him. It all started when God created humanity in His image according to His likeness (Genesis 1:26–27; cf. James 3:9) desiring a reciprocating intimate relationship with those coming into His eternal close-knit family.

126. As we take note that God has promised to conform all who love Him into the image of His Son, Jesus, the Messiah (Romans 8:29), we also realize that we are going to know God fully when we enter eternity with Him and have been made somewhat like Him (1 John 3:2). Jesus teaches that those who are striving to live out God's Word will know reality, and that by knowing reality, we will be set free from sin (John 8:31b–32). Think of that, by really knowing the facts, we become free. We are partially bound to sin by our self-induced blindness. God teaches us through Paul that when we walk with God in the future, we shall know fully as God has known us fully (1 Corinthians 13:12). This is hard to comprehend, but part of God's good work in us will be to complete us in such a way as to give us full knowledge of everything.

127. Transformed into the Image of Christ (Rom 8:29); Redemption and Being Clothed in Christ's righteousness (Gal 3:13–14; 2 Cor 5:21; 1 Peter 2:24). Presently, Jesus gives us great revelation through the New Testament enlightened by the Holy Spirit (Rom 8:38–39). Earlier, God had given partial revelation through Isaiah. He portrayed Himself as our Father (Isa 63:16; 64:8), our Husband (Isa 54:5; 62:5), and our Redeemer. God's glory (Ex 33:18–19; 34:5–7) will be seen upon Israel (God's obedient children: Isa 60:2). His word declares that anyone who will walk in His Way shall be given a place in His House with a name (relational position) better than that of earthly sons and daughters (Isa 56:4–6). God has prepared something great for those of us who wait upon Him (Isa 64:4).

128. Jesus went to the Cross for us following our heavenly Father's will: Matt 26:39; Mark 14:34–36; Luke 22:42.

129. Compare 2 Cor 6:16–18.

Jesus Is Lord as Well as Savior

130. Matt 16:16: According to Jesus, no one is to be proclaimed "teacher," "father," or "leader" except Him (Matt 23:8–12).

131. Compare: 1 Cor 8:5–6; Eph 2:10; Col 1:12–22; Heb 1:2.

132. In addition, see John 14:6, 18, 20, 26–27.

133. Compare John 14:7 from which we understand that when we look at Jesus, who is the express image of His father, we can know the Father. Through 1 John 4:12, 20, we learn that no one on earth has seen the Father in His full glory except Christ.

134. Col 1:15: In the second part of this verse, we come to understand that Jesus Christ is the first of many children in the Father's eternal family. The Greek word πρωτότοκος (*prōtotokos*) normally refers to the "firstborn son" with an understanding that this individual has the legal rights of the firstborn son. The first part of the word, πρώτως (*prōtōs*), standing alone is an adv. simply meaning "first" while the second part of the word, τόκος (*tokos*) contains the idea of multiplying (children multiplying their parents). The term normally carries with it the meaning of the rights and authority of the first born over the other children (BDAG, 894). From Scripture such as John 1:1, we know that *Jesus is not a created being*. The emphasis on this word is to highlight Jesus being *the eldest*. The Hebrew equivalent to this word is בְּכוֹר (*bekor*), which means "firstborn" with the idea of "the earliest" child, the eldest (BDB, 114).

135. Compare John 1:10; Eph 2:10, "For we are His (God's) workmanship, having been created in/through Christ Jesus for good works. . . ."; Heb 1:2; 1 Cor 8:5–6.

136. Compare 1 John 1:3; Heb 1:2.

137. Compare John 1:3, 10.

138. Compare Rev 3:14.

139. Compare John 1:1.

140. Compare Eph 1:22–23; 4:15; 5:23; Rom 12 and 1 Cor 12 and their teachings regarding the Body of Christ.

141. Compare Gal 3:13–14; Eph 1:7–10; Col 2:13–14; Heb 9:22, 28; 10:10–12; 1 Peter 2:21–24.

142. Compare Matt 25:34; Eph 1:4; 2 Tim 1:9; Titus 1:2; 1 Peter 1:19–20; Rev 13:8. When looking at Rev 13:8, the Greek text states ἐν τῷ βιβλίῳ τῆς ζωῆς τοῦ ἀρνίου τοῦ ἐσφαγμένον ἀπὸ καταβολῆς κόσμου, "in the Book of Life of the Lamb having been slain from the foundation of the world/universe." The Greek clearly places the prepositional phrase "from the foundation of the world" with the Lamb who had been appointed by the Father to be slain on humanity's behalf prior to the Lamb physically putting the universe together; a plan initiated by the Father and agreed on by the Son (Matt 26:39–44; Luke 22:42).

143. The Christ, the Son of the Living God (Matt 16:16); the Christ (Mark 8:29); the Holy One of God (John 6:69).

144. Jesus proclaims His identity through His words and actions (John 5:17, 19; 17:1); His rejection (Matt 26:63; Mark 14:61; Luke 22:70; John 5:18; 19:7); hardened hearts (Matthew 13:13–15; 21:33–46).

145.Kingdom taken from religious authorities (John 8:31–47; Matt 21:43); honor the Son (John 3:35; 5:22–23); Jesus' seeks the Father's will (John 5:30; 17:4); Jesus will have His glory restored (John 171–2; Eph 1:21).

146. Compare Mark 9:37b; Luke 9:48b; John 12:44; Gal 4:14.

147. Jesus teaches us the Father's will (Heb 1:2; John 8:28, 47; 17:8). During this age, the Church is the Light to the World even to authorities in heavenly places (Matt 5:14–16; Eph 3:10). In addition to the Father & Son being with us now through the Holy Spirit, we have God's Written Word and the same Holy Spirit who originally helped the writers write it helping us to understand it. Regarding evangelism, we are to allow God to speak through us to the World (Matt 10:20 & Mark 13:11); Christian Defense (Matt 10:20 & Mark 13:11).

148. Compare 1 John 2:17.

149. John 10:7. In the Greek, John wrote ἡ θύρα, "*the* door."

150. Compare John 14:6; Eph 2:17–18.

151. Access to the Father is through Christ (Eph 2:18). Access through Christ came with great cost, the cost of God's redeeming work on the Cross (Eph 2:13–16).

152. Striving (Matt 7:7–8; Luke 13:24). Good works assigned prior to forming the world (Eph 2:10); obeying God's Word (Rom 2:11–16); crosses (Luke 9:23).

153. Compare Acts 20:32; 26:18; Eph 5:5.

154. Some examples include: Rom 3:24; 6:11; 8:1–2; 12:5; 16:3, 7, 9, 10; 1 Cor 1:2, 4, 30; 3:1; 4:10, 15, 17; 15:18, 22, 31; 16:24; 2 Cor 2:14, 17; *5:17*; 12:19; Gal 1:22; 2:4, 17; 3:14, 28; 5:6; Eph 1:1, 3, 10; 2:6, 7, 13; 3:6; and many more.

155. See Gal 1:22; 2:4; 3:14, 26–29; 5:6. Grammatically, Paul uses the Greek preposition ἐν as a marker of close association, which follows common practice for the writers of the New Testament.

156. This teaching parallels Matthew's recorded words of Christ giving a summary of the fulfilling the Law (Matt 22:37–40).

157. In addition, see Gal 5:6, 14; 6:2, 9–10.

158. Compare part of Jesus' prayer before going to the Cross as recorded in John 17:20–23 regarding the coming glory of those who follow Christ faithfully.

159. Compare Rom 3:31 in which Paul teaches that those who live in faith fulfill the Law.

160. Phil 1:12–14; 4:22.

161. Paul uses the Greek phrase ἐν Χριστῷ, "in Christ," frequently in this letter (Phil 1:1, 13, 26; 2:1, 5; 3:3, 14; 4:7, 19, 21).

162. Eph 2:6, 7, 10, 13; 3:6, 4:32.

163. This is made possible by being "in Christ."

164. Luke 4:18–21; Isa 61:1–2. As one lives under the lordship of Christ, God produces the fruit of the Spirit in his or her life (Gal 5:22–25).

165. God teaches us to be holy (selfless caring individuals) just as He is holy (Lev 19:1–2; 20:26).

166. Compare Col 1:18; 1 Peter 3:1–8.

167. Compare Matt 22:28–30; 1 Peter 3:7.

168. Compare Rom 6:14–23; 12:1–3; 1 Peter 1:14–23.

169. Love (John 3:16–17; 1 John 4:20); Peace (Rom 5:1–5; Phil 4:4–7).

170. Our good works include exposing and correcting wrongdoing (1 Cor 6:1–5).

171. The will and the ability to carry out the good works that God has prepared for us prior to the foundation of the world (Acts 1:8; Eph 1:19; 2:10; 3:14–20; Phil 2:13; 4:13); individually assigned crosses (Luke 9:23).

172. Satan is the father of lies and deception (John 8:44). At times, Satan works among Believers through some who may even consider themselves Christians but in reality are listening to him, not God. But, some know very well that they have never committed to following Christ and are hindering some in their local churches (2 Cor 11:13–15; Matt 7:15–16).

173. Jesus teaches us that a kingdom or household divided amongst itself will fall (Matt 12:25; Mark 5:24–25; Luke 11:17).

Notes: Scripture & Church Organization

174. Consider Gal 1:6; Heb 6:4–6; and others.

175. Works of the Early Church Fathers can be found in reprints from publishers such as Hendrickson under series titles such as Ante-Nicene Fathers.

176. Bruce M. Metzger, *The Canon of the New Testament: Its Origin, Development, and Significance* (New York: Oxford University Press, 1997), 211–12, 237–38.

177. Gal 1:18–19; 2:1–10. When Paul went up to Jerusalem 17 years after his Christian conversion, he lists three existing pillars of the Christian community, the apostles James, Peter, and John. Paul lists James first, which indicates that James was the main spokesman at that time. Secondly, in Acts, after Peter had fled for his life, there is an account of both James and Peter leading a discussion about Church doctrine with members of the church at Jerusalem. At this time, James appears to be the main spokesman as he wraps up the discussion and recommends a statement for the church at Antioch. These accounts lead me to think that James had become the spokesman after Peter left Jerusalem although Peter was still alive.

178. The first expansion to leadership is recorded in Acts 6–7. We should note that those who were chosen to serve *were empowered* by God just as the existing leadership.

179. Greek: ἀπόστολος, *apostolos*. See Liddell and Scott, *Greek-English Lexicon*, rev. Jones and McKenzie (London, New York & Toronto; and many others: Oxford University Press, 1990), 220 & 1637] and Walter Bauer, *A Greek-English Lexicon of the New Testament and Other Early Christian Literature*, 3d ed., BDAG, trans. William F. Arndt & F. Wilbur Gingrich (Chicago: The University of Chicago Press, 2000), 122.

180. Prior to His ascension, Jesus had chosen twelve disciples out of which eleven would become apostles (Acts 1:13). They asked Jesus to clarify who should be the twelfth, and Matthias became the twelfth (Acts 1:21–26). Even later after His ascension, Paul is a good example of Jesus' ongoing leadership within the Church when Jesus personally called him into ministry as an apostle (Gal 1:1, 11–17, 19).

181. Gal 1:1, 19; 1 Thess 2:1, 6; Acts 18:24; 19:10; 1 Cor 1:1, 12–13; 3:4–22; 4:6,9; 9:1–2; 15:9; 16:12; 2 Cor 1:1; Titus 1;1; 3:13; Eph 1:1; Col 1:1; 1 Tim 1:1; 2:7; 2 Tim 1:1; 1:11.

182. Paul states in his second letter to the Corinthians that in addition to his ministry of proclaiming the Gospel, he is responsible to oversee the churches (2 Cor 11:28), "apart from other matters, my daily attention is with the concern of all the churches." Through the book of Acts, we observe Paul heading to Jerusalem and not having time to visit the Church of Ephesus. Therefore, Paul sends a message to the elders of Ephesus asking them to meet him at Miletus so that he could instruct and exhort them. He tells them of his concerns and prays for them (Acts 20:17, 31–32). All of Paul's letters are proof of his concern for the churches and his resulting interactions with them as they grew through God's leading.

183. Romans; 1 & 2 Corinthians; Galatians (churches-cities of Galatia); Ephesians; Philippians; Colossians; 1 & 2 Thessalonians.

184. Titus 1:5–7. In the Greek, the words πρεσβυτέρους, *presbuteros*, "presbyter/elder," and ἐπίσκοπος, *episkopos*, "overseer/bishop," are used interchangeably by Paul and the rest of the New Testament writers to signify the top leaders in the local churches.

185. In, Eph 4:11–12, Paul used the terms τοὺς ποίμενας καὶ διδασκάλους, "the shepherds (pastors) and teachers" to denote those whose primary function was to edify the Body of Christ.

186. The Greek root for deacon is διάκονος, *diakonos,* "one who serves."

187. Rom 15:8.

188. The Apostles: see Acts 6:1–2, 4. Paul: see Acts 20:24; 21:19; Rom 11:13; 15:31; 2 Cor 6:3–4; Eph 3:7; Col 1:23–5; 1 Tim 1:12; Eph 3:7. Barnabas: see Acts 12:25. Mark: see 2 Tim 4:11. Timothy: see 1 Tim 4:6.

189. Apollos: see 1 Cor 3:5; Archippus: see Col 4:17; Epaphras: see Col 1:7; Erastus: see Acts 19:22.

190. Onesimus: see Philemon 1:13; Phoebe: see Rom 16:1.

191. Stephanas: see 1 Cor 16:15. Tychicus: see Eph 6:21; Col 4:17.

192. Rom 13:4.

193. 2 Cor 11:15.

194. 1 Tim 3:2, 12; Titus 1:6. In the Greek there are three forms of the phrase μιᾶς γυναικὸς ἄνδρες, *mias gunaikos andres*, "one-woman men/husbands."

195. 1 Tim 5:9. The Greek, ἑνὸς ἀνδρὸς γυνή, *henos andros gunē*, "a one-man woman/wife."

196. A good example of Paul's ministry as an overseer to the overseers is shown as he encourages the Corinthians to complete a promise they had made regarding sending some of their resources to help their needy brothers and sisters in Jerusalem (2 Cor 8–9).

197. Peter's letters increase our knowledge of cooperation among the apostles; we observe Peter exhorting some of the churches that Paul was working with, and treating Paul's letters equal to Old Testament writings (2 Peter 3:15–16).

198. 2 Tim 3:16–17; 2 Peter 1:20–21; 1 John 2:27; Paul's letters are valued on the same level as Old Testament Scripture (2 Peter 3:16).

199. Christ's city-councils should consist only of those local church leaders who believe that the Bible is the Inspired Word of God. If they do, there will always be some uncommon ground regarding biblical understanding, but there will be no misunderstanding on Christ's primary teachings regarding: (1) His identity as the Son of God who put every part of the physical universe together; (2) the fact that He alone provides salvation through His death on a cross and suffering in Hades/Sheol; and (3) His victorious resurrection in which the Father has given Him supreme power in Heaven and on Earth until He brings His Father's creation to a point of consummation when Gods' entire eternal close-knit family will be completed (Matt 28:18–20; 1 Cor 15:28).

200. John 13:34–35; 17:21, 23; 1 John 1:7.

201. No Divisions: 1 Cor 1:10–13; 12:25–26; Eph 2:13–15; 4:1–6.

Notes: Coming to Our Senses

202. In reality, Jesus and His immediate disciples taught that we could only win spiritual battles with Jesus' assistance. When Jesus taught that we could nothing without Him, He was not saying that we could not live worldly lives without Him, but He was saying that we could not help individuals spiritually without Him. Without God, none of us could overcome the evil that is in and around us.

203. Dan 12:2; Matt 25:46.

204. In reality, open rebellion against the authority of God or any sovereign started with Satan and the rebellious angels who followed him. It is seen throughout Scripture that many do not want anyone to be king of their lives. In our western world, it is even harder to comprehend how a good-hearted benevolent ruler could be better than a ruling group elected by its citizens. What often alludes such thinking is the fact that the rule of either a monarchy or democracy is only as good as its leader(s) and in a democracy it ultimately ends up being only as good as its people. If its citizens move away from a righteous way of life so do its leaders. In George Washington's closing address of 1796 from his two term presidency, he warned the new United States of America that if they stopped listening to God, the nation would eventually fall. With a good godly king, who has the ability to lead and the power to control, the people of his kingdom will experience love, peace, and joy. God has the righteous character and power to lead His people forever in love, joy, and peace.

205. Compare 1 Tim 1:16; 2:3–4; 2 Peter 3:9.

206. Deut 30:15–19; Heb 12:1–3.

207. 2 Peter 3:9. Compare Deut 30:15–20; 2 Chron 7:14 typologically and John 3:16–17; 1 Tim 2:4; Titus 2:11 as the Messiah's Word of God for all during His messianic rule.

208. In addition to 1 Peter 1:1–2, God's foreknowledge is revealed through Scripture such as Ps 139:4, 16; Jer 1:5; Luke 11:52; Acts 2:23; Rom 1:28; 8:28–29; Gal 1:15; & 1 Tim 1:12–14.

209. In the Greek, Luke tells us that Jesus taught that for each one who was following Him, if he was οὐ μισεῖ, *ou misei*, "not regarding less," his own father, mother, wife, children, brothers, sisters, and even his own life, he was not able to be one of His disciples; he would not be born again and empowered by the Holy Spirit to witness and help bring others into God's Kingdom.

210. Compare Matt 7:21; 25:45–46; Rom 2:13; 1 John 2:3–6, 17, 19.

211. Compare Matt 7:19, 23; 25:40, 45; 2 Thess 2:10; and others.

212. John 3:14–19; Rom 10:9–13; 2 Peter 3:9.

213. Compare 2 Sam 2:4–8; Ps 86:12–14; 1 Peter 1:14–19.

214. 1 John 4:16.

215. It is important to understand that like Isaiah, we do not realize how sinful we are until we have seen God for ourselves (Isa 6:1–8).

216. Billy Graham, *How To Be Born Again,* Waco: Word Books, 1977, 152–53.

217. David is one example of many: Ps 119:67; cf. Rom 5:3–5 as a general rule even for those who follow Christ.

218. Job 27:6.

219. Compare Prov 8:1–23; 12:1; 13:1; Eph 5:11–17.

220. See also Ps 37:25; 23:6; 16:10.

221. Compare Rom 2:11–16; 8:18–19, 28–30; 1 Cor 2:9; James 1:12; 2:5; 1 Peter 1:3–5.

222. Self-centeredness (1 John 2:16–17; cf. Gal 5:19–21) vs. a God-centered love for all (John 3:16–17; 1 John 4:7, 9, 16; cf. Gal 5:24–25).

223. Matt 25:41, 46; Rom 8:6–8, 13; Rev 21:8, 27; 22:15.

224. Matt 7:21; John 7:17; 1 John 5:2–3.

225. Compare Gal 5:22–23; Rom 8:28–30; Rev 21:1–4, 7.

226. Compare Rom 8:14; 2 Cor 5:17; Phil 2:5–15.

227. Compare Rom 14:17; Gal 5:22; 1 Peter 1:8.

228. God: 2 Sam 14:14; Acts 10:34; Rom 2:11; Eph 6:9; 1 Peter 1:17. God's Desire For Humanity: Lev 19:15; Deut 1:17; 16:19; 2 Chron 19:7; James 2:1, 9.

229. Matt 27:46; John 2:19–22; 1 Cor 15:3–4.

230. Compare Acts 2:27, 31; Col 2:13–14; 1 Peter 2:24. Consider all of our various orthodox creeds that proclaim Jesus' stay in Sheol (Hades)–some say Hell. Those who were trusting God were waiting in Sheol for Jesus' redeeming work to be accomplished so that they could be made righteous through Jesus' death. See more under the subheading "Hell" in chapter 3.

231. Compare John 15:1–2; 2 Cor 5:17–19; Eph 6:10–18.

232. Compare Matt 10:38; 16:24; Luke 9:23.

233. See also Eph 2:10; Phil 2:13.

234. At the height of the Reformation, one of the major issues centered around the biblical right of those in authority within the Church to sell or grant "forgiveness of sins," which were called "indulgences." Martin Luther and others said that no one had that right. Christ had died for the forgiveness of sins for all who followed Him. Most Middle Age histories will have write-ups covering this topic.

235. Deuteronomy 30:15–20:

15 ראה נתתי לפניך היום את־החיים ואת־הטוב ואת־המות ואת־הרע:

"Look! I have given/set before you today life and goodness and death and evil (bad things),"

16 אשר אנכי מצוך היום לאהבה את־יהוה אלהיך ללכת בדרכיו ולשמר מצותיו וחקתיו ומשפטיו

"in which I have commanded you today: to love YHWH, your god; to walk (live out your lives) according to His ways; and to keep His commandments, His statutes, and His judgments,

וחיית ורבית וברכך יהוה אלהיך בארץ אשר־אתה בא־שמה לרשתה:

and you shall live and prosper; indeed, I, YHWH, your god, will bless you in the land where you are going to possess."

17 ואם־יפנה לבבך ולא תשמע ונדחת והשתחוית לאלהים אחרים ועבדתם:
18 הגדתי לכם היום כי אבד תאבדון

"But, if your heart turns (as a single entity, the nation of Israel), and you will not listen and you thrust (me) aside and bow down to other gods and serve them, I declare to you all today that you will surely perish . . . ."

236. John 14:6, "Jesus said to him, Ἐγώ εἰμι ἡ ὁδὸς ἡ ἀλήθεια καὶ ἡ ζωή· οὐδεὶς ἔρχεται πρὸς πατέρα εἰ μὴ δι' ἐμοῦ, "I am the way, the truth, and the life; no one is coming before the Father except through me."

237. Compare Luke 13:24.

238. James M. Boice, *Christ's Call to Discipleship* (Minneapolis: Grason, 1986), 139.

239. Compare the idea of life versus death as taught by God through Moses in Deut 28:12, 9, 15, and Moses' plea for Israel to "choose life" as shown in Deut 30:15–20.

240. Rom 10:4: τέλος γὰρ νόμου Χριστὸς, "for Christ is the fulfillment of law."

241. Compare Rom 6:2, 15.

242. Compare Rom 8:28–30; 2 Cor 5:21; 1 Peter 2:24; and others.

243. Compare Acts 4:12; Eph 2:18; 1 Tim 2:3–5.

244. Against all ungodliness and unrighteousness of men: Rom 1:18–24–28–32; John 8:12–19–24–28–44–47. All people disobey God on some level, and therefore, no one can be reconciled to God through the Law without Christ: Rom 3:20–23. Hardened Hearts: Matt 13:13–15.

245. The prodigal son needed something to happen in his life to show him the difference between godly love and selfishness (love of self: Luke 15).

246. Compare Matt 8:11–12; 13:40–43, 49–50; 22:12–14. Weeping/wailing and gnashing of teeth sounds similar to the way one might respond to the death of a loved one during a time of grieving. Compare Matt 25:41–46 and Rev 19:20; 20:11–15 in which God's disobedient children will be cast into an eternal fire with Matt 8:12 in which God's disobedient children will be cast into darkness and note that a physical fire produces light. We are not to take the fire of hell literally, but instead, God gives us a glimpse of the pain that eternal separation creates when our hardened hearts keep rebelling against Him.

247. See chapter 3 for information on Sheol also known as Hades.

248. Compare Gen 2:16–17; Deut 30:15–20; Isa 56:1–2; 59:1–8.

249. Compare Matt 5:14–16; 1 Peter 2:9.

250. Rom 6:23.

251. Rom 3:23.

252. Phil 3:4–11; many of Paul's countrymen were still being zealous for God just as Paul had been in the past, but they as Paul in the past were not acting according to the reality of God's plan of redemption but instead were establishing their own righteousness based on righteous works versus the righteous work of God (Rom 9:30–10:4; cf. 1:16–17).

253. Isa 6:5, . . . כִּי אֶת־הַמֶּלֶךְ יְהוָה צְבָאוֹת רָאוּ עֵינָי, "because, the King, YHWH of Hosts, my eyes have seen."

254. In the Greek text of John 3:14–15, it is clear from the word δεῖ, *dei*, "it was necessary," that Jesus die to provide salvation for πᾶς ὁ πιστεύων, *pas ho pisteuōn*, "everyone who is trusting," in God.

255. Compare Isa 53; Gal 3:13–14; Rom 5:1; Col 2:13–14.

256. Compare Matt 10:32–34.

257. Compare Isa 52:1–2; 55:3; 56:1–2; 59:1–8; Deut 30:15–20.

258. Compare Rom 1:18–2:10.

259. Compare John 3:16; 19:32–35.

260. Matt 27:57–60; John 19:38–42.

261. 1 Cor 15:1–8, 55–57.

262. Compare Matt 4:3, 6; 8:28–29 and others.

263. There are some who wanted additional proof beyond God's Word collaborating Jesus' death, burial, and resurrection. One such individual, Josh McDowell, has written a few books such as *More than a Carpenter* and *The New Evidence that Demands a Verdict* that are helpful in looking at historical evidence to show the reality of Jesus' life, ministry, death, resurrection, and work through the Church.

264. Jesus is teaching what God had Isaiah proclaim about 600 years earlier (Isa 6:9–10). Paul tried to help people understand that they needed God's help to soften their hearts when he spoke to some Jews during his Roman imprisonment (Acts 28:20–28).

265. The people of Israel whom God freed from Egypt were asked to submit to God and His ways not knowing much about what God was asking (Ex 19:3–8). They accepted His offer after seeing His ability, but many did not understand His heart nor His required holiness for all who follow Him. Submitting to God and following Christ is easier today because God has revealed the final place of peace called Heaven, an eternal paradise, for all who trust and obey Him, which has been made possible through His Son's obedient death on everyone's behalf.

Notes: Discipleship Starts with Commitment

266. Compare 1 John 2:17; John 17:3.

267. Compare John 14:21–23; 15:10–11.

268. Compare John 17:20–23.

269. Compare John 1:14; Ex 33:18–19; 34:6–7.

270. For the Hebrew word קָדֹשׁ, *qadosh*, "holy, set apart," see a Hebrew lexicon such as Brown-Driver-Briggs, 871–73; for the Greek word ἅγιος, *hagios*, "holy, dedicated, consecrated," see a Greek lexicon such as Walter Bauer's (BDAG), 10–11.

271. John 14:30–31; Phil 2:5–8; Heb 2:9–1.

272. Matt 27:11–22; Mark 15:6–13; Luke 14:13–21; John 18:37–19:16.

273. John 14:21, 23: Mark 8:34–38; Luke 9:23–26; 14:26–33.

274. John 14:12–17; 15:4, 10; 16:13; Acts 1:8 (cf. Matt 1032–33); 1 Cor 2:16; Gal 5:22–23; 1 John 2:15–17.

275. Boice, *Christ's Call to Discipleship*, 35.

276. Matt 5:12; 6:20; Mark 10:28–30; Luke 12:31–32; Acts 20:32; Col 3:23–24.

277. Matt 16:24; Mark 8:34; Luke 9:23; 14:26–27 In the scripture references, either the Greek ἀπαρνησάσθω ἑαυτόν or ἀρνησάσθω ἑαυτόν is used. In context, all three middle aorist imperatives have the same basic meaning, "let him renounce claim to himself once and for all." In other words, Jesus is saying that each one who wishes to follow Him must be willing to give up holding himself or herself as the highest priority in life and become an equal member in God's eternal family.

278. In the Hebrew Bible, the writers normally wrote out the thought of repentance with wording such as: אִם יָשֻׁבוּ מִדַּרְכֵיהֶם הָרָעִים, "if they *shuv*, 'turn,' from their evil ways." See 2 Chronicles 7:13–14. In Ezekiel, two different verb forms of *shuv* are used (qal & hiphil) to indicate both repentance and turning (Ezek 14:6; 18:30). There is another Hebrew word used at times that we translate as "repent" or "change of heart/mind." Its various forms come from the root *naham*. It has been used in places such as Exodus 13:17 & Jer 8:6; *Shuv* normally indicate "a turning" and/or "a change of heart." See Francis Brown, S. R. Driver, and Charles A. Briggs, *New Brown-Driver-Briggs Gesenius Hebrew-English Lexicon* (New York: Houghton Mifflin, 1906; reprint, Peabody: Hendrickson, 1979), 996–1000.

    In the Septuagint, a third century B.C. Greek version of Hebrew text, the translators normally used forms of the Greek words ἐντρέπω, *entrepo* or μετανοέω, *metanoeō,* for a "humbling or repenting," and ἀποστρέφω, *apostrephō,* for a "turning from"; e.g. 2 Chron 7:14; Ezek 14:6; 19:30; Jer 8:6.

    The New Testament Greek writers normally used a form of the Greek word μετανοέω, *metanoeō,* to designate the act of "repenting"; see Matt 3:2; 4:17; Acts 2:38; 3:19 and others. But, regarding "turning," various forms of the Greek verb, *epistrephō,* a verbal form of *epistrophē,* appear in the New Testament and have a range of meaning from "turning back" or "return" to "turn around" or "turn to"; see Danker, Frederick R. *A Greek-English Lexicon of the New Testament and Other Early Christian Literature.* 3d ed. BDAG. Based on Walter Bauer's Work (Chicago: University of Chicago Press, 2000), 382.

279. The various forms of the Greek verb *epistrephō* used in the Septuagint to translate the Hebrew word *shuv* into Greek match the general range of meaning used by our Greek New Testament writers.

280. Greek: μετανοεῖν καὶ ἐπιστρέφειν ἐπὶ τὸν θεόν, *metanoein kai epistrephein epi ton theon,* "to repent and turn to the (one true) God."

281. Compare Matt 11:28–30; Gal 5:22.

282. Consider 2 Cor 5:21.

283. Heb 10:10–14; 1 Peter 3:18; John 3:14–17; 17:20–23; 20:17; Rom 8:28–30.

284. George W. Bush, *Decision Points* (New York: Crown, 2010), 32–33.

285. Consider Cain who slew his brother. He slew his younger brother Abel whom he should have protected as the older brother; instead of being happy for Abel, Cain was jealous of his brother's righteousness and ongoing quality relationship with God (1 John 3:11–14; cf. Gen 4:1–10).

286. Consider also John 3:16–17; Rom 1:16–17.

287. Consider also John 1:12; Rom 8:28–29; James 2:5; Rev 3:20.

288. Compare John 1:12–13; 3:3–6; Eph 1:13–14; 1 Peter 1:1–5.

289. Compare Gal 3:13–14; Isa 53:4–6.

290. Compare Matt 16:24; Mark 8:34–35.

291. Kyle Idleman, *Not a Fan: Becoming a Completely Committed Follower of Jesus* (Grand Rapids: Zondervan, 2011), 11–13.

292. Ibid., 14–15. *Not a Fan*

293. Ibid., 158–61. *Not a Fan*

294. Heb 1:1–3; 2:9–10; 12:1–3; Rom 5:8–10.

295. Compare other Scripture such as Matt 28:18–20, John 14:23, and Eph 1:20–23 regarding Jesus' ongoing ministry.

296. God loves all people (John 3:16), and His invitation to join His family is open to all (2 Peter 3:9). Boice, in his book, *Christ's Call to Discipleship,* 41, discusses the universality of Christ's call for followers.

297. Growing Now: Phil 1:6; Rom 6:22; Eph 4:11–16. After Death: 1 Cor 13:8–13; Rom 8:16–18; Phil 3:20–21; 1 John 3:1–2; Rev 3:20–21.

298. Compare John 15:10–11.

299. Matt 26:38–44; Mark 14:34–41; Luke 22:42–44; cf. Gal 3:21.

300. Matt 27:46: ἱνατί με ἐγκατέλιπες (2nd. person sing. aorist from ἐγκαταλείπω), "for what reason have you abandoned, deserted, me?"

301. The Greek text of Luke 14:27: ὅστις οὐ βαστάζει τὸν σταυρόν ἑαυτοῦ καὶ ἔρχεται ὀπίσω μου, οὐ δύναται εἶναι μου μαθητής, "whoever is not carrying his own cross and coming after (following) me is not able to be my disciple." In the Greek, it is clear that those who refuse to carry out their assigned sufferings on behalf of others as assigned by God are not able to be Jesus' disciples; because of lack of obedience, there is no empowerment from God through the Holy Spirit. Compare what Matthew recorded from Jesus' teaching on each person carrying their assigned crosses (Matt 10:38).

302. Greek: χαίρω, "I am rejoicing"; ἀνταναπληρῶ τὰ ὑστερήματα τῶν θλίψεων τοῦ Χριστοῦ, "I am supplying the needs of the tribulations of Christ."

303. Compare 2 Cor 1:24; 11:12–15.

304. Compare 1 John 1–4.

305. Rev 3:20: I am translating δειπνήσω, *deipnēsō*, as "I will fellowship" because in context, this is what Jesus is saying when He speaks of dining with those who allow Him into their lives. Friends have meals together and enjoy each other's company; they fellowship. Enemies stay at a safe distance from one another.

306. John 17:13; 15:8–11; compare Heb 12:2.

307. Everyone has to decide to either follow God or have things his or her own way maintaining personal control. God leads Christ's followers daily and normally does not give much advance notice to what lies ahead. This is normal. Even Israel as a nation accepted God's offer for them to be a holy nation, a nation of priestly representatives, without understanding how demanding that ministry would be (Ex 19:3–8). In that respect, it is the same for Christ's followers today. We follow the leading of God through the indwelling Holy Spirit (Rom 8:14; Eph 2:10; Phil 2:13; and more) without knowing very far in advance what God will be asking of us. But, it is our pleasure and honor to serve such a faithful loving Creator and be a part in His great creation rescuing as many as possible who come to their senses and want to get off that wide road of life that leads to destruction.

308. Billy Graham, *Just As I Am: the Autobiography of Billy Graham* (New York: Harper Collins, 1997), 26–27.

309. Ibid., 28. *Just As I Am*

310. Ibid., 29–30. *Just As I Am*

311. Ibid., 30. *Just As I Am*

312. Bush, *Decision Points*, 31.

313. Ibid., 30. *Decision Points*

314. Jesus prayed that all who followed Him would experience the great joy that He was feeling as He prepared to rescue many through a terrible but atoning death on a cross for all (John 17:13; cf. Heb 12:1–2; John 15:8–13).

315. Mark 1:14–15; Luke 13:3, 5; 15:10; John 24:45–48; Acts 3:18–19; 17:30; 26:19–20; Rom 2:4; 2 Tim 2:24–25; 2 Peter 3:9.

316. Rom 1:19–20; 2:11–16.

317. John Stott, *Basic Christianity*, 2d ed. (London: InterVarsity, 1971; reprint, Grand Rapids: Eerdmans, 1999), 108, states that despite Jesus' warning for individuals to consider the conditions of discipleship carefully, many have not. This has resulted in the Christian landscape being strewn with the wreckage of derelict half-built towers. With so many not really committing to follow Christ on His terms, Christianity today is nominal for most with many trying to look respectful as they change and shape Christianity to suit their convenience. The message of Jesus was very different. Jesus never lowered His standards to make His calling more appealing to the masses. Jesus asks for a genuine commitment to follow Him, and nothing less will do.

318. John Piper, *What Jesus Demands from the World* (Wheaton: Crossway, 2006), 23–24, states that Jesus' demands are jarring to many modern readers; they appear harsh, severe, strict, stark, austere, and abrasive. But, Piper goes on to say that if we are willing to receive Him as our supreme joy [of which we all need God's help to do- my addition], His demands will not feel severe but sweet. In his book, Piper goes on to talk about 50 demands of Christ ranging from being born again to making disciples of all nations. There was and still might be a free downloadable PDF version of this book available at: http://cdn.desiringgod.org/pdf/books_bwjd/books_bwjd.pdf (05/20/2011).

319. In Luke 14:27 & 14:33, Luke uses the Greek phrase οὐ δύναται εἶναι μου μαθητής, *ou dunatai einai mou mathētēs*, "not able to be my disciple," to show that we are not able to overcome the spiritual battles nor witness effectively without the guidance and empowerment of the Holy Spirit. In Acts 1:8, Luke records Jesus telling His immediate disciples prior to Pentecost to wait for the δύναμιν, *dunamin*, "empowerment/ability," which was coming upon them through the Holy Spirit (on the Day of Pentecost)."

320. Billy Graham, *How To Be Born Again,* 147, reminds his readers that God teaches us that we must be changed from the inside out, we must be born again by God.

321. Compare Heb 1:1–4; 12:2–3.

322. Christ expects all of His followers to witness: Matt 10:32–33; Luke 12:8–9.

323. Compare 2 Tim 2:1–3.

Notes: Doing the Father's Will

324. Mal 3:10 applies to all of our activities with God not just tithing. Do we trust God enough to do what He says. Love is the foundation for Christ's followers' work: God loves us and in response we do what He commands because of a growing love for Him and others (John 14:21, 23; Gal 5:6).

325. Compare Rom 2:11–16.

326. Compare Titus 2:14.

327. Compare 1 Peter 1:3–5, 23; John 3:1–6.

328. Compare John 16:13 & Rom 8:14.

329. In the Greek text, I have translated the circumstantial participle πορευθέντες, *poreuthentes*, as "while living out your lives." This is a close interpretation of the Greek in this context. In this commissioning from Christ to His immediate and all future disciples, there is only one command (imperative): μαθητεύσατε, *mathēteusate*, "make disciples." This imperative is given in an aorist form showing ongoing action until this age is over. There are two additional present ongoing circumstantial participles that give insight into making disciples: βαπτίζοντες, *baptizontes*, "baptizing," and διδάσκοντες, *didaskontes*, "teaching."

330. In addition, see Matt 10:40; John 17:18.

331. Compare Gal 5:19–21.

332. Jesus Christ provides the "one and only" access to the Father: Matt 7:13–14; John 10:7; 14:6; Rom 6:1–14; 8:14–30; Eph 2:17–18.

333. Compare John 14:1–4; Phil 3:20; Titus 2:11–14; 1 Peter 1:3–5; 5:10.

334. John 3:16–17; 1 Tim 2:4; 2 Peter 3:9.

335. Compare Eph 6:10–12; 1 Peter 5:6–11.

336. Completion will be realized in heaven: Phil 1:6; 3:20–21; 1 John 3:1–2 and others.

337. The phrase "Body of Christ" appears in the New Testament in various grammatical forms such as τοῦ σώματος Ἰησοῦ Χριστοῦ, *tou sōmatos Iēsou Christou*, "of the body of Jesus Christ," to represent Christ's literal body (Matt 27:58; Mark 15:43; Luke 23:52; 24:3; John 19:38, 40; 20:12; Rom 7:4; Heb 10:10) or figuratively to represent His followers working together as His bodily representative throughout the Messianic age (John 17:18–20; Matt 28:18–20; Acts 1:18). There are additional references to the figurative Body of Christ stated simply as τὸ σῶμα, *to sōma*, "the Body," (1 Cor 12:12, 14, 18–19, 24–25; Eph 2:16; 4:4, 16; 5:23; Col 1:18; 2:17), ἓν σῶμα, *hen sōma*, "one Body," (Rom 12:4–5; 1 Cor 12:13, 20; Eph 2:16; Col 3:15), or τοῦ σώματος αυτοῦ, *tou sōmatos autou*, "His Body," (Eph 5:30). Greek Concordance: Kohlenberger, *The Exhaustive Concordance to the Greek NT*, 926–28.

338. Consider Matt 25:14–30; Rom 12:4–10; 1 Cor 12:7.

339. Consider 1 Cor 1:13a; Eph 4:15–16; 5:23; Col 2:16–19.

340. Paul does not consider himself more than a servant of God, a master builder, who is metaphorically like our contemporary general contractors, building up the churches in Corinth doing his part in building God's Family (1 Cor 3:9–16; cf. 1 Peter 2:4–5). Paul asked the Corinthians this rhetorical question, "Has Christ been divided (1 Cor 1:13a)?" Christ is the true leader and teacher who guides His servants such as Paul. When the Corinthian Saints say that they are of Paul or of Apollos, they are forgetting their relationship with Christ and speaking as people without God, worldly (1 Cor 3:4).

341. Greek: τὸ μεσότοιχον τοῦ φραγμοῦ, *to mesotoichon tou phragmou*, "the dividing middle-wall."

342. James B. Joseph, "No More Walls! The Nonobligatory Ordinances Contained in the Law and the Creation of One New Man in Christ: Ephesians 2:11–22" (Ph.D. diss., Southeastern Baptist Theological Seminary, 2004), 26–45.

343. Greek: ἐκκλησία, *ekklēsia*, "assembly" or "church." *Ekklēsia* normally denoted regularly summoned gatherings of people whether religious, political, or general. See Bauer's *Greek-English Lexicon* (BDAG), 303–04.

344. Greek: μέλη ἐκ μέρους, *melē ek merous*, "a member of a part of the whole." See Bauer's *Greek-English Lexicon* (BDAG), 628, 633.

345. Greek: καὶ ὅσοι τῷ κανόνι τούτῳ στοιχήσουσιν, εἰρήνη ἐπ᾽ αὐτοὺς καὶ ἔλεος καὶ ἐπὶ τὸν Ἰσραὴλ τοῦ θεοῦ, "and as many as are living according to this rule, peace and mercy be upon them, the Israel of God." The third καὶ of this verse is epexegetical describing those who are conducting themselves according to Christ's κανών, *kanōn*, "canon/rule." These are truly the τὸν Ἰσραὴλ τοῦ θεοῦ, "the Israel of God."

346. One of Max Lucado's new books, *Out Live Your Life: You Were Made To Make a Difference* (Nashville: Thomas Nelson, 2010), has a thought provoking chapter on tearing down Satan's divisive walls called "Blast a Few Walls" starting on page 121.

347. Matt 28:18–20; Eph 2:10; 1 Cor 3:9; Titus 2:14.

348. Lucado, *Out Live Your Life*– see end note # 346 above.

349. John 13:34–35; 15:12–13: 17:20–23; Eph 2:11–22; 4:1–6; Rom 8:1–4, 14; and others.

350. Joy is a key response to being in God's family and seeing people's lives being transformed by God; when individual's whom you love are blessed, you experience great joy (1 John 1:4; John 15:8–11; 17:13; Heb 12:2; cf. God and His angels: Luke 15:7, 10, 22–24).

351. Greek: κοινωνίαν, *koinōnian,* "having things in common, fellowship."

352. 1 John 4:10–11, 18–20; cf. 1:7; John 13:34–35; 15:12–17.

353. Gordon D. Fee and Douglas Stuart, *How To Read the Bible for All Its Worth,* 3d ed. (Grand Rapids: Zondervan, 2003).

354. Billy Graham, *The Journey,* 62.

355. John 16:33; Rom 5:1–2, 8:1–2; Eph 2:8–9; 2 Tim 1:9.

356. Josh McDowell and Bob Hostetler, *Beyond Belief to Convictions* (Carol Stream: Tyndale House, 2002), 296.

357. Compare Isa 9:1–4; Matt 4:12–17.

358. Prior to the Cross, individuals such as David listened to God and desired His instructions, His light (e.g. Ps 18:28; 27:1). David said that God's words were sweeter than honey to him (Ps 119:103; cf. 119:1–8, 81, 97–106).

359. Property & Control of Resources: Acts 5:4. Owning Personal Houses: Acts 12:12. Relinquishing Ownership: Luke 14:33. Being a Good Steward of possessions placed under your authority: Matt 25:14–30; Luke 16:10–13.

360. Paul's missionary work in Athens (Acts 17:22–31) is a good example of how we all should work on building mental bridges in order to help those whom we are helping move more easily from their contemporary world views to an accurate godly view of themselves and their surrounding world.

361. In the Greek text (Rom 10:14), Paul asks how the unsaved will hear without a κηρύσσοντος, *kērussontos,* "proclaimer." We normally translate this as "preacher" but that gives the false idea in our society that preachers are responsible for telling about God's love. In reality, all of Christ's followers are in some form or fashion also "proclaimers" of God and His work of salvation for as many as will listen.

362. Dietrich Bonhoeffer, *Letters & Papers from Prison,* rev. ed., ed. Eberhard Bethge (New York: Simon & Schuster, 1997), 411.

363. Ibid., 369–70. *Letters*

364. Luke 12:51–53. During His thousand year reign, Jesus, the Messiah, will force the world to abide in peace. It should be noted that as soon as Satan is released at the end of Jesus' thousand year reign, he will be able to gather a large

army to go against Jesus—man's sinful nature will still enslave many even when a world-wide peace has been enforced for generations. See Rev 19:11–20:10.

365. Graham, *The Journey*, 74–76.

366. Ibid., 77–78. *The Journey*; for a practical introduction to discipleship, consider working through Henry Blackaby's 13 week course, *Experiencing God*, rev. ed. (Nashville: Broadman and Holman, 2008).

367. Compare Cor 14:26; 1 Tim 4:13; 2 Tim 2:2; Titus 2:3–5.

368. Everyone who has a true desire to know and do the will of God and takes time to study and implement His Word will come to know Him and His Creation more fully. If one knows God more fully, he or she knows reality more fully (John 8:31b–32; Rom 12:1–2; 2 Tim 3:16–17).

Bibliography

Primary Sources

Biblia Hebraica Stuttgartensia. 3d ed. Stuttgart: Deutsche
 Bibelgesellschaft, 1987.

The Greek New Testament. 3d UBS ed. Stuttgart: Biblia-Druck,
 1988.

The Septuagint with Apocrypha: Greek and English. London:
 Samuel Bagster & Sons, 1851. Reprint, Peabody:
 Hendrickson, 2001.

Reference Works

Bauer, Walter. *A Greek-English Lexicon of the New Testament and
 other Early Christian Literature.* Rev. and ed. Frederick W.
 Danker. 3d ed. Chicago: The University of Chicago Press,
 2000.

Brown, Francis, S. R Driver, and Charles A. Briggs. *The New
 Brown-Driver-Briggs-Gesenius Hebrew-English Lexicon.*
 Peabody: Hendrickson, 1979.

Kohlenberger III, John R., Edward W. Goodrick, and James A.
 Swanson. *The Exhaustive Concordance to the Greek New
 Testament.* Grand Rapids: Zondervan, 1995.

Liddell, Henry George and Robert Scott. *A Greek-English
 Lexicon.* Rev. & augmented by Henry Stuart Jones and
 Roderick McKenzie. 9th ed. Oxford: Oxford University
 Press, 1940. Reprint, 1990.

General References

Blackaby, Henry. *Experiencing God*. Rev. ed. Nashville: Broadman and Holman, 2008.

Boice, James M. *Christ's Call to Discipleship*. Minneapolis: Grason, 1986.

Bonhoeffer, Dietrich. *Letters & Papers from Prison*. Rev. ed. New York: Simon & Schuster, 1997.

Bush, George W. *Decision Points*. New York: Crown, 2010.

Chan, Francis and Preston Sprinkle. *Erasing Hell: What God Said about Eternity, and the Things That We Have Made Up*. Colorado Springs: David C Cook, 2011.

Corts, Mark C. *The Truth about Spiritual Warfare: Your Place in the Battle between God and Satan*. Nashville: Broadman & Holman, 2006.

Dodd, C. H. *The Interpretation of the Fourth Gospel*. New York: Cambridge University Press, 1953. Reprint, 1958.

Fee, Gordon D. and Douglas Stuart. *How To Read the Bible for All Its Worth*. 3d ed. Grand Rapids: Zondervan, 2003.

Graham, Billy. *How To Be Born Again*. Waco: Word Books, 1977.

_____. *The Journey: How To Live by Faith in an Uncertain World*. Nashville: W Publishing, 2006.

_____. *Just as I Am: The Autobiography of Billy Graham*. New York: Harper Collins, 1997.

Hybels, Bill. *Just Walk Across the Room: Simple Steps Pointing People to Faith*. Grand Rapids: Zondervan, 2004.

Hybels, Bill and Mark Mittleburg. *Becoming a Contagious Christian*. Grand Rapids: Zondervan, 1994.

Idleman, Kyle. *Not a Fan: Becoming a Completely Committed Follower of Jesus.* Grand Rapids: Zondervan, 2011.

Innes, Dick. *I Hate Witnessing: A Handbook for Effective Christian Communications.* Rev. ed. San Clemente: Acts Communications, 2003.

Joseph, James B. "No More Walls! The Nonobligatory Ordinances Contained in the Law and the Creation of One New Man in Christ: Ephesians 2:11–22." Ph.D. diss. Southeastern Baptist Theological Seminary, 2004.

_____. "Unity and Obedient Discipleship in John 17." M.A. Wake Forest University, 1993.

Lucado, Max. *Out Live Your Life: You Were Made To Make a Difference.* Nashville: Thomas Nelson, 2010.

McDowell, Josh. *A Ready Defense.* San Bernardino: Here's Life, 1990. Reprint, 1991.

McDowell, Josh and Bob Hostetler. *Beyond Belief to Conversion.* Carol Stream: Tyndale House, 2002.

Metzger, Bruce M. *The Canon of the New Testament: Its Origin, Development, and Significance.* New York: Oxford University Press, 1997.

Milne, Bruce. *The Message of John.* Downers Grove: InterVarsity, 1993.

Piper, John. *What Jesus Demands from the World.* Wheaton: Crossway, 2006.

Scouteris, Constantine. "The People of God– Its Unity and Its Glory: A Discussion of John 17:17–24 in Light of Patristic Thought." *The Greek Orthodox Theological Review* 30, no. 4 (Winter 1985): 399–414.

Stott, John. *Basic Christianity.* 2d ed. London: InterVarsity, 1971.

Index A: General References
(References Are Taken Only from the Body–Not Notes)

215

Index B: Scriptural References
(Only the Start of Each Scripture is Referenced)
(References Are Taken Only from the Body–No Notes)
("Q" Represents a Block Quote)

www.ingramcontent.com/pod-product-compliance
Lightning Source LLC
Chambersburg PA
CBHW030916090426
42737CB00007B/213